ABOUT ISLAND PRESS

Island Press is the only nonprofit organization in the United States whose principal purpose is the publication of books on environmental issues and natural resource management. We provide solutions-oriented information to professionals, public officials, business and community leaders, and concerned citizens who are shaping responses to environmental problems.

In 2004, Island Press celebrates its twentieth anniversary as the leading provider of timely and practical books that take a multidisciplinary approach to critical environmental concerns. Our growing list of titles reflects our commitment to bringing the best of an expanding body of literature to the environmental community throughout North America and the world.

Support for Island Press is provided by The Nathan Cummings Foundation, Geraldine R. Dodge Foundation, Doris Duke Charitable Foundation, Educational Foundation of America, The Charles Engelhard Foundation, The Ford Foundation, The George Gund Foundation, The Vira I. Heinz Endowment, The William and Flora Hewlett Foundation, Henry Luce Foundation, The John D. and Catherine T. MacArthur Foundation, The Andrew W. Mellon Foundation, The Moriah Fund, The Curtis and Edith Munson Foundation, The New-Land Foundation, Oak Foundation, The Overbrook Foundation, The David and Lucile Packard Foundation, The Pew Charitable Trusts, The Rockefeller Foundation, The Winslow Foundation, and other generous donors.

The opinions expressed in this book are those of the author(s) and do not necessarily reflect the views of these foundations.

Understanding Environmental Administration and Law

Understanding Environmental Administration and Law

Third Edition

Susan J. Buck

ISLANDPRESS Washington • Covelo • London

ISLAND PRESS is a trademark of the Center for Resource Economics.

Library of Congress Cataloging-in-Publication Data

Buck, Susan J.
 Understanding environmental administration and law / Susan Buck. — 3rd ed.
     p. cm.
Includes bibliographical references.
ISBN 1-59726-035-5 (cloth : alk. paper) —
ISBN 1-59726-036-3 (pbk. : alk. paper)
1. Environmental law—United States. 2. Environmental policy—
United States. I. Title.
KF3775.B83 2006
344.7304'6--dc22
                                    2006009304

Printed on recycled, acid-free paper ✪

Manufactured in the United States of America

10 9 8 7 6 5 4 3 2 1

*With love and gratitude for nearly forty years
of friendship, this book is dedicated to
Ted R. Powers, Sr.*

CONTENTS

Chapter Seven: International Environmental Policy and Law   190

PREFACE

This book springs from the premise that environmental managers need to understand the legal context of their work. Of course, most environmental managers understand the laws and regulations affecting their own jobs. However, they usually view these as constraints on their own autonomy. As the Boatman in *A Man for All Seasons* says, lamenting that the fee is the same for rowing upstream as down: "whoever makes the regulations doesn't row a boat." Most managers are taught their professional and scientific disciplines first, and their training for administration takes place on the job. Thus they learn the "right" way to measure floodways or to harvest trees, and when state budgetary constraints preserve inaccurate maps or leave a prime stand of trees uncut, managers are outraged because they have not been taught that political factors are as valid as a basis for decisionmaking as scientific measurements.

Setting aside the question of whether political issues *ought* to be considered, the fact remains that they *are* considered. Good managers need to understand how the legal and political processes operate in order to anticipate political changes and perhaps to channel their impacts in ways that are helpful to the managers' own professional goals.

Environmental managers deal with the law every day. At the very highest level, statutes and executive orders define the boundaries of job responsibilities. At the lowest level, rules and regulations provide guidance and, at times, restrictions on bureaucratic activities. Somewhere in between is the middle manager, that fabled creature who must translate the larger commands into operations. At the middle manager's level, the law is both friend and master. The law is flexible, and a good manager learns how to use it to achieve the organization's policy goals.

Typically the middle manager has come up through the technical ranks and, as a reward for good technical skills, has become an administrator. At this point, the infamous Peter Principle may come into play: employees rise to their level of incompetence. Administration is a skill, as much art as science, and it has its own special tools. One of the most important tools for environmental managers is the law. The managers' interest in the law is practical; their concerns are not those of a lawyer or law student. For example, in the case of *National Audubon Society v. Department of Water and Power of the City of Los Angeles* (1983), a California court held that a public trust protected the waters of Mono Lake. Los Angeles was required, under this decision, to reconsider its use of water from the lake. To a lawyer, this case is of great legal interest. To an employee of the Los Angeles water department, the case is a nightmare, providing no useful guidelines on whether, when, or how water may still be diverted from Mono Lake for the urgent water supply needs of the city.

The purpose of this book is to show how the policy process is infused with the legal process. I hope to demystify the law, to translate it from the law books, and to make it accessible to the nonlawyer. The law is like chess: a finite number of pieces, each with its own moves, resulting in infinite combinations and strategies. Here I hope the readers will find the pieces pictured and the moves defined. They must play their own game.

THE THIRD EDITION

This edition has been revised and updated to include developments in environmental law and policy during the William J. Clinton and George W. Bush administrations through the summer of 2005. I have added discussion cases; their purpose is to help readers wrestle with practical applications of legal principles. At one point I considered calling them "Where the Rubber Meets the Road," because they are real-world examples of environmental law in action. However, good taste prevailed, and now each case has its own heading. They are based on actual law cases, but I have taken some liberties with details, so readers should not view them as case briefs. (I am especially grateful to Frona Powell for her excellent book *Law and the Environment* [West, 1998]. Several of the cases I used for discussion points first came to my attention when I was teaching from this book.)

ACKNOWLEDGMENTS

As was true for earlier editions, I have been fortunate in having able and dedicated students to help with this writing project. Steve Hawryluk read the entire manuscript, pointing out places where the language was unclear or the mechanics flawed. He also verified all the case citations, the bibliography, acronyms, and newly added legislation. Steve was thorough and meticulous; he caught errors I'd read over a dozen times. He did a superb job. Amanda Latham researched policy changes since 1995 and verified all the legislative citations from the second edition. Marian Kshetrapal, a friend and attorney here in Greensboro, revised and updated the material on "Finding Case Law." Susan Cockrell was the copyeditor for this edition; she was meticulous and made many helpful suggestions.

As always, I am thankful for the support and friendship of Todd Baldwin, editor-in-chief of Island Press. This is the third book we have worked on together, and it is a real comfort to have an editor who reads with care and attention and whose suggestions are always right on target. He makes my work easier and better. Two other people at Island Press were also extraordinarily helpful. Shannon O'Neill shepherded the book through the writing phases with careful attention to detail and good humor. Jessica Heise was the production editor; she has kept us all on schedule and has an enormous supply of patience. It was a pleasure to work with them all.

For the second edition, John Ehmig verified the case and statutory citations and wrote the section on "Finding Case Law." Also for the second edition, Nancy Carlson prepared the case on Fisheating Creek and Christen Compton prepared the material on the environmental policy in the European Union.

Several students helped with the research for the first edition. David Cushing's work was essential; without his efforts with interlibrary loan, the manuscript would have been years late. Dana Dooley prepared the bibliography and list of cases, saving me much time and trouble. Megan Schmid provided the full citations for the legislation. Three other students, Jeff Bimmer, Paul Bivens, and Joe Morgan, chose to write annotated bibliographies for this book in lieu of research papers; their excellent research eased my own task considerably. I am also grateful to two colleagues, Marlene Gaither and Harley Hiett, who wrote about cases that presented a practitioner's view of environmental law.

CHAPTER ONE

The American Legal System

While legal scholars over the centuries have offered many definitions of *law*, the definition that meets with the approval of most Americans is that of the nineteenth-century jurist John Austin: the law is the command of the sovereign backed by a sanction. In other words, the law is whatever the government says it is, and if we choose not to comply, the government will punish us. For citizens whose encounters with the law are largely limited to traffic police or the IRS, such a definition is adequate. But citizens whose daily work is bounded by a governmental structure of rules and regulations see more to the law than simply commands. Who gives the sovereign the right to issue commands? Are there areas of public or private endeavor in which the sovereign has no rights to issue commands? What is the range of penalties for noncompliance? Does it matter if the noncompliance is accidental, or unavoidable? How does a citizen *discover* the latest governmental command?

All of these questions are pertinent to environmental managers. The scope of their administrative authority and the intent of the legislature in giving them that authority are important parameters. They must also adapt to changes in political authority. Managers in regulatory enforcement must know when they may or should compromise and when they must bring their full enforcement powers to bear on a violator. Resource managers must maintain the delicate balance between resource protection and resource use. Their arsenal is not restricted to the "sanctions" of the sovereign. They have persuasion, political pressure, and incentives on their side as well. To understand these managerial tools, managers must also understand the system in which they wield them.

This chapter explores the legal system in which American environmental managers must operate. The first section discusses the English roots of American common law and how this body of law became accepted in the new United States. It also discusses the other sources of law: statutes, rules and regulations, and the Constitution. How judges apply this law is discussed in the second section. The impact of our complex federal system on environmental administration and law is discussed in the third section.

SOURCES OF LAW

Western public law is based on one of two systems: English common law and the European civil law tradition, also called continental or codified law. The simplest way to distinguish between these two systems is to look at the judicial decision-making process. Common law is based on the idea of precedent: like cases are decided alike. Judges base their decisions not only on the applicable statute but also on how other courts have interpreted the statute. In some areas of the common law there are no controlling statutes, only rules set forth by appellate courts. By contrast, in the continental or civil system, the law is spelled out in detailed civil codes; the specific rules laid out in *Leviticus* are a familiar example of the civil code approach to the law. In the civil system, the judge locates the appropriate section of the code and then applies it to the situation at hand.

The Common Law

The common law system developed in the thirteenth century.[1] When the English feudal system began to weaken and modern cities began to develop, the king sent royal judges to decide controversies in his name. This was done primarily to increase the king's power and authority as the power and authority of his feudal lords waned. Each feudal manor had its own customs, and the judges would weigh their own perceptions of fairness, the existing customs, and the political repercussions in reaching decisions. As we might expect, the decisions were often based on unclear reasoning, and cases that appeared similar might be decided in completely contradictory ways. The clerks accompanying the judges began to record decisions and reasoning;

congregating back in London they compared notes, and gradually judges started to refer to the decisions of their colleagues as another basis for decisions. Eventually, recording decisions became routine, and judges were required to set out their reasoning for the formal record. Any deviation from precedent had to be justified. In this way the common law—the system of law common to the entire country—was established.

Today we take the English basis of our legal system for granted. In the early days of the republic, when the former colonies did not have their own cases to determine the precedents for judicial decisionmaking, judges drew on the same English law that had governed their decisions prior to the American Revolution.[2] At the time of the Revolution, there was debate about whether the new country would follow the English tradition; in some quarters feelings were very strong that a complete break from England was the only correct approach. The legal system that was suggested to replace the common law tradition was the civil law approach that prevailed on the continent of Europe and was used by allies such as the French. The French colonies had retained the continental legal system, and even today Louisiana, a former French possession, is still governed by such a system.

Despite the radical proposals to change the law, the English system prevailed. Colonial lawyers and judges were trained in the common law, and contracts, property transfers, and all forms of legal transactions were already in the English style. Besides, despite the outpourings of anti-English sentiment immediately following the Revolution, most colonists still thought of themselves as English in spirit. Edmund Burke, the English statesman and philosopher, excused the American Revolution on the grounds that good Englishmen *should* rebel when treated unfairly. Common sense and common law prevailed, and the American legal system was based upon the English one.

One of the earliest environmental cases resting on common law traditions appeared before the United States Supreme Court in 1842. *Martin v. Waddell* originated with the contention by a New Jersey riparian landowner, Waddell, that he had exclusive rights to take oysters from the Raritan River. He based his assertion on a grant made by King Charles in 1664 to the Duke of York, which gave the Duke "all the powers of government." Waddell claimed that his rights to the mudflats were directly descended from property rights transferred by the Duke of York and his managers. Waddell's opponent, Martin, argued that the King held certain resources (among them, mudflats) in trust for the people, and that the King's grant to the Duke of York required the Duke to hold these resources in trust as well. Thus, he argued, despite language that might be interpreted otherwise, the Duke did not have the power to transfer the mudflats to private ownership any more than the King did. The Supreme Court agreed with Martin that the original grant did not include the *exclusive* right to fish the adjacent waters. Of course, in the interim since the grant had been given to the Duke of York, the State of New Jersey had formed a new government, so the second question before the Court was whether New Jersey was similarly prohibited from granting private, exclusive rights to lands that under common law were public trust lands. Justice Taney (the same justice whose decision in *Dred Scott* helped precipitate the Civil War) found that the public trust doctrine had survived the Revolution:

> [W]hen the people of New Jersey took possession of the reins of government, and took into their own hands the powers of sovereignty, the prerogatives and regalities which before belonged either to the crown or the Parliament, became immediately and rightfully vested in the State.[3]

Although *Martin v. Waddell* is not the only case in which courts articulated the continuance of English traditions, it is one of the clearest. Of course, the changing social and economic situations in the United States led to many and frequent diversions from the English law, but the basis was firmly established.

In addition to the common law, which continues to develop, statutes, rules and regulations, and the Constitution are rich sources of American law.

Statutes and Ordinances

Statutes are the formal acts of legislation passed by Congress or the state legislatures. Similar enactments passed by county and city governments are often called ordinances or local laws. Sometimes statutes are very specific, for example, setting time limits on Superfund damage claims or the maximum permissible automobile emission levels. At other times, however, legislatures establish broad guidelines and leave the details to the executive branch.[4] This is done for several reasons. First, the legislators have neither the time nor the expertise to hammer out the details of implementation. Second, the legislative process is slow and cumbersome; it is designed that way so that the decisions are as free from circumstantial pressure as possible. Administrative actions are comparatively speedy, as will be seen in chapter 5. Finally, by passing the responsibility for detailed implementation to the executive branch, the legislature avoids much of the political repercussions of unpopular decisions. For example, when the Bureau of Land Management (BLM) proposed raising the cost of federal-land grazing permits to market levels, the resulting firestorm engulfed the BLM bureaucrats and not the Congress that had given them the authority to raise fees.

Rules and Regulations

Another source of American law is the rules and regulations promulgated by administrative agencies. Technically, under the Constitution only the legislature has the authority to make laws. However, in the American system, the legislature has delegated some of its law-making authority to the executive agencies. From the late nineteenth century through the middle of the New Deal, the constitutionality of legislative delegation of authority was questioned, and even today some commentators argue that the Congress in particular cannot give rule-making powers to the executive branch without very clear and restrictive guidelines. In practice, however, federal and many state agencies have the power to make rules and regulations that have the force of law. These rules must meet two constitutional standards: *procedural due process* (Did the agency follow the legal requirements of notice and hearing?), and *substantive due process* (Is the agency operating within its designated policy boundaries?). This will be discussed more fully in chapter 4. It is, however, important to note that any rule or regulation that is formulated with the proper procedures and is within the statutory authority of an agency has the same legal status as legislation passed by the legislature and signed by the executive.

CASE DISCUSSION 1.1

Cover Crops

In 1938, the federal government created the Federal Crop Insurance Corporation (FCIC) to provide a safety net for farmers who suffered losses from "unavoidable causes, including drought." In February 1945,

(continued)

CASE DISCUSSION 1.1 (*continued*)

the FCIC published its wheat regulations in the *Federal Register*. The following month, Merrill and others applied for insurance for their wheat crop in Bonneville County, Idaho. The County Agricultural Conservation Committee was the FCIC's agent in Bonneville County; Merrill and friends told the Committee that they were planting 460 acres of spring wheat, 400 acres of which had previously been seeded with winter wheat. The Committee told them the entire crop would be covered and recommended that the FCIC office in Denver accept the application. The written application did not mention that any of the acreage was reseeded. In May, the insurance application was accepted.

The summer of 1945 was very dry, and in July, drought caused most of the crops to fail. When Merrill and friends filed their insurance claims, they were told that under the February regulations, reseeded wheat was *not* covered, and that portion of the claim was denied.

- Under Idaho state law, a private insurance company in similar circumstances would be bound by the agent's word.

Should the crop losses of Merrill et al. be covered?

(Source: *Federal Crop Insurance Corporation v. Merrill et al.*, 332 U.S. 380 [1947])

The Constitution

The Constitution plays a vital part in environmental regulation. For example, the common urban practice of zoning raises the constitutional question of whether zoning is a "taking" of an individual's property. We are accustomed to thinking of zoning as a way to regulate and to protect the welfare and orderly development of a community. However, the Constitution clearly states:

> No person shall . . . be deprived of life, liberty, or property without due process of law; nor shall private property be taken for public use, without just compensation. (Amendment V)

Is zoning the equivalent of taking a person's property "for public use"? Suppose the zoning significantly reduces the value of the property or makes it unusable? Must the owner be compensated? Or is the act of zoning the use of "due process of law" and therefore exempt from paying just compensation? Until recent years, zoning has been consistently interpreted by the courts as a legitimate exercise of a state's police power: the obligation to protect public health, safety, and welfare. But court decisions in the 1980s and 1990s have found some forms of zoning to be a taking; this is partially a result of the increasing number of conservative justices now in the legal system following the Reagan and George H. W. Bush years (1981–1993).[5]

Another constitutional issue in environmental law is the legitimacy of agency rulemaking. Prior to the New Deal, agency rulemaking was viewed with deep suspicion by the legal profession. Some questioned the authority of Congress to delegate its legislative powers; others questioned the wisdom of allowing bureaucrats, who are not directly responsible to the people, to make binding rules and regulations. The issue seemed to be settled with the New Deal, the passage of the Administrative Procedure Act in 1946, and subsequent challenges to delegation that generally resulted in agency victories. In recent years, the Supreme Court has become more conservative, and a majority of justices may choose to return to the position that Congress is neglecting its duties when delegating its legislative authority. Dissenting in *American Textile Manufacturers v. Donovan* in 1981, Justice Rehnquist wrote that, in delegating rule-making responsibility for cotton-dust standards to the Occupational Safety and Health Administration (OSHA),

> Congress simply abdicated its responsibility for the making of a fundamental and most difficult policy choice. . . . That is a "quintessential legislative" choice and must be made by the elected representative of the people, not by nonelected officials in the Executive Branch . . . in so doing Congress unconstitutionally delegated its legislative responsibility to the Executive Branch.[6]

Justice Scalia is also inclined to encourage Congress to give clearer policy directions to the agencies.[7] Throughout the history of administration, this tension between delegation (when Congress shares decisionmaking with administrative agencies) and administrative discretion (the need for agencies to exercise administrative expertise) has been a key issue that is based on the constitutional concepts of separation of powers as well as checks and balances.

Other constitutional issues arise within agency procedures for appeals, investigations, and hearing procedures. These will be looked at again in the discussion of the Administrative Procedure Act in chapter 5.

JUDICIAL DECISIONMAKING

In deciding the cases brought before them, judges are required to interpret the relevant statutes and regulations, to follow common law precedents, and to apply constitutional principles. One of the more difficult areas for judicial review is statutory interpretation.

Statutory Interpretation

Unlike the common law, which rests on facts and the idea of precedent, statutory law is the result of negotiations and debate. When, for example, a citizen challenges official behavior based on the accusation that the official has violated a statute, the first chore for the reviewing court is to determine just what the statute means. The court can do this by several techniques. First, the court may examine the intent of the lawmakers in the language of the statute itself and as it is shown in the legislative history. The legislative history is the formal record of the evolution of the statute: testimony offered in support or opposition to the statute, or to parts of the statute; the debates on the legislation; and the amendment sequence. The best source of legislative history is the House, Senate, or Conference report that accompanies the bill to the final floor vote.

Interpreting legislative history may sound simple, but it can be a judicial morass. First, the testimony is often conflicting. Second, the debates are *real* debates, during which legislators may become convinced that the position of the opposition has merit, so that on one day the legislator holds one opinion and on the next day a different opinion. Because the legislative history is the chronological history of the act, it may record ideas or motivations that were ultimately utterly abandoned by the members. Third, the *Congressional Record*, which is the official organ of the Congress and records these testimonies and debates, is given to the members for correction prior to publication. This was originally intended to allow members to correct grammatical slips of the tongue, but now the *Record* may be substantially edited for the home constituents, and what is printed in the *Record* may bear only a superficial resemblance to what was said on the floor of the Congress. In the 1990s, the conservative members of the Supreme Court were less anxious to delve into the legislative history and sought to decide the cases wherever possible based on the plain language of the act.

In interpreting statutes, the courts also look at contemporary administrative interpretations. The courts presume that if the agencies were very far off the mark in their application of the statute, the legislature would have corrected the mistake. In theory this is so, but in fact, only those aberrations that are brought to the attention of an elected representative with both the interest to do something and the position within the legislature to accomplish it are likely to be corrected. Nevertheless, the courts often continue to defer to agency interpretations of their own statutes, especially where the language is ambiguous and the agency interpretation has been consistent. This is known as the *Chevron doctrine*, after a case decided in 1984.[8]

The courts will also consider nonlegislative changes that have taken place since the statute was enacted. For example, the Federal Communications Commission (FCC) was established long before cable television existed, but courts are required to determine the cable industry's compliance with the regulatory apparatus put in place by the FCC. The courts must look beyond the direct language of both the statute and the legislative history to find the *intent* of the legislature. This can be a very complex task. For example, when the Forest Reserve Act was enacted in 1891, the legal concept of "endangered species" had not been imagined. In 1989 and 1990, the spotted owl controversy forced legislators, judges, and Forest Service administrators to reconcile the 1891 Act with the Endangered Species Act (1973) requirements and with the demands of the troubled logging industry and environmentalists. How successfully this was accomplished may be indicated by the 1995 Supreme Court decision[9] that supported federal regulation of private land to protect endangered species, and continuing efforts to amend the Endangered Species Act.[10]

Finally, the courts examine past judicial opinions on the statute, partly to search out the reasoning of other courts (in obedience to the dictates of the common law) and partly again on the assumption that the legislature would move to correct any misplaced judicial opinions.

Judicial Precedents

The theory underlying common law interpretation is deceptively simple: judges determine the facts and then, finding previous cases with similar facts, reason from analogy to reach their conclusions. In practice, of course, this can be an amazingly complex process. Astute attorneys will find cases that parallel their client's position, while the opposing attorneys, working from the same set of facts, will offer as precedent an entirely different set of cases that support an entirely opposite judicial conclusion. This is why common law decisions are often referred to as "judge-made" law: judges use their own discretion to choose between the competing precedents. For example, in an Arizona case, *Spur Industries v. Del Webb Development* (1972), Del Webb's company developed his Sun City housing community toward Spur's feedlot. Webb sued to close the feedlot on the grounds that it was a public health hazard (i.e., a public nuisance). Spur relied on the common law protection that Webb was "coming to the nuisance" (or, in kindergarten terms, Spur was there first). There was no statute to help the judge decide, and because this was a controversy between two private parties and hence had no government involvement, there was no constitutional question to be resolved. The court exercised the wisdom of Solomon, ordering Spur to move and Webb to pay for the move.

Application of Constitutional Principles

In cases that raise constitutional issues, the court must first consider the language of the Constitution itself. For example, the First Amendment states:

> Congress shall make *no law* respecting an establishment of religion, or prohibiting the free exercise thereof; or abridging the freedom of speech, or of the press; or the right of the people peaceably to assemble, and to petition the Government for a redress of grievances. (Emphasis added.)

Supreme Court justices Hugo Black and William O. Douglas were known as "absolutists" because they refused to accept any restriction on First Amendment freedoms: they insisted that "no law means no law." Their colleagues on the bench did not accept this position, relying instead on another facet of constitutional interpretation: the intent of the Framers as reflected in documents from the Constitutional Convention and from the private and public papers of the men who wrote the Constitution. From these documents and papers, it is clear that the Framers intended to protect political speech and broadsheet-pamphlet types of literature. The Framers would probably be surprised to find their amendment protecting salacious photographs and the *National Enquirer.*

Most judges and legal scholars agree that the Constitution is a "living document" that must be allowed to change with changing conditions. For example, there is no right to privacy written into the Constitution, yet the Supreme Court has held that the Constitution confers such a right. This right to privacy was first announced by Justice Douglas in *Griswold v. Connecticut* (1965) when he concluded that the guarantees in the Bill of Rights implied a right to privacy because they could not be achieved without it.

CASE DISCUSSION 1.2

Bird's Eye View

Dow Chemical Company owned a 2,000-acre manufacturing complex in Midland, Michigan. This facility had numerous buildings connected by piping conduit and equipment, all of which was visible from the air. Dow imposed strict security around its plant. The entire 2,000 acres was surrounded by an eight-foot chain link fence posted with security guards and closed-circuit cameras, an alarm system, motion detectors, and a strict prohibition on photographs. To restrict public views of the area, Dow also investigated any low-level flights over the facility by recording the identification number and description of the plane and then by working with the Michigan State Police and local airport authorities to locate the pilot. If the pilot had taken any photographs, Dow asked for the film and retained any negatives and prints of the facility. If unable to recover the film, Dow sued the pilot. The purpose of all this security was to protect trade secrets.

In 1978, U.S. Environmental Protection Agency (EPA) inspectors came into the facility with Dow's consent to inspect two power plants in the complex for compliance with Clean Air Act requirements. Dow refused permission for a second inspection, and EPA did not try to get an administrative search warrant. Instead, EPA took to the skies. They used a commercial aerial photographer to record the facility at 12,000, 3,000, and 1,200 feet. All the flights were within lawful airspace. When Dow found out about the photographs, Dow sued,

(continued)

CASE DISCUSSION 1.2 (*continued*)

claiming that the search violated Dow's Fourth Amendment rights and exceeded EPA's power of investigation.

- "The right of the people to be secure in their persons, houses, papers, and effects, against unreasonable searches and seizures, shall not be violated, and no Warrants shall issue, but upon probable cause, supported by Oath or affirmation, and particularly describing the place to be searched, and the persons or things to be seized." U.S. Constitution, Amendment IV.
- The common law doctrine of "curtilage" considers the outbuildings connected to a dwelling or in close proximity to it, and the land and grounds surrounding the house that are used by the family, as subject to the same search and seizure protections as the dwelling. *Black's Law Dictionary*, 1990
- The "open fields doctrine" permits government officials to enter and to search a field— "any unoccupied or undeveloped area outside of the curtilage" (*Black's Law Dictionary*, 1990)—without a warrant. *Oliver v. United States*, 466 U.S. 170 (1984)
- Although commercial businesses are generally protected from unreasonable searches, some administrative searches do not require warrants: businesses that are traditionally closely regulated, such as liquor stores (*United States v. Biswell*, 406 U.S. 311 [1973]); social workers checking on families receiving Aid to Families with Dependent Children (*Wyman v. James*, 400 U.S. 309 [1971]); safety inspections at mines (*Donovan v. Dewey*, 452 U.S. 594 [1981]).

Did EPA need a warrant to take the aerial photographs? Does it matter that they did not notify Dow of their intent? Should they have had a warrant even if one were not required?

(Source: *Dow Chemical Company v. United States*, 476 U.S. 227 [1986])

In 2001, based on a tip, local narcotics agents used a thermal imager to detect an area of excessive heat inside a private residence. Suspecting the heat indicated high-intensity lights for growing marijuana, agents obtained a warrant and arrested the resident for growing marijuana. Was that a legal search? *Kyllo v. United States*, 553 U.S. 27 (2001)

FEDERALISM

One of the most important characteristics of our political system often gets lost in our focus on national government activities. The United States is a federal system: it is an intergovernmental system of state governments and the national government.[11] Each level has some degree of autonomy, although the national level has been increasing in power for the last century, and the states no longer have the same independence they once had. This can be attributed to several factors.[12] First, presidential candidates for the past century have believed in and campaigned for a strong national government; members of Congress achieve—often inadvertently—the same goals as they provide services to their constituents and thus earn reelection. Second, there has been widespread disillusionment with the state governments. Many states are dominated by rural interests, and the cities suffer in legislative allocations; as a result, the cities seek federal relief and further enlarge the national power. Third, the United States has had a series of national crises that were clearly beyond the abilities of the states as single government entities: World War I, the Great Depression, World War II, several "police actions" during and since the cold war, and now terrorism. The expansion of federal social programs to cope with the Depression and the increase in defense spending from both active military engagements and the cold war has increased the power of the national government at the expense of the states. Since the mid-1980s, conservatives in the national government have advocated shifting responsibilities for some policy areas to the states; the states have often been reluctant because they are concerned about bearing the costs of these programs, especially since the renewed emphasis on federalism is often linked to a national budget reduction. However, some environmental policies are still set primarily at the state level; for example, certain aspects of wildlife management, such as setting hunting seasons, are state prerogatives, although several federal laws restrict state autonomy in this area. (See chapter 6 for a full discussion of the relationship between the federal and state governments in wildlife management.)

Federalism is especially important in environmental law because, typically, federal agencies rely upon the states to enforce environmental regulations. Even in nonregulatory areas, the federal presence of such agencies as the Bureau of Land Management, the Forest Service, and the National Park Service affects the states. These agencies manage most federally owned land, and in some states (especially in the West) large tracts of undeveloped land are owned by the national government. Over half the land in Alaska, Colorado, Oregon, and Utah belongs to the federal government; 86 percent of Nevada is federally owned.[13] This has a substantial impact on economic development, tourism, recreation, and the tax base of state and local governments.

Another reason that federalism is so important in environmental issues is that so many environmental problems cross political boundaries; for example, transboundary air pollution was addressed by the 1990 Clean Air Act Amendments, which created regional ozone transport commissions to deal with smog problems on a multistate basis. Interstate compacts, described in the Constitution and subject to Senate ratification, provide another vehicle for state cooperation in many environmental areas. For example, the Potomac River Fisheries Commission is the regulatory body formed in 1963 from the Potomac River Compact (1958) between Maryland and Virginia. Under the compact, the river fisheries were originally managed in accordance with Maryland laws, but more recently the commission has adopted new regulations to govern fishing. Although commission regulations may be challenged in court, the commission has never lost a court challenge; regulations may be changed or revoked by a joint resolution of both the Maryland and Virginia legislatures, but this process has never been used. Many other jurisdictions across the country that must deal with transboundary issues such as water quality, air quality, wildlife management, bridges, harbors, and conservation choose to use interstate compacts.[14]

Federalism has other, less obvious, effects on environmental law. Lobby groups find their influence increased through federalism because multiple governments provide multiple points of access. State policymakers may be more vulnerable to lobbying because their state economies are more fragile. One western state, for example, decided not to comply with the state natural resource trustee requirement of the Superfund Amendment and Reauthorization Act (SARA) for fear of alienating one of the major businesses in the state; that particular business would have been a likely candidate for state resource damage suits were a trustee to be appointed.[15] During the 1970s, business lobbies often favored state control of pollution enforcement because they thought states were more vulnerable to economic pressure. In the 1980s, as the Republican administrations of Reagan and Bush began to ease the federal burden on business, businesses found that many states were exceeding federal standards, creating an administrative nightmare for those companies with plants and offices in several states. By the early

1990s, they were back in Congress, advocating federal regulations that would set the ceiling (rather than the floor) for state actions. Of course, states can, and often do, operate independently of the federal government. For example, in 2004–2005, nine western state legislatures passed energy-related laws to encourage development and use of alternative sources of energy and to regulate the fossil fuels industry. They have also gone their own way on other issues: Utah has banned some forms of nuclear waste, while Wyoming has not only protected landowners from oil and gas companies that own subsurface mineral rights but has also established a state fund for wildlife and habitat preservation.[16]

Another federal factor that increases the access points for lobbyists is the staggered election campaigns in a federal system. With national elections held every two years for the House of Representatives, every four years for president, and every six years for the Senate, plus the various gubernatorial and state house elections, busy lobbyists can be permanently involved with helping or hindering election prospects of candidates at all levels of government. Lobbyists can then pick and choose the races and the candidates that will be the most helpful to their organizations' goals.

It is no accident that the national terms of office are so staggered. The Constitution is designed around a federal system. The House, allocated by population (the larger a state's population, the more representatives it has) is balanced by the Senate, which has two senators per state regardless of the state's land mass or population.[17] This compromise, struck during the Constitutional Convention, was needed to accommodate concerns that each state be fairly represented. One unanticipated result has been that, at times, this balances the states so well that they cancel each other out, leaving a clear field for the president and his national policies.

Our national culture has changed from the predominately agrarian times of Jefferson. Globalization, urbanization, development of national transportation networks, international communications, and problems such as homelessness, drug use, and AIDS are beyond the states' capacities to manage or even to coordinate. The civil rights movement, which never could have succeeded without federal judicial and legislative involvement, has also changed the relationship between the states and the national government. Since the mid-twentieth century, state politicians have often found it easier to get money from the federal government than to raise state and local taxes and thus endanger their own chances for reelection.[18] The national government can also influence state policies by offering federal money to pay for state programs, such as wildlife management. In intergovernmental relations (as well as practically everywhere else), he who pays the piper calls the tune.

The *Tangier Sound* case, discussed below, provides a good illustration of the complexities of intergovernmental involvement in resource management. This case also illustrates some of the points to be discussed in chapter 6: the state ownership of wildlife doctrine, conflicts with federal law, and limitations on state and federal authority to regulate.

CASE STUDY: *TANGIER SOUND WATERMEN'S ASSOCIATION V. DOUGLAS* (1982)

Tangier Sound is an area of the Chesapeake Bay that is especially rich in crab habitat. Unfortunately, the Virginia-Maryland state line runs through Tangier Sound; the crabs tend to live in Virginia while the local crabbers live in Maryland.

Prior to 1982, Virginia imposed a residency requirement on anyone seeking a license to fish in Virginia waters. This meant that the Maryland crabbers could not legally follow the crab supply out of their state jurisdiction. The Watermen's Association argued that the residency requirement created an improper barrier to interstate commerce ("Congress shall have Power . . . to regulate Commerce with foreign Nations, and among the several States. . . ." [Article I, § 8]), and it was therefore unconstitutional. They further argued that the only justification for such interference with interstate commerce would be a legitimate and compelling state interest such as conservation, and Virginia clearly had no conservation interest since there was no limit on the number of Virginia residents allowed to have crabbing licenses. The watermen stated that the privileges and immunities clause of the Constitution ("The Citizens of each State shall be entitled to all Privileges and Immunities of Citizens on the several States," [Article IV, § 2]) and the equal protection clause ("No state shall . . . deny to any person within its jurisdiction the equal protection of the laws," Fourteenth Amendment) protected their rights to work in Virginia water. Finally, the watermen noted that many of their fishing vessels were federally licensed and were therefore exempt from state restrictions.

Virginia argued that the state had a compelling state interest to allow the residency requirement to stand. First, effective enforcement of regulations required that only residents be allowed to crab. That enabled Virginia inspectors to check boats unloading in Virginia and to ensure court appearances of violators who otherwise must be either arrested or extradited. Second, the requirement was essential for conservation measures. By limiting crabbing to residents, each resident could use the most efficient possible gear, thus maximizing his catch. If nonresident crabbers were permitted, restrictions on gear would be required to protect the crab resource from stress. This in turn would reduce each crabber's catch, which would interfere with the state's legitimate authority to protect an internal industry. As an aside, Virginia offered a federalism defense: by restricting a state's control of its resources, the state was restrained from trying "novel social and economic experiments without risk to the rest of the country."[19]

In dismissing the constitutional claims advanced by the watermen, Virginia argued that the commerce clause was not violated because the residency requirement was not a barrier to *trade*; watermen were allowed to buy or sell crabs and to transport them in, out, or through the state. The only prohibition was against catching them in the state. The privileges and immunities clause was not violated; Maryland watermen were not restricted from lawfully pursuing their trade because the trade itself was not lawful. In a desperate attempt to stave off the inevitable, Virginia advanced the trespass defense: since crabbing by necessity disturbs the bottom, any taking of crabs was also a trespass on state-owned land. (The states do own the submerged lands; it is navigation on the water above that is given into federal jurisdiction.)

Of course, what was truly at issue here was Virginia's desire to keep out-of-state crabbers (and in particular, Maryland crabbers, with whom a centuries-old feud existed) from profiting in Virginia wildlife. Virginia was really asserting state independence from federal interference in natural resource management. The federal presence in fisheries management in the Chesapeake Bay was felt in two areas: legal constraints on state regulations, and in certain species-specific (for example, striped bass) management plans.

In 1982, neither state was particularly eager to enter into cooperative management plans. Maryland was so reluctant that it entered the *Tangier Sound* case on the side of Virginia and against its own citizens. The arguments raised against cooperative management had four bases. First was the difference in political philosophy between the two states: Virginia was more reluctant to impose and to accept regulation than was Maryland, but once regulatory authority was delegated, the Virginia legislature was willing to rely upon administrative expertise. Second, Maryland's economic and political base was more dependent on fisheries than was Virginia. This reduced Maryland's willingness to negotiate and to compromise. If Maryland and Virginia were to formalize a cooperative agreement through, for example, an interstate compact, some state control would be lost and a new center of power developed. The states were understandably reluctant to risk this.[20] Third, the regulatory structures in place and the implementation strategies used varied greatly between the two states; they did not agree on season, catch limits, size limits, or even legal gear. Finally, the portion of the Chesapeake Bay under Maryland jurisdiction is biologically homogeneous to a great extent. In contrast, Virginia has separate ecosystems in each major river in addition to the great difference between the mouth of the Chesapeake Bay and the areas closer to the Virginia-Maryland state line. The Bay is a marine environment in its lower reaches that blends to a brackish one as it approaches the Susquehanna. Even if the Chesapeake were within only one political jurisdiction, its size and variability would make management difficult.

In 1982, the Federal District Court in Richmond decided in favor of the Watermen's Association, finding the residency requirement to be a violation of the Commerce Clause. Virginia did not appeal, and one more area of state autonomy was reduced in favor of broader resource management objectives.[21]

SUGGESTED READING

Carter, Lief and Thomas Burke. *Reason in Law*. 7th ed. New York: Longman, 2004. An elegant and pithy explanation of how judges think, and how they *ought* to think.

Garraty, John, ed. *Quarrels That Have Shaped the Constitution*. New York: HarperCollins Children's Books, 1987. Sixteen landmark Supreme Court cases are presented in a "We were there" format. They are highly readable and give an indelible understanding of the cases. Especially relevant for environmental law are "The Dartmouth College Case," "The Steamboat Case," and "The Charles River Bridge Case."

Knight, Alfred H. *The Life of the Law*. Oxford: Oxford University Press, 1998. Unlike Garraty's book, which focuses on cases, this book addresses legal concepts. It is more opinionated and therefore a bit livelier. Readers who already have some background in legal history will particularly enjoy it.

Nice, David. *Federalism: The Politics of Intergovernmental Relations*. 2nd ed. Belmont, CA: Wadsworth Publishing Company, 1995. Academic but thorough.

Scheberle, Denise. *Federalism and Environmental Policy: Trust and the Politics of Implementation*. 2nd ed. Washington, DC: Georgetown University Press, 2004. A thorough examination of the intergovernmental aspects of program implementation in five areas: asbestos, coal, drinking water, radon, and wellhead protection

NOTES

1. For a brief introduction to the history of the development of the common law system, see Alfred Knight, *The Life of the Law* (Oxford: Oxford University Press, 1996), chapter 4.

2. The common law system is indeed *English* rather than *British*. Scotland, which joined England in 1707, has a form of law based on the continental system, a reflection of the long Scottish association with France.

3. *Martin v. Waddell*, 41 U.S. 367 (1842), at 416.

4. However, since the 1970s, enabling legislation for "second-generation regulators" that serve as both regulatory and service delivery agencies, such as the Environmental Protection Agency (EPA), which provides water quality and solid waste disposal assistance to state and local governments, is often less flexible.

5. In September 2005, Congressional debates over critical habitat provisions of the Endangered Species Act addressed this very issue: If the government restricts use of private property to protect endangered species, should the government compensate the landowner?

6. *American Textile Manufacturers Institute et al. v. Donovan, Secretary of Labor et al.*, 452 U.S. 490 (1981), at 547–548.

7. See, for example, Scalia's dissent in *Mistretta v. United States*, 488 U.S. 373 (1989).

8. *Chevron U.S.A. v. Natural Resources Defense Council*, 467 U.S. 837 (1984).

9. *Babbitt v. Sweet Home Chapter of Communities for a Greater Oregon*, 515 U.S. 687 (1995).

10. As this is written, the House of Representatives has passed a bill with dramatic revisions of the Endangered Species Act that is, at least in part, clearly a response to the decision in *Sweet Home.*

11. Examples of other federal systems are Canada, Australia, and Switzerland.

12. The following discussion is drawn from William Keefe, Henry Abraham, William Flanigan, Charles O. Jones, Morris Ogul, and John Spanier, *American Democracy: Institutions, Politics, and Policies* (Homewood, IL: Dorsey Press, 1983), chapter 2.

13. Tom Arrandale, *The Battle for Natural Resources* (Washington, DC: Congressional Quarterly, 1983), 47.

14. V. Randall Tinsley and Larry Nielsen, "Interstate Fisheries Arrangements: Application of a Pragmatic Classification Scheme for Interstate Arrangements," *Virginia Journal of Natural Resources Law*, 6 (2) (Spring 1987): 265–321.

15. Susan J. Buck and Edward Hathaway, "Designating State Natural Resource Trustees under SARA," in *Regulatory Federalism, Natural Resources and Environmental Management*, edited by Michael Hamilton, 83–94 (Washington, DC: ASPA, 1990).

16. Ray Ring, "As Washington Waffles, Western States Go Green," *High Country News*, 25 July 2005, 5–6.

17. Until 1913, senators were not even popularly elected but were instead chosen by their own state legislatures.

18. Federal mandates that require state action but provide no financing are another critical issue in discussions of federalism, but they are more an exercise of increased federal power than a cause of it.

19. *New State Ice Co. v. Liebmann*, 285 U.S. 262 (1932), at 311, Justice Brandeis dissenting.

20. Given the long-term success of the Potomac River Compact, we might expect less reluctance. However, the economic stakes are much higher in the Chesapeake Bay.

21. An article that elaborates on the *Tangier Sound* case is Susan J. Buck, "Interjurisdictional Management in Chesapeake Bay Fisheries," *Coastal Management* 16 (1988): 151–166.

CHAPTER TWO

Environmentalism in the United States

While American environmentalism is rooted in the works of philosophers such as Thoreau, preservationists such as John Muir, and politically active conservationists such as Theodore Roosevelt and Gifford Pinchot, the contemporary American emphasis on environmentalism as regulatory policy is of fairly recent origin. This chapter traces the environmental movement in the United States from the 1960s through 2005, after George W. Bush was reelected president. The first section summarizes the beginnings of the modern environmental movement in the 1960s, which culminated in the passage of the National Environmental Policy Act (NEPA) in 1970. The second section discusses the major provisions of NEPA. The third provides an overview of major legislation and environmental changes during the 1970s. The fourth and fifth sections do the same for the decades of the 1980s and 1990s. The sixth section, "Past the Millennium I: George W. Bush," identifies some environmental milestones of Bush's terms in office. The final section, "Past the Millennium II: Challenges to Old Environmentalism," briefly introduces a new perspective on environmental strategies for the future.

BEGINNINGS: THE 1960s

In the fall of 1962, Rachel Carson's book *Silent Spring* was published with little fanfare. Formerly a biologist with the U.S. Fish and Wildlife Service,

Carson had written wonderful, lyrical books about nature. This book was different: it took on the chemical industry in much the same way as Ralph Nader's *Unsafe at Any Speed* would take on the auto industry three years later. The chemical industry predicted an early demise for the book: "It is fair to hope that by March or April *Silent Spring* no longer will be an interesting conversational topic."[1] They were mistaken. The American imagination was caught by the vision of spring devoid of birdsong or katydids or bullfrogs bellowing in the night. Over forty years later, Carson's book is still an interesting conversational topic. Its effects were larger than just reducing the use of pesticides or saving the bald eagle. The book was a catalyst for the entire environmental movement because it mobilized the average American. Biocide was in everyone's backyard.

There were other forces at work in the sixties. The Vietnam War was provoking intense controversy and conflict in American society, and the related counterculture movement was prompting a romantic, back-to-nature perspective. The financial prosperity of the 1950s, coupled with increasing mobility and leisure time, regenerated interest in outdoor activities. Causes were "in," and the environment, with its appeal to health and aesthetics and its underlying antibusiness philosophy, became an enduring political value.

Looking back through the fifties and sixties, we can see the inexorable building of American consciousness toward the first Earth Day in 1970. A New York case, *Scenic Hudson Preservation Conference v. Federal Power Commission* (1955), for the first time admitted scenic and recreational criteria in legal actions. In 1963, the Clean Air Act authorized federal hearings on *potential* air pollution problems; in 1964, the Wilderness Act set aside tracts of land and barred them permanently from development. In 1966, an early version of the Endangered Species Act was passed, and in 1968, the spectacular American Apollo space flight that circled the globe produced moving photographs of a fragile planet.

Early in 1969, a major "trigger event" shocked the American public into demanding immediate action to protect the environment. On January 28, 1969, Union Oil Company's Platform A off the coast of California began to disgorge oil. Over an eleven-day period, 235,000 gallons of crude oil spread out, ruining forty miles of Santa Barbara's beautiful Pacific beaches. Thousands of birds and mammals died; one dramatic photograph showed an oil-soaked bird surrounded by debris and gazing in a doomed stupor over the surf. The spill became a national event, searing the public conscience with images of ruined water and pathetic, dying animals. Five months later, industrial debris and oil in the Cuyahoga River in Ohio caught fire. One of President Nixon's aides wrote that the political mood in Washington engendered by the public outcry could only be captured by the word *hysteria*. On January 1, 1970, President Nixon signed the National Environmental Policy Act (NEPA), arguably one of the most important pieces of environmental legislation in the century. It presented a national policy that became a model statute for the states and the United Nations. In the Environmental Impact Statement (EIS), NEPA created a venue for citizens and interest groups to affect national environmental policy from planning through implementation.

NATIONAL ENVIRONMENTAL POLICY ACT (NEPA)

Congress passed a bill with goals that were lofty but amazingly imprecise for a law with no agency to implement it. NEPA's purpose was spelled out in Section 2:

> To declare a national policy which will encourage productive and enjoyable harmony between man and his environment; to promote efforts which will prevent or eliminate damage to the environment and biosphere and stimulate the health and welfare of man; to enrich the understanding of the ecological systems and natural resources important to the Nation; and to establish a Council on Environmental Quality.[2]

NEPA's greatest impact has come from both the universal federal mandate to take environmental concerns into account and the action-forcing procedures exemplified by the EIS requirement. The first objective of NEPA was to provide a clear mandate for all federal agencies, regardless of their mission or position within the government, "to create and maintain conditions under which man and nature can exist in productive harmony."[3] There were no exemptions for any federal agency; all were expected to comply and to cooperate with other agencies. The second objective of the act was to establish action-forcing procedures for the federal agencies. The most influential provision was the requirement that agencies write an Environmental Impact Statement (EIS) for all federal projects and to circulate the statements to local and state governments and to other federal agencies for their comments.[4] The EIS requirement exploded into a powerful weapon used by citizen lobbies to stop or delay numerous projects.

The first court decision to examine the underlying intent of NEPA and the EIS requirement was *Calvert Cliffs Coordinating Committee, Inc. v. United States Atomic Energy Commission* (1971).[5] This case arose when the United States Atomic Energy Commission (AEC) issued rules governing the granting of construction and licensing permits for nuclear power plants. The AEC claimed that its rules complied with the procedural requirements of NEPA. However, the Calvert Cliffs Coordinating Committee, a Maryland public interest group trying to halt the licensing of a partially constructed nuclear plant on the Chesapeake Bay, sued on the basis that the AEC had not adequately considered environmental issues when the rules were promulgated.

One of the most important aspects of Judge Skelly Wright's decision was the distinction he drew between the goals laid out in NEPA's Section 101 (42 U.S.C. 4331) and the procedural requirements of Section 102 (42 U.S.C. 4332), which contains the EIS provision. Section 101, he wrote, provided a broad, substantive mandate to all federal agencies to "use all practicable means and measures" to protect the environment. Judge Wright found this mandate to be flexible, giving wide discretionary powers to the agencies. In contrast, he found the procedural requirements of Section 102 to be very strict, compelling agencies to consider environmental factors,

> to the fullest extent possible. . . . We must stress as forcefully as possible that this language does not provide an escape hatch for footdragging agencies; it does not make NEPA's procedural requirements somehow "discretionary." Congress did not intend the Act to be such a paper tiger. Indeed, the requirement of environmental consideration "to the fullest extent possible" sets a high standard for the agencies, a standard which must be rigorously enforced by the reviewing courts.[6]

The importance of this ruling can hardly be overestimated. By the time the EIS issue reached the U.S. Supreme Court, Judge Wright's opinion had been cited as precedent over 200 times. The early legal sophistication of the environmental lobbies is rooted in their response to the power of the EIS. NEPA changed from a bill viewed by most of its proponents as a "motherhood and apple pie" measure to an act that delayed the B-1 bomber and the

Alaska oil pipeline. Major environmental groups and citizen plaintiffs have used NEPA and the EIS to force federal agencies to consider all environmental factors when any federal action, however loosely defined, is contemplated. In 2005, even in the aftermath of 9/11, a proposed Navy Outlying Landing Field in Washington and Beaufort counties in North Carolina was halted by the federal district court for failing to provide an adequate EIS.[7]

Another objective of NEPA was the creation of the Council on Environmental Quality (CEQ).[8] This council of three members appointed by the president is subject to Senate confirmation and has statutory obligations such as data collection and an annual report to the president that forms the basis of *The President's Annual Report on Environmental Quality*. President Reagan tried to abolish the CEQ early in his first administration but was thwarted by the NEPA requirement for the Council. The election of Democrat Bill Clinton twelve years later did not presage a return to the glory days of the Carter administration when the CEQ was held in high regard. Indeed, early in his administration, Clinton proposed eliminating the CEQ and replacing it with an environmental policy adviser. This was not done, and the CEQ has regained some staff, but "it has long ceased to be a major player in White House politics."[9] However, the CEQ still wields some power in its oversight of the EIS process. For example, in 1999, the CEQ approved a Forest Service request to bypass NEPA requirements for emergency timber clean-up following severe storms in the Boundary Waters Canoe Wilderness in Minnesota.[10]

NEPA is largely administered by the Environmental Protection Agency (EPA). In 1970, President Nixon created EPA by executive order. Nixon's advisers saw EPA as a coordinating agency that would cut across existing agency lines to provide a coherent national policy for the environment. However, EPA's responsibilities have gone far beyond NEPA. EPA has complete or partial jurisdiction over air pollution, water pollution, drinking water contamination, hazardous waste disposal, pesticides, radiation, and toxic substances. It covers thirteen major environmental laws, portions of many more, and participates in the implementation of many laws administered by other agencies at both the national and state levels.

EPA is unique in its organization: all other regulatory agencies (as opposed to regulatory commissions that are not headed by a single political appointee) are housed administratively in a cabinet-level department, such as the departments of the Interior or Agriculture. The EPA administrator is appointed by the president and oversees the Washington staff and ten regional offices. EPA is relatively independent and has control over its own information sources. Bureaucratic theory supports the prediction that such a mega-agency would fall victim to interagency battles for resources. EPA does not have an exclusive advocate in the cabinet; it regulates powerful businesses, and its supporting constituencies must spread their resources across many other agencies. It has regulatory responsibility for too many statutes, because these statutes address a wide range of technical issues that may contain incompatible goals. Added to this are a chronic shortage of staff and funding, impossible legislative timetables and deadlines, and an exponential increase in new technologies and chemicals. Given all these constraints, EPA does a remarkable job.[11]

Although most Western nations have a cabinet-level environmental department, it is doubtful that EPA will ever return to the halcyon days of cabinet-status possibilities. In 1993, President Clinton proposed elevating EPA but could not get the bill through the House of Representatives. The agency is confronted with "a profound legislative distrust permeating almost all the Agency's congressional relationships,"[12] and policy implementation at the agency is often driven by the need to comply with court orders.[13] To succeed in meeting its many congressional mandates, EPA needs a massive infusion of resources, which, given its poor record in meeting statutory deadlines and its lack of success with such programs as Superfund, seems unlikely.

EPA is caught in the political crossfire between presidential expectations and administrative responsibilities: the George W. Bush White House has strong policy preferences that are often at odds with scientific opinion and EPA's statutory obligations.[14] By 2005, the Bush administration had apparently won. Eric Schaeffer, former director of EPA's Office of Regulatory Enforcement, said EPA was becoming an "orphan" in the Bush Administration: "'Under Clinton and [George H. W.] Bush, it had a fair amount of independence,' says Schaeffer. . . . Now, he says, 'the White House basically runs the EPA.'"[15]

THE ENVIRONMENTAL DECADE: THE 1970s

The 1970s have been called the environmental decade. Major pieces of legislation were put into place during the ten-year period between NEPA and the first Reagan administration. In 1970, the Resource Recovery Act (Solid Waste Disposal Act) was passed, the Clean Air Act was amended, and EPA was established. The first Earth Day, April 22, 1970, was celebrated by millions of Americans who were also celebrating the apparent end to American involvement in Vietnam. In 1971, Barry Commoner published *The Closing Circle*, an influential examination of the environmental crises, and the Alaska Native Claims Settlement Act authorized federal nomination of "national interest lands." In 1972, the Federal Water Pollution Control Act, the Federal Environmental Pesticide Control Act (a major amendment to the Federal Insecticide, Fungicide, and Rodenticide Act of 1947), the Marine Protection, Research and Sanctuaries Act, and the Coastal Zone Management Act were all passed. After this point, legislation was more often refined than initiated; the last major legislative achievement of the decade was the flawed Comprehensive Environmental Response, Compensation, and Liability Act (CERCLA or Superfund, 1980).

Nonlegislative landmarks of the 1970s included the United Nations Conference on the Human Environment, which led to the United Nations Environmental Programme, and publication of *Limits to Growth* by the Club of Rome and *Small Is Beautiful* by English economist E. F. Schumacher. However, the environmental accomplishments of the seventies were over-shadowed by the tragedies of Love Canal (1977) and Three Mile Island (1979), and by the 1973 oil crisis. In October 1973, the Organization of Petroleum Exporting Countries (OPEC) voted to cut oil production by 5 percent, and Saudi Arabia halted its oil exports to the United States, threatening to maintain the embargo until the Nixon administration changed its pro-Israel stance. Fuel prices at the gas pump shot up, and Americans old enough to have been driving in 1973 remember long lines and restrictions on gasoline purchases. The "crisis" continued in one form or another through the Ford and Carter administrations; even when petroleum products were reasonably plentiful, the fear of a recurrence drove federal energy policy. Reagan was committed to deregulation even in energy policy, believing that a free market and regulatory relief would be most beneficial for the beleaguered energy industry. This brought his administration into direct conflict with environmentalists as he opened, or proposed to open, federal lands and the outer continental shelf to oil exploration.

ENVIRONMENTAL ACTION IN THE 1980s

As with many of Reagan's policies, what was perhaps bad for the environment was good for the environmental movement. During the seventies, environmental concerns became routinized and the dramatic events of the sixties faded from public memory. In the Reagan administration, scandals in EPA under Anne Gorsuch Burford and the antienvironmental stance of Reagan's Secretary of the Interior James Watt reignited general public concern and mobilized renewed support for environmental activists and their causes. During Burford's administration, EPA became politicized, or at least it was perceived to be politicized, causing damage to its effectiveness with both the regulated industries and the Congress, neither of which now trusted EPA's findings or accepted its decisions.

Despite these problems, several important pieces of legislation were passed or renewed during Reagan's tenure. In 1986, Superfund was reauthorized in the Superfund Amendment and Reauthorization Act (SARA). SARA did more than simply continue the 1980 Superfund legislation. It added, among other provisions, a community right-to-know provision that required companies to notify local communities about the location, nature, and volume of certain hazardous materials within their jurisdictions.

Reagan's heir in the White House, George H. W. Bush, promised to be the environmental president. In retrospect, this promise was largely a campaign decision triggered by national events such as the forest fire in Yellowstone National Park.[16] Early signs were encouraging as he appointed William Reilly, former president of the World Wildlife Fund and Conservation Foundation, to head EPA. His choice of Michael Deland, former director of EPA's Region I office in Boston, as chairman of the CEQ was also widely supported by the environmental community. However, with the notable exception of William Reilly, most Bush appointees favored regulatory reform over strong environmental programs. Bush's other nominations to environmental positions were not as well received. For example, James Cason, Bush's nominee to head the Forest Service, was not confirmed by the Senate because of charges he was biased toward mining and oil interests, and the appointment of Manuel Lujan from New Mexico as Secretary of the Interior sent a strong signal that it would be business as usual in the West. The Reagan legacy of conservative judicial appointments was beginning to roll back environmental gains, and a national economic slump caused many voters to question the cost of environmental enforcement.[17]

The optimism of environmentalists in 1990 soon faded. Vice President Dan Quayle chaired the White House Council on Competitiveness, a new organization used to weaken environmental regulations by imposing stringent cost-effectiveness criteria. Although serious environmental issues, such as wetlands protection and the 1989 *Exxon Valdez* spill in Alaska's Prince William Sound, arose during the Bush administration, perhaps the most critical problem came from the clash of environmental values and economic growth posed by the Endangered Species Act (ESA). The collision between the timber industry and the northern spotted owl occurred on George Bush's watch. In 1989, the Secretary of the Interior listed the spotted owl as an endangered species, raising the ire of loggers who saw old growth forests not as habitat but as economically unproductive timber ripe for harvest. To defend his administration's decision to log in old growth forests, Bush convened the "God Squad," the special panel empowered to loosen ESA restrictions on a case-by-case basis, but only a few sales survived the hearings, and even those were cancelled when Clinton became president.

In his efforts to promote environmentalism, Bush was partly hampered by budget concerns; perhaps this is one reason he did little to prove that his pro-environment campaign position was more than just political rhetoric. With the federal deficit perceived by a majority of Americans as the most severe problem facing the country, and energy sources increasingly uncertain, generous environmental budgets were unlikely. As a good conservative, Bush favored market solutions to environmental problems and thus encountered opposition for his new programs from a largely Democratic Congress. Although he seemed to prefer regulatory reform over deregulation,[18] budgetary constraints inhibited the flexibility of either the president or the Congress to commit needed resources.

The environmental high point of Bush's presidency was passage of the 1990 Clean Air Act Amendments, which strengthened and extended the Clean Air Act. Bush's leadership was essential for their passage. This was the only major environmental legislation passed during his term, and in the last two years of his term, many environmental laws were weakened or themselves endangered. For example, despite Bush's campaign promise of "no net loss of wetlands," a new federal wetlands manual—written with the help of Quayle's Council on Competitiveness—redefined wetlands to permit some destruction.

By the end of the 1992 presidential campaign, public opinion polls showed a high disapproval rating for Bush's record on the environment. During 1991 and 1992, Bush had opposed the reauthorization of most major environmental laws. This had the effect of delaying reauthorization of the Clean Water Act, the Resource Conservation and Recovery Act, and the Endangered Species Act, which pushed the reauthorization fights into the Clinton administration.[19]

SEALING THE CENTURY: THE 1990s

Clinton and Gore promised to strengthen environmental policies, and "green" voters provided overwhelming support.[20] The administration got off to a strong start. Just as Bush's appointment of William Reilly seemed auspicious, Clinton's appointment of Bruce Babbitt as Secretary of the Interior was greeted with quiet jubilation by environmentalists. Then, in April, 1993, Clinton signed the Biodiversity Convention, which had opened for signature at the Rio Conference; however, the convention stalled in the Senate Foreign Relations Committee and never came to a vote.[21] Soon other problems arose: Clinton backed down from his support for Babbitt's proposed increase in public lands grazing fees,[22] and he also supported the North American Free Trade Agreement (NAFTA), seen by many environmentalists as a license to take pollution across the border into Mexico rather than stopping it in American territory.

After the midterm elections of 1994, Clinton was hampered by a recalcitrant Congress. In the Senate, majority leader Bob Dole had one eye on his presidential campaign, while the House, under the leadership of Speaker Newt Gingrich, was interested primarily in passing its "Contract with America." The Republicans targeted environmental regulation as antigrowth. However, very few of the Republican proposals were actually passed; the most impressive were a moratorium on listing new endangered species and a rider that opened northwest forests to salvage logging.[23] Clinton relied on his veto power to stop Republican proposals that he felt would harm the environment. In 1995, he vetoed an appropriations bill that contained dramatic cuts in the Park Service budget, and in 1999 he vetoed another budget bill that did not include full funding for several environmental programs.

Clinton inherited more than just the reauthorization fights from the Bush years. He was also left with the extremely volatile issue of environmental justice (also called environmental equity): the problem that locally undesirable land uses (LULUs) are sited disproportionately in low income and minority communities.[24] To respond to these and related issues, President Clinton issued Executive Order 12898, requiring each federal agency to identify and address, "as appropriate, disproportionately high and adverse human health or environmental effects of its programs, policies, and activities on minority populations and low-income populations."[25] This executive order provided neither funding nor enforcement language, so it is largely a paper tiger, albeit one with symbolic significance.

Clinton's second term did not accomplish any milestone legislation, but he did use the administrative regulatory process to tighten existing environmental standards.[26] The most dramatic actions were a flurry of activity in the final year of his presidency, when Clinton used his executive powers to create nineteen new national monuments and to enlarge three existing ones. However, the picture of Clinton's presidency is framed by two international failures. At the beginning was the failure to ratify the Biodiversity Convention, and at the end was America's failure to participate in the Kyoto Protocol.

PAST THE MILLENNIUM I: GEORGE W. BUSH

George W. Bush, elected in 2000, has not been a friend to the environment.[27] Almost immediately he renounced the Kyoto Protocol on climate change; it went into effect without American participation in 2004 when Russia acceded to the treaty. Bush moved quickly to limit the impact of Clinton's last-minute regulatory changes and executive orders, For example, EPA suspended Clinton's new, lower arsenic standards (although these were eventually reinstated), and snowmobile restrictions in Yellowstone National Park were lifted. The president also sent a clear message with his new political appointments. Republicans have traditionally favored energy and mining interests, but the political connections between the Bush administration and those interests have been unprecedented in recent history. Bush comes from a Texas oil family, and his vice president, Dick Cheney, had been head of Halliburton, an oil exploration company. Other sectors of corporate America have also been well represented in the White House: the White House chief of staff had been the chief lobbyist for General Motors, and the new chairman of the CEQ had represented industry in fights with EPA over toxic waste cleanup.[28] This influence has extended throughout Bush's presidency. For example, in June 2005, the British newspaper *The Guardian* reported that ExxonMobil had an "active involvement" in the president's decisions on climate change policy.[29]

The 9/11 disaster gave an enormous advantage to the energy and mining interests, which already had substantial presidential support. For example, approvals for permits to drill for oil and gas on public land increased 74 percent from 2001 to 2004.[30] In April 2005, Bush advocated building new nuclear plants, streamlining nuclear licensing procedures, and placing new oil refineries on obsolete military bases.[31] His budget proposal requested $6.7 billion in tax breaks for the energy industry.[32] Other agencies within the federal government have taken advantage of the focus on national security to get around environmental regulations. For example, in 2003 the Pentagon received broad exemptions from many environmental laws, including the Endangered Species Act, Marine Mammal Protection Act, Clean Air Act, and Superfund.[33] Further changes, proposed in May 2005, would allow additional air pollution from training exercises, cap financial liability under Superfund, and exempt explosives, weapon materials, and munitions from "solid waste" definitions.[34] Bush has also aimed the budget guns at EPA. In FY2001, the EPA budget was $7,832,212,000, with a workforce of 18,000; the requested budget for FY2004 was 7,626,537,000 for a workforce of 17,850, a budget reduction of 3 percent.[35] This may not seem to be dramatic change, but since 9/11, EPA has been given new responsibilities for homeland security issues, so the actual impact of loss of funding for pre-9/11 programs is substantial.

What distinguishes the Bush administration from its predecessors is its masterful use of the courts and administrative process to achieve environmental goals. To give just one example: Chinook salmon and delta smelt are protected under the Endangered Species Act. Between 1992 and 1994, the state of California withheld irrigation water from farmers near Bakersfield in order to protect the fish. Local farmers sued the federal government under the takings clause of the Fifth Amendment, and in 2003, the federal claims court awarded them $14 million plus interest. The Bush administration did not appeal (leaving the claims court decision as precedent) and instead settled the case for $16.7 million.[36] By not appealing, the administration has given the green light to similar suits in the Klamath Irrigation District and elsewhere.

Sometimes the strategies are more subtle. In January 2005, EPA issued new rules that allow owners of Concentrated Animal Feeding Operations (CAFOs) to sign up for voluntary air pollution monitoring studies; this then immunizes them from prosecution for violations of the Clean Air Act.[37] In June 2005, EPA and the Army Corps of Engineers issued a permit to dump mine tailings into Lower Slate Lake near Juneau, Alaska.[38] Although the 1972 Clean Water Act prohibits dumping mine waste into streams and lakes, in 2002 EPA had changed the definition of chemically processed mine "waste" to "fill" and set up a permit system for fill to be discharged into lakes. Other tactics to achieve policy goals involve timing as well as substance. For example, on Christmas Eve 2002, the Department of the Interior released rules to allow states to develop new roads from existing trails and streambeds, thus removing the areas from potential wilderness designation.[39] The timing of this release was not accidental; the administration often releases controversial announcements on Fridays and during holiday weeks.[40]

The Bush administration is also under fire for pressuring scientists to change data or to modify their conclusions. These accusations are not unique to the current Bush administration: in 1980, the congressional testimony of NASA scientist James Hansen was edited by the White House Office of Management and Budget (OMB) to downplay the evidence of global warming.[41] However, in George W. Bush's administration, evidence is mounting of a general disdain for scientific autonomy and accuracy. As early as July 2003, former administrators were accusing the administration of distorting scientific evidence on climate change.[42] In February 2004, sixty-two senior scientists (including several Nobel laureates) released a statement that charged "widespread and unprecedented 'manipulation of the process through which science enters into its decisions.'"[43] The Union of Concerned Scientists followed up with two reports that found (1) a "well-established pattern of suppressions and distortion of scientific findings by high-ranking Bush administration political appointees across numerous federal agencies"; (2) efforts to manipulate the scientific advisory system; (3) censorship of government scientists; and (4) that "the scope and scale of the abuse of science by the Bush administration are unprecedented."[44]

Some 44 percent of U.S. Fish and Wildlife Service science professionals report they have been ordered to suppress information; 20 percent have been "directed to inappropriately exclude or alter technical information."[45] Scientists at the National Oceanic & Atmospheric Administration Fisheries Service have similar experiences: 37 percent have suppressed information and 24 percent have been told to change data. Over half have knowledge of inappropriate commercial and political influence on fisheries decisions.[46] Partly as a result, some scientists are leaving federal service. For example, in 2005, two long-term BLM scientists resigned, in part, over frustrations with BLM's rewriting of a report on revised grazing regulations.[47]

As this is written, George W. Bush has more than three years left in his second term. He has pulled the United States out of the Kyoto process (see chapter 7), and his new energy bill will apparently have almost everything he wanted except authorization to drill in the Arctic National Wildlife Refuge (ANWR). His popularity in the polls has dropped precipitously, but with a Republican Congress, gasoline prices at a historic high, economic uncertainty, and terrorist attacks around the globe, he is likely to be able to continue on the pro-industry path that has characterized his first five years in office, unless the midterm elections in 2006 change congressional dynamics.

PAST THE MILLENNIUM II: CHALLENGES TO OLD ENVIRONMENTALISM

In 2004, as climate change moved to the forefront of environmental concerns, Michael Shellenberger and Ted Nordhaus released their controversial essay "The Death of Environmentalism."[48] This is a persuasive essay that covers old ground: by failing to define the problem of climate change properly as, perhaps, an issue of global trade or poverty or energy efficiency, American environmentalists are missing the true root causes and therefore also miss potentially viable solutions.[49] The authors' argument is that the economic and political strategies that have worked since the 1970s have failed to adjust to the changed conditions of the twenty-first century. Trying to solve the climate change problem by simply passing legislation to reduce carbon emissions will not work, they say, because the obstacles to passing or implementing such legislation (see chapter 3) must be addressed before legislation is passed. And these obstacles are preceded by other obstacles that are not amenable to national legislation, such as treaty obligations or dependence on fossil fuels. Those obstacles are in turn preceded by other obstacles that are. . . . It is an argument of infinite regression.

"The Death of Environmentalism" provides a provocative challenge to a well-entrenched environmental community that has seen many successes over the past hundred years. The instinctive reaction of the mainstream environmental community was like a hedgehog: roll into a ball to protect vital organs and show only prickles to the outside world. Movements for policy change face many resource constraints, and the environmental community may need to develop new goals and benchmarks for success. However they choose to confront the challenges of the next century, environment managers and activists may want to model the ecosystems they try to preserve by adapting and evolving to meet new challenges.

SUGGESTED READING

Clark, Ray, and Larry Canter, eds. *Environmental Policy and NEPA: Past, Present, and Future.* Boca Raton, FL: CRC Press, 1997. Clark is the former associate director of the CEQ; Canter is professor emeritus at the University of Oklahoma and an expert on Environmental Impact Assessments. This collection of essays examines the origins, impact, and future possibilities of NEPA.

Clarke, Jeanne Nienaber, and Daniel McCool. *Staking Out the Terrain: Power Differentials among Natural Resource Management Agencies.* Albany: State University of New York Press, 1985. An excellent study of bureaucratic behavior of seven main federal resource agencies (Army Corps of Engineers, Forest Service, Bureau of Reclamation, Park Service, and the Fish and Wildlife Service). The authors develop a useful model of bureaucratic power that is based on the ability of agencies to expand resources and their jurisdictions.

Kaufman, Herbert. *The Forest Ranger: A Study in Administrative Behavior.* Baltimore: Johns Hopkins University Press, 1967. The classic study of socialization of professionals into the bureaucratic norms of the Forest Service.

Nash, Roderick. *American Environmentalism: Readings in Conservation History.* 3rd ed. New York: McGraw-Hill, 1990. Superb collection of original documents in American conservation history with clear introductory comments. Be sure to get the third edition, as the first two are not edited as crisply.

Vig, Norman, and Michael Kraft, eds. *Environmental Policy: New Directions for the Twenty-First Century.* 6th ed. Washington, DC: CQ Press, 2006. An excellent collection of essays by knowledgeable scholars on the changes facing American political institutions in both the domestic and international arenas.

Vogel, David. "The Politics of the Environment, 1970–1987: A Big Agenda." *Wilson Quarterly* 11(4) (Autumn 1987): 51–68. A graceful summary of the political influences on major environmental actions during the seventies and eighties.

NOTES

1. Ted Williams, "'Silent Spring' Revisited," *Modern Maturity*, October–November 1987, 48.

2. 42 U.S.C. §4321.

3. 42 U.S.C. § 4321(a).

4. Agencies were also required to consider qualitative information, to protect the global environment "where consistent with the foreign policy of the United States," and deliberately to seek the least damaging alternatives. This latter provision has conflicted with efforts of presidents from Reagan to G. W. Bush to impose

cost-benefit analysis on environmental regulations. (The central conflicts between cost-benefit analysis and environmental regulation and protection are twofold: first, differing political and statutory objectives, and second, technical difficulties. A thorough discussion of these issues is found in Phillip J. Cooper, *Public Law and Public Administration*, 3rd ed. [(Itasca, IL: Peacock, 2000)], 354–359.) The act also stipulated that the social sciences were to be integrated into the decision processes; no longer were relatively simple physical data sufficient. This provision is still not fully utilized.

5. *Calvert Cliffs Coordinating Committee, Inc. v. United States Atomic Energy Commission* (1971), 449 F. 2d 1109 (D.C. Cir.).

6. *Calvert Cliffs*, at 1114.

7. The OLF would overfly Cape Lookout National Seashore and four national wildlife refuges.

8. The CEQ website is http://www.whitehouse.gov.ceq. An aside: the website for the NEPA Task Force, convened by CEQ in 2002, is http://ceq.eh.doe.gov/ntf/. I have been unable to discover why the task force website should be part of the Department of Energy site, but conspiracy theorists could have a field day with this.

9. Walter A. Rosenbaum, *Environmental Politics and Policy*, 6th ed. (Washington, DC: CQ Press, 2005), 89.

10. Jacqueline Vaughn Switzer, *Environmental Politics: Domestic and Global Dimensions.* (Belmont CA: Thomson/Wadsworth, 2004), 126–127.

11. For a thorough, if depressing, assessment of EPA's missions and resources, see Walter A. Rosenbaum, *Environmental Politics and Policy*, 6th ed. (Washington, DC: CQ Press, 2005), 81–88. See also Walter A. Rosenbaum, "Improving Environmental Regulation at the EPA: The Challenge in Balancing Politics, Policy, and Science," in *Environmental Policy: New Directions for the Twenty-First Century*, 6th ed., edited by Norman Vig and Michael Kraft (Washington, DC: CQ Press, 2006), 169–192.

12. Walter A. Rosenbaum, *Environmental Politics and Policy*, 3rd. ed. (Washington, DC: CQ Press, 1995), 115.

13. Rosemary O'Leary, *Environmental Change: Federal Courts and the EPA* (Philadelphia: Temple University Press, 1993).

14. For a trenchant discussion of EPA's current problems, see Walter A. Rosenbaum, "Improving Environmental Regulation at the EPA," in *Environmental Policy: New Directions for the Twenty-First Century*, 6th ed., edited by Norman Vig and Michael Kraft (Washington, DC: CQ Press, 2006), 169–192.

15. Laura Paskus, "Bush's Second-Term Shake-ups," *High Country News*, 7 February 2005, 3.

16. Norman Vig, "Presidential Leadership and the Environment: From Reagan and Bush to Clinton," in *Environmental Policy in the 1990s*, 2nd ed., edited by Norman Vig and Michael Kraft (Washington, DC: CQ Press, 1994), 80.

17. Nancy Kubasek and Gary Silverman, *Environmental Law*, 5th ed. (Upper Saddle River NJ: Pearson Prentice Hall, 2005), 138–139.

18. One might argue that not much remained to deregulate, leaving only reform as an alternative anyway.

19. Norman Vig, "Presidential Leadership and the Environment: From Reagan and Bush to Clinton," in *Environmental Policy in the 1990s*, 2nd ed., edited by Norman Vig and Michael Kraft (Washington, DC: CQ Press, 1994), 86.

20. An excellent discussion of the Clinton presidency and the early years of George W. Bush's term is found in Norman Vig, "Presidential Leadership and the Environment," in *Environmental Policy: New Directions for the Twenty-First Century,* edited by Norman Vig and Michael Kraft (Washington, DC: CQ Press, 2003), 103–125.

21. Reluctance to ratify the Biodiversity Convention is connected to ESA reauthorization. The convention is modeled in part on the ESA, and ratification would provide a federal treaty obligation to protect endangered species and habitats in ways that closely parallel the ESA. Conservatives have long argued that the ESA infringes on states' rights. If they were to be successful in passing legislation to weaken the ESA, the precedent set in *Missouri v. Holland* (see chapter 6) might undo their efforts.

22. This is a battle that no one ever wins, despite the fact that public-land grazing fees are substantially below market value, and federal grazing programs are losing money every year. The problem is, as always, politics. Western legislators have enormous incentives to keep fees low, and no members of Congress care enough to risk alienating western colleagues and perhaps to lose votes for their own bills.

23. Kubasek and Silverman, *Environmental Law*, 143.

24. The Bush administration had, to its credit, tackled this thorny issue as early as 1990, when William Reilly appointed an EPA task force to investigate charges of inequity. It issued a report in 1992 that confirmed the possibility of discriminatory decision making (see USEPA, Office of Policy, Planning and Evaluation, *Environmental Equity: Reducing Risk for All Communities, Vol. 1: Workgroup Report to the Administrator* (Washington, DC: EPA, June 1992), cited in Walter A. Rosenbaum, *Environmental Politics and Policy*, 3rd ed. (Washington, DC: CQ Press, 1995), 182, n. 58.

25. 59 FR 7629, 16 February 1994 (signed 11 February 1994).

26. Norman Vig, "Presidential Leadership and the Environment," in *Environmental Policy: New Directions for the Twenty-First Century*, edited by Norman Vig and Michael Kraft (Washington, DC: CQ Press, 2003), 114.

27. Bush's record during his first administration was so clearly prodevelopment that, in the second election, some westerners who invariably vote Republican actually changed their coats to vote with Democratic environmentalists to

protect the federal lands on which they hunt and fish. Writing in *High Country News*, Tom Reed (a self-avowed registered Republican, lifelong westerner, and founding member of Backcountry Hunters and Anglers) writes that he was seeing "Sportsmen Against Bush" bumper stickers during the election. "They are concluding that this president has done more damage to our wildlife heritage than any other president, Republican or Democrat, in the history of modern wildlife management." Tom Reed, "Hunting: It's Not About the Gun," *High Country News*,11 October 2004, 19.

28. Norman Vig, "Presidential Leadership and the Environment," in *Environmental Policy: New Directions for the Twenty-First Century,* edited by Norman Vig and Michael Kraft (Washington, DC: CQ Press, 2003), 117.

29. John Vidal, "Revealed: How Oil Giant Influenced Bush," *Guardian* [Manchester], 8 June 2005. http://www.guardian.co.uk/international/story/0,,1501632,00.html (accessed 2 July 2005).

30. Beth Daley, "On Energy and Environment, a Vast Divide," *Boston Globe*, 19 October 2004, A. 20.

31. Laura Paskus, "Congress Touts 'Green Energy,' but Bill Is Black and Blue," *High Country News*, 16 May 2005, 2.

32. Paskus, "Congress Touts 'Green Energy.'"

33. Louis Bayard, Ryan Cree, Barbara Elkus, Betsy Loyless, Mary Minette, and Chuck Porcari, eds., *2003 National Environmental Scorecard*, (Washington, DC: League of Conservation Voters, February 2004), 12–16.

34. Michael Janofsky, "Pentagon Is Asking Congress to Loosen Environmental Laws," *New York Times*, 11 May 2005, A16.

35. http://www.epa.gov/history/org/resources/budget.htm.

36. Matt Jenkins, "The Public Pays to Keep Water in a River," *High Country News*, 4 April 2005, 6.

37. "Follow-up," *High Country News*, 7 February 2005, 3. See also the Weston A. Price Foundation Action Alert at http://www.westonaprice.org/federalupdate/aa2005/actionalert_021005.html.

38. Lower Slate Lake is in the Tongass National Forest. The gold mine will endanger the entire Berners Bay watershed. Earthworks. "Gold Mine to Dump Mine Waste in Pristine Alaskan Lake," *Yubanet*, 24 June 2005, http://yubanet.com/artman/publish/printer_22140.shtml (accessed 29 July 2005).

39. Jennifer Hattam, "Highway Robbers: Make-Believe Roads Threaten Real Wilderness," *Sierra*, July/August 2003, 11; "Casualty Friday," Sierra, July/August 2003, 13.

40. "Casualty Friday," 13.

41. Walter Rosenbaum, *Environmental Politics and Policy*, 5th ed. (Washington, DC: CQ Press, 2002), 44–46.

42. Jeremy Symons, "How Bush and Co. Obscure the Science," *Washington Post*, 13 July 2003, B4. Symons was a climate policy advisor in EPA.

43. Union of Concerned Scientists, "Scientific Integrity in Policy Making," http://www.ucsusa.org/global_environment/rsi/page.cfm?page ID=1641 (accessed 23 July 2005).

44. Union of Concerned Scientists, "Scientific Integrity." Scientific abuses include deleting science-based recommendations on endangered salmon, suppressing information on the effects of mercury, withholding "an analysis of the benefits of a bipartisan alternative to President Bush's Clear Skies Act," suppressing research on airborne bacteria from farm waste, and replacing scientists recommended by staff to serve on a Lead Poisoning Prevention Panel "by appointees with financial ties to the lead industry." See Union of Concerned Scientists, "Specific Examples of the Abuse of Science," http://www.ucsusa.org/global_environment/rsi/page.cfm?page ID=1398 (accessed 23 July 2005). See also J. M. McCord, "'Sound Science' in Doubt at Yucca Mountain," *High Country News*, 18 April 2005, 3.

45. Union of Concerned Scientists, "U. S . Fish & Wildlife Service Survey Summary" (February 2005), http://www.ucsusa.org/global_environment/rsi/page.cfm?page ID=1601 (accessed 23 July 2005). See also the story of fisheries scientist Mike Kelly in Laura Paskus, "'Sound Science' Goes Sour," *High Country News*, 23 June 2003), 7–12.

46. Union of Concerned Scientists, "Summary of National Oceanic & Atmospheric Administration Scientist Survey," http://www.ucsusa.org/global_environment/ rsi/page.cfm?page ID=1804 (accessed 23 July 2005).

47. Erick Campbell, who had worked for BLM for thirty years, resigned because "the Bush administration is just rolling back any advances made in the last 30 years. We are going back to the 19th century." Bill Brooks, a 25-year veteran, had similar concerns. The new rules, which BLM acknowledges are intended to support ranchers, require lengthy, detailed, and expensive monitoring before BLM can require ranchers to remove cattle to protect range health. Ranchers will also have property rights in range improvements; earlier regulations gave ownership of fencing, wells, and other improvements to the federal government. (Under common law, permanent improvements made by a tenant, such as wells and roads, are the property of the owner, while movable improvements can be taken by the lessee when the lease expires. This had also been the rule for BLM lands.) To be fair, however, some of the new rules show promise for range improvement; for example, ranchers can leave allotments idle indefinitely without losing their permits, and the rangeland health standards remain the tougher standards put in place under Clinton. (Tony Davis, "New Grazing Rules Ride on Doctored Science: Veteran Scientists Leave the BLM in Frustration," *High Country News*, 25 July 2005, 3.)

48. http://www.thebreakthrough.org/images/Death_of_Environmentalism.pdf. This essay was first made public at a meeting of the Environmental Grantmakers Association in October 2004.

49. For a classic article that makes a similar point, see Mark Sagoff's brilliant essay on category mistakes: "At the Shrine of Our Lady of Fatima *or* Why Political Questions Are Not All Economic," in *Environmental Ethics: Readings in Theory and Applications*, edited by L. P. Pojman (Boston, MA: James and Bartlett, 1994), 443–450.

CHAPTER THREE

The Public Policy Process

Beloved by social scientists, models of how the world works are only approximations at best. Public policy process models are no better—and no worse. The process described in this chapter appears to be elegant and linear, but be forewarned that public policy is in reality a complex, confused, and confusing Rube Goldberg device into which an infinite variety of ingredients are poured and out of which comes . . . a surprise.

Still, as a heuristic device, a linear description of public policy can be helpful. The four types of public policy and their relationship to environmental policy are discussed in the first section of this chapter. The remainder of the chapter examines the policy process, beginning with the second section, which uses the 1969 Santa Barbara oil spill to provide an overview of the process. The third section discusses agenda setting; the fourth, policy formulation and legitimation; the fifth covers implementation. The final section discusses evaluation.

TYPES OF PUBLIC POLICY

Domestic public policy can be divided into four major categories: distributive, protective regulatory, redistributive, and competitive regulatory.[1] Many policies have characteristics of more than one of these policy types; nevertheless, the categorization is useful because it highlights the different policy actors and policy processes associated with each type.[2] As might be expected, agencies that cope with overlapping policy types face especially difficult administrative problems. Since each policy type involves different sets of actors, the complexities of political bargaining, budget protection, and client services are multiplied. The troubles of the Environmental Protection Agency (see chapter 2) are partly caused by such dual responsibilities, since the EPA administers grants and contracts (distributive) as well as enforces regulatory statutes (protective regulatory).

Distributive Policy

Distributive policy supports private activities that are beneficial to society but would not usually be undertaken by the private sector. For example, certain kinds of medical research are expensive and have little, if any, financial reward for the companies involved; the government may subsidize such research. Farmers need support through the bad times if they are to produce agricultural products on a regular basis; in response, the federal government instituted price supports. In the nineteenth century, settlement of the American West was physically dangerous and economically risky; the government, eager to encourage western expansion, gave away land and leased federally owned lands at below-market prices. This subsidy of western cattle ranchers continues today.

Government policies in which the government acts as a private party may also be distributive policies. The U.S. Forest Service, originally established to provide a stable source of affordable timber, is an example of distributive policy, as are the national parks and BLM programs to lease federal grazing lands.

Distributive policies usually have low visibility. The people involved (e.g., ranchers and BLM officials) maintain cordial relations, and unless some unexpected event triggers media interest, the decisions governing this sort of policy are usually made by *subgovernments*, also known as *iron triangles*. A subgovernment is a coalition of three groups of actors: the affected interest group, the relevant agency in the executive branch, and the appropriate congressional committees or subcommittees. They are quiet and stable networks of policy actors with similar interests and goals; they may exist in any type of policy but they are most prevalent in distributive policy. When an issue is more visible, *issue networks* may be the driving force. Issue networks are "webs of influence [that] provoke and guide the exercise of power."[3] They are quite fluid, with participants moving in and out, and without clear leadership. Network members are policy experts who pool their expertise to achieve policy outcomes, but there is no formal organization, and neither schedules nor methods of communication are routinized.[4]

Distributive policy is not often the focus of public controversy, and in distributive policies, subgovernments are king. When controversy does arise, subgovernments disintegrate, only to re-form when the dust settles. During the first Reagan administration, some western states attempted to obtain control of the federal lands within their state boundaries. This "Sagebrush Rebellion" pitted the BLM against their normal allies, the cattlemen. In previous times, the environmentalists and BLM had been bitter enemies, the environmentalists claiming that poor management and overgrazing were ruining the public lands of the West. One BLM official told me off the record that he would never have believed a year before the Sagebrush Rebellion started that he would be leaking advance information to the environmental lobby. However, the environmentalists were, for once, on the same side as BLM as they both fought to keep the federal lands out of the control of what they perceived as rapacious state developers. Once the controversy subsided, the environmentalists and BLM found themselves again on opposite sides of the fence, figuratively if not literally.[5]

Protective Regulatory Policy

This form of policy protects the public by regulating private activities. Unlike the other forms of policy, this may be an active policy, not only prohibiting certain actions (such as emitting sulfur dioxide into the atmosphere) but also requiring some activities (building tall smokestacks or inspecting automobiles or recycling waste). When a banker tells his loan customers the total price of a car (including interest), he does so because of protective regulatory policy, not because he has a big heart. As with distributive policies, when government activities parallel private sector activities, they may fall under protective regulatory policies. The air pollution standards for which the Pentagon requested waivers (discussed in chapter 2) are an example of protective regulatory policy (Clean Air Act) imposed on a federal agency.

The main actors in the protective regulatory policy are the committees and subcommittees of the Congress (the full House and Senate), executive agencies, and business interest groups. Many of these policies cannot be relegated to a subgovernment level: for example, an announcement that some prescription pain medications increase the dangers of heart attacks or strokes is front-page news. Usually, however, these policies have only moderate visibility, and the parties involved work out their decisions through bargaining and compromise. Issue networks, discussed earlier, often have considerable influence in this type of policy.

Environmental policies that deal with issues such as pollution, hazardous and toxic materials, mining, or energy development fall into the protective regulatory category. Some observers of the environmental scene blame the slow improvement of the nation's environment on the federal choice of protective regulatory policy as a vehicle for compliance, rather than distributive policies. By defining pollution control as punitive (allowing certain amounts of pollutants to be released or generated and stored, and then punishing any excess), the federal government provides corporate America with little incentive to develop waste reduction policies or to look for alternate production methods. Critics suggest that more progress would be made by rewarding recycling and encouraging material conservation and waste reduction rather than by continuing an adversarial, litigious approach.

Most environmental policy fits either the protective regulatory policy category (air and water pollution policies) or distributive policy (national parks). Sometimes a policy may overlap categories. For example, the burros at Grand Canyon National Park were a nuisance and also destroyed habitat needed for native species. Unfortunately for the Park Service, burros are cute; one in particular, Brighty, had been the subject of a very popular children's book and had a statue erected to him on the South Rim.[6] In order to preserve the canyon ecosystem, the Park Service decided to shoot the wild burros, prompting an avalanche of protest. The Park Service ultimately compromised, allowing animal protection groups to rescue many of the burros before shooting the rest. The Park Service, usually categorized as a distributive policy agency, was engaged in protective regulatory policy when it decided to destroy wild burros to protect native species.

Redistributive Policy

The most controversial type of public policy is redistributive, which seeks to change the allocation of valued goods or services—money, property, rights—between social classes or racial groups or genders. It is the most controversial because, in this policy, unlike the others, there are usually clearly defined winners and losers. Most often the winners are from disadvantaged groups in society; for example, environmental justice issues are often redistributive policy.[7] Because of the high visibility of this type of policy, the political actors also have high visibility: the president, congressional leaders, and large interest groups.

Sometimes astute politicians can sell a program as one politically acceptable form of policy, knowing all the while that the real impact will be otherwise. Urban renewal is such a program. Advertised as a redistributive program to help the poor of the inner cities, in fact the poor were pushed out, and high-rise offices and expensive condominiums replaced the slums. The poor simply shifted to more crowded and less convenient tenements. Instead of being redistributive, the program was distributive, subsidizing urban real estate speculators.

Competitive Regulatory Policy

The control of radio broadcasting by the Federal Communications Commission (FCC) is an example of competitive regulatory policy. Several parties *compete* for the right to broadcast on a certain frequency; the successful applicant is then *regulated* by the agency. Thus, competitive regulatory policy limits the provision of specific goods and services to a few who are chosen from a group of competitors, and the selected few are then regulated. Other examples are television station licensing and, in the pre-Reagan days of intense industry regulation, airlines and trucking company route assignments. The regulation of trucking companies was so extensive at one time that trucking lines were told specifically which goods could be carried between two points and in what direction. Airlines had to agree to service feeder lines in order to be awarded major, profitable runs.

Since deregulation, the importance of competitive regulatory policy has diminished considerably, and environmental policies are not usually found in this category.[8] These are usually low-visibility policies, and decisions are made at the bureau level, or by independent regulatory commissions, such as the FCC or the Securities and Exchange Commission, or by the courts. Often the regulated industries have a great deal of input into the regulatory decisions. This leads to the problem of the *captured agency*, an agency that identifies so closely with the interests of the regulated industry that it forgets its responsibilities to society. For several years after the commercial development of cable television, the FCC was accused of being a captured agency in thrall to the Big Three of broadcasting: ABC, CBS, and NBC.

Critics of the agency attribute the slow acceptance of cable television to the networks' ability to influence FCC decisions.

THE PUBLIC POLICY PROCESS:
INTRODUCTION

One of the unfortunate truths about the depth of our political concerns is that we care most about those incidents that are closest to us. When an airplane crashes on an international flight, the media reports the number of American dead or injured, and if the plane is filled entirely by foreign nationals, the crash has only the briefest mention on the national media and is then forgotten. Just so do environmental issues come into the national consciousness. For most Americans, the first really big oil spill was the January 1969 Santa Barbara spill off the coast of California. However, on 18 March 1967, the *Torrey Canyon*, a 970-foot tanker with 117,000 tons of crude oil in its storage tanks, ran aground fifteen miles west of Land's End in Cornwall, northeast of the Isles of Scilly. Initially, about 40,000 tons of oil were released by the ruptured tanks, but salvage efforts were futile, and all 117,000 tons of oil spilled into the western end of the English Channel. Eventually the oil washed up on the holiday coasts of England and France.

American environmentalists were a small but hardy band in the late 1960s, and they watched the *Torrey Canyon* incident with horror. Oil experts, however, noted the narrowness of the Channel, the peculiarity of the prevailing winds and currents, and assured the American public that such an accident would not happen in American waters. Environmentalists received similar assurances about oil wells off the Pacific coast. The general public was not very worried, but the environmental activists were, and when the Santa Barbara well blew, they were quick to take advantage.

An interest group called GOO (Get Oil Out) was rapidly formed. The American media were much more concerned with the destruction of forty miles of Southern California beaches than with the holiday sites of France and England. Within three days, GOO had collected more than 50,000 signatures on petitions asking President Nixon to stop deep-sea coastal oil drilling. Attention focused on the federal outer continental shelf (OCS) oil leasing program administered by the Bureau of Land Management (BLM), although two other federal agencies—the U.S. Geological Survey and the

Federal Water Pollution Control Administration—were also involved. The leasing program was temporarily halted by Interior Secretary Walter Hickel.

The incident also drew attention to the growing problem of other forms of marine oil pollution. Estimates about the relative importance of various oil sources vary. There is general agreement that most of the oil comes from operational discharges from shipping and land-based sources, while natural oil seepage from the ocean floor contributes 7 percent to 10 percent.[9] However, the American National Research Council estimates natural seepage at 46 percent. Offshore production is responsible for a very small percentage, ranging from 2 percent to 7 percent.[10]

The public uproar over the 1969 Santa Barbara spill led to passage of the National Environmental Policy Act in December of the same year; it was signed into law on 1 January 1970. It had long-term repercussions for the federal oil-leasing programs. Despite the oil crisis in the early seventies, OCS leasing goals were never met. The coastal states and communities were reluctant to have oil rigs drilling off their coastlines, and political pressures caused by a constant stream of small spills and a few major disasters such as the *Exxon Valdez*, which poured 11 million gallons of oil into Prince William Sound in Alaska, kept the public interested in the impact of oil development in the marine environment. In 1978, the Outer Continental Shelf Leasing Act Amendments incorporated the coastal states into the planning process for OCS development. Until recently, although the OCS oil production exceeds that of the dry lands, the states have prevented massive exploitation of the OCS. In 1990, George H. W. Bush signed a ten-year moratorium on new leases, and Bill Clinton added another twelve years. However, shortly after the 2000 elections, with rising gasoline prices and instability in the Middle East, the George W. Bush administration began to reconsider the OCS leases, and in 2003 exploratory drilling was authorized.[11]

Here we have a microcosm of the policy process. A trigger event (the Santa Barbara spill) is used by policy initiators or policy entrepreneurs (environmental lobbyists) to induce policy formation and legitimation (passage of NEPA) to achieve policy goals (de-emphasis on OCS wells and reemphasis on environmental protection) that are implemented throughout the country (EPA regulations and state involvement in OCS planning).

The environmental policy process is exceedingly complex. What appears as a relatively straightforward process is actually an iterative process. Evaluation, or predicting impacts and outcomes, begins with the agenda-setting process, and interest groups dissatisfied with the predicted outcomes begin immediately to reforge the agendas. Formulation and legitimation are shaped in a fluid system that reflects the constant activities of interest groups and bureaucracies, both of which are conscious of the possibility of judicial intervention. Evaluation strategies are chosen and rejected on the basis of their projected political outcomes.

What is necessary to negotiate the political process successfully? Political experience, flexibility, an acceptance of the validity of political decision-making, and above all, the realization that nothing is ever final. The next three sections discuss in more detail the various stages in this process, beginning with the setting of the public policy agenda.

AGENDA SETTING

Why do citizens strive to get their issues on the public agenda? Why not be satisfied with convincing their own circle of friends and colleagues of the correctness of their position? They strive to have their preferences turned into public policy for three reasons. First, public policy is legitimate. Government policies are usually regarded as legal obligations that citizens have a duty to uphold. The big exceptions—speed limits, Prohibition—are notable because they are exceptions. Nongovernmental groups and institutions may generate important policies (for example, corporate investment guidelines or PGA tour eligibility) and those policies may be regarded as binding on the members of the organizations, but these policies have no authority for people who are not members. Only government policies are *legally binding*, and only government policies are legitimate almost automatically.

A second characteristic of public policy that encourages citizens to work for their own preferences is the universality of government policies. Membership in other policy-generating groups is voluntary, and these groups make policy only for their own members. But government policy applies—or may apply—to everyone.

Finally, only the government has the power to force compliance with its policy decisions. Government has a monopoly on coercion in society; other organizations can legally exercise only limited sanctions. Only government can imprison (or even execute) individuals for refusing to obey its directives.[12]

So, because government actions are legitimate, enact societywide policies, and enforce these policies, people work to have their policy preferences become public policies.

Systemic and Institutional Agendas

In public policy there are two basic forms of agendas: systemic agendas and institutional or decision agendas.[13] The *systemic agenda* consists of all the issues that a political community agrees need to be resolved and that it also agrees are within governmental authority. These are the issues that wax and wane in the public attention until finally the issue recurs often enough or becomes sufficiently problematic that it can no longer be ignored. When this occurs, policymakers place the issue on their *institutional agenda*: the list of issues they plan to consider actively and seriously.

Systemic agendas are fairly abstract and fluid. Issues may appear on the systemic agenda for years before actually reaching the institutional agenda; some issues never do make it. Systemic agendas identify problem areas but rarely propose concrete alternatives and solutions. As a general rule, the more people are interested in and concerned about an issue, the more likely that issue is to reach the systemic agenda and perhaps the institutional agenda as well. Rarely, however, does an issue suddenly become a topic of general conversation; dramatic trigger events (discussed later) such as Three Mile Island and the Chernobyl reactor disaster are the exception. Although some issues reach the systemic and institutional agendas by the actions of issue networks, most often concern for an issue moves first through predictable stages of public awareness.

The narrowest kind of public is the *identification group*, people with a detailed awareness of specific issues. Local groups concerned about stopping a nuclear reactor in their neighborhood form identification groups. *Attention groups* focus on the broader implications of the issues concerning identification groups: antinuclear power groups are attention groups. Unlike the identification group, which is interested only in the reactor threatening their community, the attention group opposes nuclear reactors everywhere. The *attentive public* is the generally informed and educated layer of society. These are the people who, once they are convinced that an issue is important, inform the wider public. They may not have a passionate opposition to nuclear power, but Three Mile Island and Chernobyl have convinced them that nuclear power is a danger. They will write articles, make speeches, join protests, lobby their elected representatives, and discuss the issue at church suppers. The combined effect will be to bring the issue to the attention of the general public. The general or *mass public* is the last segment of the public to become involved in placing an issue on the systemic agenda. These people are less active, interested, and informed than any of the other kinds of public. Getting their attention requires highly generalized and symbolic issues, and keeping their attention for any length of time is difficult. However, without their concurrence, reaching the systemic, and then the institutional, agendas is difficult.

Institutional agendas are the formal lists of issues a governmental body is considering; they are specific, concrete, and limited. They identify the problem and its alternative solutions; often institutional agendas work within strict time constraints. Usually an issue must first be placed on the systemic agenda, although sometimes an issue is so critical that it moves immediately to the institutional agenda. It is, however, important to note that some issues are on the institutional agenda without passing through this process each time. The Congress (and indeed, most legislatures) deals with four kinds of problems: chronic problems, such as the federal budget that recurs annually; sporadic problems, such as reauthorizing environmental legislation; crisis problems, such as widespread western forest fires in 2003 and 2004, and, finally, discretionary problems.[14] This discretionary agenda is chosen by legislators for many reasons: perhaps they have an ideological commitment to the issue, like Paul Rogers of Florida, who struggled for strong emission standards during the fight over the 1977 Clean Air Act amendments; or there are rewards to be gained in the political fray (paying old debts or creating new ones) or in subsequent elections (Rogers, for example, represented a south Florida constituency deeply concerned with respiratory problems of the elderly).

Reaching the Institutional Agenda

Issues reach the institutional agenda in a variety of ways. One way is through individuals or coherent groups working deliberately to have their concerns addressed by government;[15] another is less deliberate, seeing policy proposals as ingredients in a "policy primeval soup" in which ideas and solutions blend, then sink to the bottom or rise to the top before being skimmed off by government and served up on the decision agenda.[16] Often the agenda is reached by a combination of the two. To extend the metaphor, individuals may stir the soup, vary the ingredients, or add a few spices to tempt the appetites of decisionmakers.

According to the instrumental view, there are four ways to create issues and four corresponding categories of initiators or policy entrepreneurs (people who use situations to place issues on the agenda); these categories may overlap. "Readjustors" may perceive an inequality that affects them; they then strive to have the inequality reduced. For example, rural residents, who do not themselves generate low level nuclear waste, fight to stop nuclear waste disposal sites being placed in their communities. "Exploiters" manufacture issues for their own gain. In 1988, when George H. W. Bush used the pollution in Boston Harbor to discredit his Democratic opponent for president, he was probably acting as an exploiter. "Circumstantial reactors" take advantage of unanticipated events or "trigger events" to create or to magnify issues. For example, the Santa Barbara oil spill was used to halt OCS development; the crash of a fixed-wing aircraft filled with tourists led to regulations prohibiting below-rim sightseeing flights in the Grand Canyon; the terrible forest fires that ravaged Yellowstone National Park in 1988 led to a reevaluation of the controlled burn policies of the federal resource management agencies. Finally, "do-gooders" use events to publicize issues but gain no personal benefit from the issue. They may use inequalities or unanticipated events, but their motivation differs from the readjusters or circumstantial reactors. The Greenpeace activists arrested in 1995 for protesting French nuclear testing in the Pacific were not motivated by private gain or perceived inequalities.

Some issues never reach the mass public and yet manage to be placed on the institutional or decision agenda. This often requires desperate measures by the identification and attention groups. Issues that are confined to an identification group gain the institutional agenda when the group members threaten to disrupt the system; an example of such disruption is "monkey-wrenching," carried out by radical environmental groups who despair of the traditional political process. Issues that are confined to attention groups are brought to the decision agenda by threatening legislators with legitimate sanctions such as recalls and withholding contributions or votes. When an issue can only reach the attentive public, access is easier because the attentive public tends to have political power by virtue of their social and economic status. Here political brokerage techniques or controlling the media will bring an issue to the institutional agenda. The media is, of course, available to, and used by, the identification and attention groups, but the attentive public often has formal control of the media.

Timing is critical in gaining the attention of the policy decisionmakers. Policy problems may exist for quite a long time before a politically acceptable solution is found, and even then, if the decisionmakers have other priorities, the issue may not make it to the decision agenda. All three of these "process streams" of problems, policies, and politics must meet for an issue to reach the agenda of government.[17] When they do—often because an initiator has taken some critical action—a window of opportunity is opened, and the issue is under active and serious consideration by government officials. The passage of the Endangered Species Act in 1973 is an example of the three streams coming together to open a window of opportunity. Its passage resulted from a fortunate combination of circumstance: a powerful environmental lobby backed by an aroused public, a legislative urge for association with environmentalism, enormous ignorance about the political consequences of its implementation, growing scientific advocacy of species protection, and (no trivial matter) the threatened extinction of the American bald eagle, the national symbol.[18] Small wonder that the Endangered Species Act passed almost unanimously.

POLICY FORMULATION AND LEGITIMATION

While the entire policy process is political, the formulation and legitimation phases are the most intensely political. Many actors are involved in the formulation stage. The bureaucracy, although most involved in the implementation phase of public policy, has a role in formulation by suggesting policies to the legislature and providing information on the strengths and weaknesses of proposed solutions. Bureaus are given this role because they have, or are perceived to have, technical expertise that the elected officials and their staff lack, although bureaus often have their own organizational needs to be satisfied by the policy process (budgetary constraints, personnel demands, program protection and expansion). The federal bureaucracy most often reflects the president's policy position, but the president and the bureaucracy may have separate goals in the policy process. Many times during the Reagan administration, for example, the EPA staff were at odds with the goals and initiatives of the political appointees and the president. In fact, the accusation that the bureaucracy could not be trusted with the conservative agenda was a constant plaint of the administration. It took powerful and clear messages from the mass public to convince President Reagan that commitment to a protected and healthy environment was a fixture in American values.

The media are also involved in formulation and legitimation as well. While they may create issues, as they did in the Watergate scandal, and often do on television programs such as *Sixty Minutes*, the media are most often used by other actors to influence public or political opinion. Special interest groups watch the process carefully and intervene in those issues that affect their own concerns.

Problem Definition

One of the first difficulties in policy formulation is problem definition: legislators must first agree on the parameters of the problem before they can begin to formulate solutions. This is an intensely political process. An example of the difficulties in problem definition may be found in the issue of tropical rain forest destruction. This destruction occurs in four main stages: road building and lumbering; colonization (made easier by the development of roads and the clearing of timber tracts) and crop planting (since the new settlers cannot live off the forested areas); soil exhaustion (because there is no dormant season); and grass planting and cattle grazing (inefficient, marginally profitable, and a contributing factor to soil erosion). Assuming that the governments having jurisdiction over the rain forests want to halt the destruction, or that the developed countries are convinced that this issue is important enough to justify interference in the activities of a sovereign nation, how might this problem be defined? The problem definition will guide the solutions to be attempted.

As a start, this might be defined as a timber problem. Obviously, one incentive to reduce rain forest destruction would be to reduce the world market for rain forest lumber. In a world where even expensive eyeglass frames are made from mahogany, reducing the demand for fine furniture seems unlikely. A second definition might be as a problem of population pressures. If the developing countries with rain forests could house, feed, and employ their own populations within the urban or already existing rural environments, these people would not need to move into the rain forest areas denuded by the lumber companies. Unfortunately, there seems to be little political will to reduce populations; the developing countries sometimes perceive attempts to require reductions in the birth rate as hidden genocide.

Perhaps the rain forest destruction is a problem of agricultural techniques. The indigenous people of the forest survive very nicely without destroying the trees; the new settlers might be taught the indigenous farming practices. However, unlike the new settlers, the native peoples are unaccustomed to the luxuries of urban life: soft drinks, blue jeans, boom boxes. Their farming methods are labor intensive and generate little cash crop. The food they do produce is neither familiar nor appealing to the settlers' palates. What about replenishing the soil so it does not become exhausted? Fertilizers are expensive and bring their own potentially harmful environmental effects.

Finally, the problem might be defined again as a market problem. By reducing world beef consumption (although hogs or sheep would do equally well—or poorly—on deforested land) or banning beef grown on deforested land (much as the European Union banned American beef fed growth hormones), the final stages of deforestation might be avoided.

None of these problem definitions or problem solutions alone seem useful. As the issue of the rain forest becomes expanded to wider publics, policymakers are going to be forced to find some way to address and define the issue. "Stop the destruction of the rain forest" is an agenda-setting strategy with emotional appeal; *how* to stop the destruction becomes the formulation problem.

Formulation

Once a problem has been defined, the solution that emerges is the result of bargaining and compromise by various government factions, each of which believes it has the answer to the problem. When a problem appears intractable, the appointment of a study commission is one way to delay, and perhaps ultimately to avoid, a decision. Another strategy is to pass resolutions condemning the undesirable activity, while actually doing nothing. Negotiations may hinge on issues not directly related to the policy problem; congressional logrolling—trading political favors—frequently influences policy formulations. The process of negotiation and bargaining does not stop with passage of initial legislation; it continues in the formulation of subsequent amendments and reauthorizations of the original legislation. The 1977 amendments to the Clean Air Act are a good example of this continual renegotiation process.

In 1977, Congress considered amendments to the 1970 Clean Air Act.[19] At issue was the auto industry's attempts to delay by five years their compliance with the auto-emission standards imposed by the original act. They had already had three one-year extensions. Democrats led both sides of the battle in the House. Paul Rogers of Florida, chairman of the House Subcommittee on Health and the Environment, pushed for compliance within the extended time limits already agreed upon. John Dingell, representing Detroit with its blue-collar autoworkers and their threatened jobs, was joined by a majority of the Republicans in asking for the extension. Dingell usually was on the side of environmental legislation, but in this case his constituents' needs were paramount.

Rogers defined the issue in terms of health: respiratory problems in the elderly, developing respiratory problems of children. Dingell defined it as jobs and the protection of an essential American industry. By the time it emerged from the subcommittee, the issue had been defined as "how can we clean up the air at the lowest possible cost?" This was a substantial victory for the auto industry: Rogers really didn't care how much it cost, but in order to get the opposing forces to compromise, he accepted their definition of the problem. By the time the final vote came on the floor of the House, Rogers had been forced to give even more ground. President Carter's energy policy had fueled Dingell's allies, and the automakers and sellers had exerted great lobbying pressure on all members of the House. Dingell's forces carried the day, although their victory was somewhat diminished by the subsequent changes made in Conference Committee with the Senate.

By defining the problem and then using negotiation and compromise, the policy was formulated. It was also legitimated by the same process. Although no one member of either the House or the Senate was truly satisfied with the outcome, all accepted it as legitimate because in the American political system, the public generally accepts as legitimate the decisions made by the government.

CASE DISCUSSION 3.1

Touch-and-Go

In September 2003, the Navy announced its decision to site an Outlying Landing Field (OLF) in rural, coastal North Carolina. The Navy would use the 30,000 acre site to train Super Hornet fighter pilots; the Navy contends that, because pilots need to practice landings on aircraft carriers before deploying, in the current state of national emergency they must have additional facilities for training. The training would reserve 900 square miles of airspace for combat training; this area overlaps four national wildlife refuges (Pocosin Lakes, Lake

(continued)

CASE DISCUSSION 3.1 (*continued*)

Mattamuskeet, Swanquarter, and Alligator River). Jets would fly about 16,000 "touch-and-go" simulated landings per year; approximately 4,000 would be between 10 p.m. and 7 a.m. Airplanes would be flying in the OLF area about eight hours per day.

The actual runway area is within five miles of the Pocosin Lakes National Wildlife Refuge. Established in 1963, the refuge includes wetlands and open water. During the winter, almost 100,000 waterfowl rest and feed in the refuge. Over half of these birds are tundra swans or snow geese. The Super Hornet flight pattern would be within 0.2 miles of the refuge, with planes flying between 2,000 and 2,500 feet. In December 2005, a jet on a test run had to bank sharply to avoid colliding with a flock of tundra swans.

Most residents in the area chosen for the OLF are poor. Almost one-quarter of the residents live below the poverty line, and the median annual income is below $29,000. Almost half of the residents are African-American. The Navy already has an OLF at Naval Auxiliary Landing Field Fentress in Chesapeake County, Virginia, where residents have complained about noise from jet aircraft and oppose expanding the field. At that site, only about 7 percent of the residents live in poverty, the median annual income is over $50,000, and 29 percent of the residents are African-American.

Who are the major stakeholders? What are their professional interests? Cultural? Social? Economic? Political? Personal? In terms of resources? Who benefits from this decision? Who might lose? How would the various stakeholders define the problem? How would they change their definitions to suit different audiences? If you were deciding whether or not to approve the Navy decision to site the OLF here, how would you define the issue? What additional information would you need? How would you collect it?

(Sources: *Washington County, North Carolina v. Department of the Navy*, 357 F. Supp. 2d 861 [2005]; Southern Environmental Law Center [www.southernenvironment.org]; Hampton Roads.com/PilotOnLine.com. I cannot resist including two of my favorite acronyms that appeared in the law case: BASH [Bird Aircraft Strike Hazard] and BAM [Bird Avoidance Modeling].)

Legitimation

Legitimate policies have the authority of the state (in the American system, the authority of the people) attached.[20] Legitimacy is "a belief on the part of citizens that the current government represents a proper form of government and a willingness of the part of those citizens to accept the decrees of that government as legal and authoritative."[21]

Legitimacy is largely psychological. There is nothing that the government can do to force citizens to accept its policies as legitimate. Legitimacy is substantive as well as procedural; there are certain areas in which citizens feel the government should not meddle, although examples of these areas are increasingly difficult to find.[22] An unrealistic example: a legislative decision to ban red meat production would not be perceived as legitimate, regardless of any predicted positive impact on world food supplies, tropical rain forests, and American coronary disease rates. Finally, legitimacy is variable. Governments that are either consistently outside the areas of public acceptance or that violate the public trust may become illegitimate; loss of legitimacy was a major factor in the resignation of President Nixon.

In the American system, legitimacy is achieved through the legislative process, the administrative process, the courts, and—rarely—through direct democracy. The legislature is the source of primary legislation. Elected by the people, legislators are expected to represent their constituencies.[23] As long as they collectively do not violate the wishes and expectations of the electorate, and they follow the procedural guidelines for their own legislative bodies, the laws they pass are legitimate to the voters.

The administrative process, being of fairly recent origin and handicapped by not being mentioned explicitly in the Constitution,[24] has been subject to criticisms of its legitimacy from the earliest days of the administrative state. However, the rulemaking process ("secondary legislation") is generally accepted as legitimate. If the agencies follow the correct procedures, usually as laid down in the Administrative Procedure Act, their rules have the force and effect of legislative law. There is frequent opportunity for public input and influence in the administrative decision process, and while citizens may complain about a "fourth branch of government," administrative decisions are usually accorded legitimacy.

Court decisions, while subject to appeals or changes due to changing circumstances, are also legitimate. Federal court decisions are especially powerful because they have a direct constitutional connection and judges are, at most levels, less vulnerable to political pressures. Judges rarely need to compromise. The decisions of the United States Supreme Court are particularly influential in legitimating government decisions because they are *not* subject to further appeal and the justices may rule on the constitutionality of the actions of another branch of government. Only Congress can nullify a Supreme Court decision, either through legislation or by removing a disputed issue from the Court's jurisdiction.[25]

The final source of legitimacy is direct democracy, most often expressed in referenda or initiatives. In recent years, stringent demands have been placed on many state budgets by taxpayer initiatives, and these have had an inevitable effect on state environmental programs.

IMPLEMENTATION

Implementation occurs when the policy goals are translated into governmental actions that affect other branches of government or the citizens. It is in implementation that bureaucracy shows its greatest influence.[26] Although implementation may be hampered by poor policy design or a lack of commitment by policymakers, once responsibility for the policy passes to the hands of the administrators, other factors come into play. Bureaucratic resources and administrative discretion are two of the most important factors.

Bureaucratic Resources

The resources available to bureaucracies are considerable. The initial source of their powers comes from their legal authority to implement legislation. Congress delegates its legislative authority to agencies, thus providing the legal justification for administrative rules and regulations. Bureaucratic power is also enhanced by the indispensable nature of the bureaucratic activity: modern government would be impossible without the agencies. The agencies are also empowered by their technical expertise and support of their constituencies.

The technical expertise of senior or midlevel agency administrators is especially important in the environmental agencies; usually these administrators are first trained in their substantive fields and then promoted to increasingly important administrative posts. In the U.S. Park

Service, for example, the interpretation and historic preservation employees are trained in history, journalism, and related fields, while the management employees have degrees in forestry, marine biology, environmental science, and similar technical areas. Superfund site administrators must be knowledgeable about chemical, physical, and biological processes. Many of the environmental agency staff have graduate degrees in their professional areas. Although rarely trained in administrative skills, the technical expertise of the bureaucrats and the intimate knowledge of their own policy areas far outreach the knowledge base of the most well-informed congressional staff. Despite the information available from the Congressional Research Service and the Office of Technology Assessment, Congress is almost forced to rely upon information and analyses provided by the bureaucracy.

There is a negative side to the issue of technical expertise. Because agency personnel rarely have professional administrative experience, they often view the interjection of values or political ideas as a corruption of the decision-making process. This rejection of political influence is not limited to the agencies. Environmentalists deplore the political influence used by lumber companies in the Pacific Northwest to bring pressure on Congress and the Forest Service to allow them to clear-cut. Timber companies ridicule the efforts of Native Americans and environmentalists to protect rare animals with no apparent commercial value. And government specialists, trained in the sciences, are outraged that Superfund sites take years to clean because state and local governments insist on approving all EPA and responsible party agreements. This is one area in which professional socialization is needed for environmental administrators. Political factors are a reality, and in a representative democracy, political factors are a legitimate balance to the technical side of the decision process.

The constituencies that each agency develops are a second resource. This is the reverse side of the "captured agency" coin. Any regulatory or management agency works closely with interest groups. These groups become accustomed to the working habits of the agency and learn effective patterns of negotiation and compromise. "Better the devil you know than the devil you don't" is their operating theory. They are reluctant to upset the stable relationships they have developed, and so a threatened agency may rely on its interest groups for protection in times of budgetary crisis or changing political leadership. These client groups often have prestige and political influence, and they are a powerful factor in consolidating the positions of the agencies. While they are not often called upon to defend the agency or to exercise influence on the agency's behalf, their very existence increases the authority of the agencies.

Administrative Discretion

A third factor that cannot be underestimated is the discretionary power of the agencies. [27] While some commentators would like to limit discretion as much as possible, or even to eliminate it entirely, discretion is essential for an effective administration. Legislatures cannot possibly draft legislation in the detail that is necessary for implementation. They lack the technical expertise that is such a powerful resource for the bureaucracy. And even if they had the necessary staff and expertise, the cumbersome legislative process of negotiation and compromise would bog down the governing process.

Discretion also gives administrators leeway to fit policy decisions to individual cases, to "humanize" the governmental process. It enhances their flexibility, allowing administrative law to evolve incrementally and to be checked or changed without the fanfare that accompanies legislative activity. Finally—and this is especially true in environmental administration—discretion accommodates changing technology. As scientific data accumulates, or drought endangers national forests, or new species are discovered, the discretionary powers of administrators allow rapid and responsive change.

This is not to say that governing necessarily continues to improve as discretionary powers increase. Too much discretion can lead to corruption, favoritism, or simple confusion and be as harmful as too little discretion. The advantages of bureaucratic government rest in part on the regularity and predictability of government activity. A good administrator is able to strike a balance.

Administrators make three kinds of discretionary decisions: substantive, procedural, and complex. *Substantive* discretionary decisions are those in which an administrator makes a decision or promulgates a rule on a policy issue. These substantive decisions are one method for agencies to distribute benefits to their client groups. Agencies exercise this discretion in several ways. They decide, for example, where to locate research stations or unit headquarters that frequently are major sources of employment in small communities. In the late 1980s, the Forest Service proposed consolidating the administrative offices of the Prescott and Coconino national forests in northern Arizona. The impact on the town of Williams, a very small community already endangered by an interstate bypass, was enormous, and the political fallout was great enough that the Forest Service shelved its plans, at least temporarily. A more subtle use of substantive discretionary power is in wording rules and regulations either to create client groups or to shape the benefits for which they are eligible. Sometimes discretion is at the "street level." In granting wetland permits, for example, state investigators have wide latitude in interpreting potential soil erosion or habitat destruction.

Procedural discretionary decisions relate to the selection of the processes used to gather information or to make decisions. A procedural discretionary decision might be whether to hire consultants or to use in-house personnel to develop a forest plan. Finally, *complex* discretionary decisions, such as the hybrid rule-making process discussed in the material on the Administrative Procedure Act in chapter 5, combine the features of both substantive and procedural decisions. For example, will a forest plan be based on timber industry data or agency data or a combination of both? Administrative officials are given wide latitude in their decisionmaking and actions; this increases their flexibility and improves the efficacy of the administrative state. However, administrative officials can exceed their authority or misuse it. When this occurs, they may be individually liable in tort actions brought against them by citizens.

Under the ancient common law doctrine of sovereign immunity, government and its employees were absolutely immune from prosecution for actions related to their governmental functions. The doctrine has its origins in the ancient divine right of kings: God ordains the king, and since God can do no wrong, the king can do no wrong. However, even divine kings recognized that their subordinates could make mistakes (or that, for political reasons, the king might want to dissociate himself from some subordinate's action), and so the custom evolved that the king could give permission for his agent who represented the government to be sued. Under American law, sovereign immunity still protects governments at all levels although government employees may not have the same immunity. Thus a town can invoke sovereign immunity to bar lawsuits involving city vehicles, while the driver of the vehicle may be individually liable in a civil suit. Immunity of government officials from liability suits ranges from absolute immunity (for such activities as legislating) to none (no more immunity than is borne by a private citizen). In the middle range is qualified immunity: an employee acting in "good faith" is immune from individual tort actions.

Variables Affecting Implementation

Successful implementation is very difficult, partly because it involves a number of interdependent actions that must be accomplished almost simultaneously.[28] Implementation actions include acquiring resources such as money, land, personnel, or equipment; interpreting directives, rules, and regulations; planning programs; organizing activities; and extending benefits and applying restrictions.

The implementation process is characterized by many complicating factors. First is the multiplicity of actors. At a minimum, federal bureaucrats are responsible to two masters: the president (or his political appointee) and Congress, which has authorized the agency's existence and continues to hold the purse strings. Bureaucrats must also satisfy their client groups or, failing that, be able to defend their actions to the elected officials who receive the complaints of the client groups. Some agencies have advisory groups with various degrees of influence on agency activities. There is always the possibility of judicial review that even for the victorious agency is a process that consumes time and resources and perhaps even political goodwill.

Another complicating factor is the federal context of environmental administration mentioned in chapter 1. Each of the fifty states has its own bureaucratic organization to cope with environmental policy. In some states, there are as many as eight state agencies with some environmental responsibilities. This obviously complicates efforts by the states or the federal government to encourage intergovernmental coordination in environmental administration. In addition, the state bureaucracies, although often given implementation responsibilities for federal programs, must also respond to the political pressures of their own state legislatures.

Because of the numerous agencies and policy-making bodies involved, goals for any one policy may be diffuse, multiple, and competing. For example, the Forest Service is often frustrated by its multiple-use mandate. Trained as silvaculturists, foresters may view trees as a crop, to be nurtured and then harvested when mature. The Forest Service was established partially to ensure a steady, affordable, flexibly priced source of timber for the American construction industry. Being forced to allow old stands of timber to decay for habitat protection, when by forestry standards they should have been cut years ago, goes against the grain of traditional foresters. Equally dismayed is the entrepreneur who invests in patents for a new biological form of pest control only to find that, while one federal agency grants him a patent, another refuses to let him sell his product. Or take the case of power plant operators forced to change reactor design long after approved construction has taken place. This "ratcheting" (incremental tightening of regulations) afflicts many industries subjected to EPA regulations.

Finally, there are unforeseen circumstances—hurricanes and floods, broken dams, decreasing ozone layers, economic recessions, the September 11, 2001, attacks on New York and Washington—that can skew the best designed and best intentioned implementation strategies. Flexibility is key to effective implementation, but too much flexibility allows unacceptable waivers and weak enforcement.

Implementing Environmental Policy

The two most common types of environmental policies are distributive policy and protective regulatory policy. Each policy type generates its own set of issues during implementation.

Although generally stable and dominated by subgovernments, *distributive policy* may erupt into conflict and difficulties for the implementing agencies. One problem arises when new responsibilities are added to existing, well-established policies, for example, adding recreation and wildlife habitat to the Forest Service's mandate. From the agenda setter's perspective, new issues may be easier to pass by tacking them onto existing remedies, often without much concern for the fit. From the implementer's perspective, this shakes up comfortable coalitions, brings in new client groups, and usually necessitates redistribution of resources. Another problem may occur when the elected officials change priorities.[29] In theory, bureaucrats should be responsive to the political will of the electorate that is expressed to them by the political appointees. However, responsive changes are difficult to accomplish after years of sunk costs and interest group expectations.[30] This becomes especially complicated when the will of the executive differs from the will of the legislature. Finally, changes in society, either through technological advances or resulting from socioeconomic differences, may force bureaucrats to rethink their allocation of distributive benefits.

Protective regulatory policy is inherently controversial and highly visible, a real tinderbox for bureaucrats implementing the policy. As technology and economic conditions change, routines for enforcement must also compensate. Congress remains closely involved in implementing protective regulatory policy because its members hear so frequently from their regulated constituents. The president is also likely to become involved, as the first President Bush did over spotted owl habitat protection. Bureaucrats find themselves under pressure from industry and businesses to cut back on enforcement, while the environmentalists push for enforcement that may seem punitive.

EVALUATION

Evaluation is not simply the end stage of the policy process during which analysts measure actual outcomes against desired ones; it occurs throughout the policy process.[31] Evaluation is of two types: formative and summative. *Formative evaluation* takes place while the policy is being formulated and implemented. It allows midcourse corrections if the original policy goals have been forgotten or if new and unintended consequences seem imminent. It is flexible and encourages policy outcomes that fit policy intentions. *Summative evaluation* is used when a policy or program is completed. Analysts isolate the goals of the program and then observe how closely the program achieved the goals.

As complicated as implementation may be, evaluation can be even more problematic. It is difficult to isolate the precise, actual goals of many policies. Perhaps the legislation was vague, or the goals were impossible to attain, given existing technology. The action-forcing provisions of NEPA discussed in chapter 2 raise just such problems: How should progress toward goals be evaluated if the goals required inputs that did not exist? Policy goals may change between the time the policy reaches the systemic or institutional agendas and the time it is evaluated. Other management programs and directives may affect goals and outcomes by addressing goals that compete with or cancel out another agency's mandates. They may also accidentally enhance or damage each other's programs. Even if achieved, goals may have unintended consequences: did Congress really intend the Endangered Species Act to be used to halt a federal project such as the Tellico Dam that had already cost over $100 million?[32] Finally, stated goals may not be the true goals of a policy. For example, in 1984, the state of Maryland declared a moratorium on catching striped bass. One possible explanation for the controversial moratorium was a recent state initiative to reduce pollution in the Chesapeake Bay. The moratorium would increase striped bass populations, which is an indicator in the public mind of water quality, regardless of the effectiveness of the cleanup program. Thus the state program (and the governor) would appear effective even if the cleanup effort were unsuccessful.[33]

A second set of problems involves measurement of outcomes. Some environmental activities have no direct market value and various techniques of shadow pricing must be used to derive their monetary value. How, for example, does an evaluator put a price on a day at Yellowstone National Park? Most people would agree that there are some values that cannot be measured, such as the utility of a life or the last dusky seaside sparrow, but the demands of regulatory analysis may require that some market value be assigned.

Bureaucrats must also deal with a third set of problems: the dynamic between efficiency and effectiveness. It is often easier to measure efficiency in delivery than effectiveness in achieving goals. A park may increase its visitor-days and claim legislative applause for serving more citizens per dollar spent. However, if the purpose of the park—or even its partial purpose—is to provide a satisfying experience of the natural environment, information on simply the number of citizens served is not an adequate measure of success.

Coping with the values of individuals and organizations involved in the policy process is the last problem in evaluation and is perhaps the least amenable to solution. Organizations have values (for example, the Park Service traditionally supports preservation values while the Forest Service advocates conservation and use); professions within organizations have values (such as the silvaculturists' desire to cut old timber); and clients and the general public have values (such as the preservation of wilderness and simultaneous access to the wilderness). Even evaluators have their own values and expectations.

SUGGESTED READING

General public policy

Kingdon, John W. *Agendas, Alternatives, and Public Policies*. 2nd ed. New York: Longman, 2002.

Mazmanian, Daniel, and Paul Sabatier. *Implementation and Public Policy*. Glenview, IL: Scott, Foresman & Company, 1983.

Ripley, Randall, and Grace Franklin. *Congress, the Bureaucracy, and Public Policy*. 4th ed. Homewood, IL: Dorsey, 1991.

Ripley, Randall, and Grace Franklin. *Policy Implementation and Bureaucracy*. 2nd ed. Chicago, IL: Dorsey, 1986.

Environmental policy

Rosenbaum, Walter A. *Environmental Politics and Policy*. 6th ed. Washington, DC: Congressional Quarterly, 2005. Primarily an undergraduate text, this furnishes an excellent overview of several areas of environmental policy: air pollution, water supply and pollution, toxic and hazardous wastes, energy, and public lands. The discussions on the relationships between science and politics, alone, make the book worthwhile.

Sussman, Glen, Byron Daynes, and Jonathan West. *American Politics and the Environment*. New York: Longman, 2002. Environmental policy in the traditional political science context: federalism, public opinion, parties and interest groups, Congress, the presidency, bureaucracy, and courts. It is very concrete and loaded with current examples.

Vig, Norman, and Michael Kraft. *Environmental Policy: New Directions for the Twenty-First Century*. 6th ed. Washington, DC: Congressional Quarterly, 2006. This book provides recent analyses of environmental activity in Washington. Most of the articles are specialized but rewarding, if one perseveres.

NOTES

1. The material that follows is drawn primarily from Randall Ripley and Grace Franklin, *Congress, the Bureaucracy, and Public Policy* (Homewood, IL: Dorsey Press, 1984), esp. chapter 1.

2. Some policies are transformed from one type to another: for example, the federal food stamp program is now redistributive, but it originated as a distributive program to support farmers by buying surplus crops during the New Deal. Some internal agency actions don't fit into one of these categories at all. Personnel issues, recurring budgets, and agency reorganizations usually have no direct impact on policy outcomes and are rarely driven by policy expectations. Of course, at the highest levels of government, decisions about such things as personnel or budgets can have enormous policy implications.

3. Hugh Heclo, "Issue Networks and the Executive Establishments," in *The New American Political System*, edited by Anthony King (Washington, DC: American Enterprise Institute, 1978), 87–124, esp. 102.

4. Heclo, "Issue Networks."

5. Another perspective on the temporary coalition of BLM and environmentalists is found in Susan J. Buck, "Cultural Theory and Management of Common Property Resources," *Human Ecology* 17 (1989): 101–116.

6. Marguerite Henry, *Brighty of the Grand Canyon* (New York: Rand McNally, 1953).

7. For example, the state-of-the-art landfill in Greensboro, North Carolina, had capacity for another ten years. Using the reserved areas of the landfill would have shifted waste disposal activity closer to a new subsidized housing project. The city decided to close the landfill early and to use more expensive transfer stations to ship the city's solid waste to a neighboring county. This protects the property values of a small group of primarily minority citizens and shifts a much larger, long-term cost to all property owners.

8. I can't think of any competitive regulatory policies that are strictly environmental, although some, such as railroad expansion in the nineteenth century, certainly had unintended environmental consequences.

9. Global Marine Oil Pollution Information Gateway, "Sources of Oil to the Sea," http://oils.gpa.unep.org/facts/sources.htm (accessed 1 August 2005). This site is part of the United Nations Environmental Programme.

10. Global Marine Oil Pollution Information Gateway, "Sources of Oil to the Sea."

11. Nancy Kubasek and Gary Silverman, *Environmental Law*, 5th ed. (Upper Saddle River, NJ: Pearson, 2005), 348–350.

12. We do have laws that protect us from the government using coercion arbitrarily; for example, the Fifth Amendment states that no person (not *citizen*, but *person*) "shall be . . . deprived of life, liberty, or property, without due process of law."

13. The material on agenda-setting is from Roger Cobb and Charles Elder, *Participation in American Politics* (Boston: Allyn and Bacon, 1972), esp. chapters 5–9; and from John Kingdon, *Agendas, Alternatives, and Public Policies* 2nd ed. (New York: Longman, 2002).

14. Jack Walker, "Setting the Agenda in the U.S. Senate," *British Journal of Political Science* 7 (October 1977): 423–445.

15. Cobb and Elder, *Participation in American Politics*, esp. chapters 5–9.

16. This charming analogy is from Kingdon, *Agendas, Alternatives*, chapter 6.

17. Kingdon, *Agendas, Alternatives*, chapter 4.

18. Walter A. Rosenbaum, *Environmental Politics and Policy*, 3rd. ed. (Washington, DC: CQ Press, 1995), 333.

19. This material comes from an excellent documentary, *An Act of Congress* (Learning Corporation of America, 1979).

20. The discussion of legitimation that follows is drawn from Guy Peters,

American Public Policy: Promise and Performance, 2nd ed. (Chatham, NJ: Chatham House Publishers, 1986), chapter 4.

21. Peters, *American Public Policy*, 63 (notes omitted).

22. One of the side effects of consumer rights and the incredible expansion of personal injury litigation has been involvement of government agencies into personal lives in ways even our grandparents would find incredible. To force an unwilling store owner to prohibit smoking on his premises—to assign financial penalties for illegitimate children—to pass a leash law for *cats*—all of these are responses to demands that government do something about everything. This is not what the Framers had in mind for limited government. As a result, there are fewer areas in which American citizens will not accept government activity.

23. This is known as the "delegate" theory of representation: that the elected representatives vote their constituents' wishes. An opposing view is the "trustee" theory of delegation, which assumes that legislators, having access to better information, should vote their own consciences, regardless of the wishes of the folks back home.

24. Of course, the writers of the Constitution knew about administration. Among the president's powers are that he may appoint "officers of the United States" (Article II, § 2 [2]), and that "he shall take care that the laws be faithfully executed" (Article II, § 3), which, even in 1787, would have been impossible without an administrative bureaucracy.

25. Congress is, of course, subject to constitutional checks in this process.

26. The discussion that follows on bureaucratic resources and implementation, unless otherwise noted, is drawn from Ripley and Franklin, *Policy Implementation and Bureaucracy*, esp. chapters 1 and 2.

27. This is an extremely complex part of administrative law, and immunity depends on a wide array of circumstances. See Cooper, *Public Law and Public Administration*, 3rd ed. (Itasca, Ill: Peacock, 2000), 527–548.

28. A very clear explanation of the implementation process is found in Daniel Mazmanian and Paul Sabatier, *Implementation and Public Policy* (Glenview, IL: Scott, Foresman & Company, 1983), esp. 22.

29. Judicial review (see chapter 4) is often based on congressional intent at the time legislation was passed, and this is the standard to which federal bureaucrats are held. However, if party control changes, bureaucrats may be faced with a Congress that prefers outcomes that don't match the intent of the original Congress, and it is this new Congress that now controls the agency budget.

30. One excellent definition of *sunk costs* is found in NEPA, § 102(C)(v), which refers to it as "irreversible and irretrievable commitment of resources."

31. This discussion of evaluation is from Peters, *American Public Policy*, chapter 7.

32. *Tennessee Valley Authority v. Hiram Hill et al.*, 437 U.S. 153 (1978).

33. This speculation on the motives underlying the moratorium is based on numerous conversations, between 1985 and 1988, with resource managers in the Chesapeake Bay and with political analysts interested in Maryland-Virginia conflicts.

CHAPTER FOUR

Legal Concepts in Environmental Law

Every discipline has basic techniques and skills. A miter joint is the same for a picture frame as for a house. Basic stitches must be mastered before sewing a hand towel or a suit. So it is with the law. This chapter explains the basic stitches of the law.

The chapter is divided into four parts. The first explains how to read a case to distinguish between the facts of a case and the point of law the case establishes.* Briefing or summarizing a case is the best way to distinguish between facts and law. A brief for *Tennessee Valley Authority v. Hill* (1978) is used to illustrate how to write a law school brief.

The second section discusses due process, which is at the heart of the administrative process. It is the set of rules that arbitrate between exercise of government power and rights of individuals. Included here are procedural due process, substantive due process, and a discussion of the "due process explosion." The third section covers standing, a common law legal concept that has been adapted to fit administrative law. The fourth section discusses the common law doctrines that are the basis for much of environmental law: nuisance, property, and the public trust doctrine.

*Readers who need to locate particular cases should consult "Finding Case Law," by Marian Kshetrapal, at the end of this book.

UNDERSTANDING CASE LAW

One of the most difficult ideas to grasp in following legal cases is that often the facts of the case are less important than the point of law decided by the court. Facts provide the context for the decision, such as the policy area, the precedents that might be followed, or mitigating circumstances. They frequently tell a tantalizing story, and it is frustrating to ask for "the rest of the story" and be unable to discover what happened to the parties in the case.[1] However, readers of court opinions are often looking for legal "holdings," or the legal precedents that are set. The holding or "point of law" is the core of the case; it is critical to learn how to find the point of law for each case. Perhaps the easiest way to remember how cases should be used is to place ourselves in the role of a prosecuting or defending attorney. How would this case support our argument?

To illustrate the importance of the point of law and the lesser importance of the facts of the case, consider two cases, *Boyce Motor Lines v. United States* (1952) and *Dalehite v. United States* (1953). Boyce Motor Lines was a trucking firm that transported, among other things, explosives. The regulations of the Interstate Commerce Commission (ICC) prohibited carrying explosives through tunnels, for the obvious reason that a tunnel, explosion not only endangers more lives than an explosion on an open highway, but in an underground or—even worse—an underwater tunnel the damage would be extensive. Unfortunately for Boyce, the ICC also had a rule that required trucks carrying explosives to move between the pick-up and delivery points as quickly as possible, which usually meant traveling by the shortest route. Boyce, a New York City firm, chose to take carbon bisulfide, an explosive, through the Holland Tunnel in Brooklyn, reasoning that avoiding the tunnel would put the truck on the road for significantly more miles and a longer time than was safe. The third time Boyce used the tunnel, the load exploded and about sixty people were injured. Boyce was indicted for violating ICC tunnel regulations; the district court dismissed the indictment but the appeals court reinstated it. Boyce appealed to the Supreme Court, arguing that the two rules were conflicting: the ICC had not given clear guidance, and it was impossible to transport explosives into Brooklyn without traveling on some dangerous, congested thoroughfare. The basis of Boyce's argument was that the regulations were impermissibly vague; the Court disagreed. Although three members of the Court dissented, the majority upheld the ICC and thus Boyce's indictment.

A second case dealing with explosives is *Dalehite v. United States* (1953). Both explosives and fertilizer contain ammonium nitrate, and after the Second World War the Army converted fifteen of its ordinance plants to fertilizer production as part of the American effort to rebuild the agriculture of Europe and Japan. In 1947, the harbor of Texas City, Texas, exploded: two ships loaded with the Army's fertilizer caught fire and blew up. Five hundred and sixty people were killed and over three thousand more injured; Texas City practically disappeared. In a class action suit, Dalehite and others sought damages from the government, claiming the government had acted negligently in its handling of the potentially explosive materials. In 1953, when the case finally reached the Supreme Court, existing law exempted the government from liability when the government was performing discretionary actions; to do otherwise would be to discourage government officials from making decisions with any element of risk in them at all. The Army argued successfully that the procedures it had followed in labeling and shipping the materials were discretionary, and Dalehite lost the case. Congress later redressed the damages by passing a relief bill.

At a superficial level, these two cases seem similar. They both deal with explosions and with the safe transportation of explosives. Yet they cannot be categorized as "explosives" cases. The legal issue in *Boyce* is the alleged vagueness of two ICC regulations, while the legal issue in *Dalehite* is government liability for accidents that result from the exercise of legitimate discretion. The harm in *Boyce* is caused by a private carrier; the harm in *Dalehite* is caused by the government. Although a perfunctory reading of these two cases might find them to be similar, their legal impact is quite different. A careful reading that tried to distinguish the precedent established by each case would distinguish between regulatory vagueness and administrative discretion.

One way to ensure that cases are understood is to make a *case brief*. There are two kinds of briefs: lengthy legal memoranda written by lawyers and filed with the courts to support motions, and the standard law school brief, which is a written summary, in a standard format, of the important facts and decisions of each case. The law school brief is a useful practice for managers to summarize key facts and the legal holding of each case. Briefing a case helps the reader grasp the essentials of the law determined in the case. While managers do not need all the information in a case brief, the habit of briefing is useful in a profession that rests so much on administrative law. Learning to brief a case may seem to be only an academic exercise, but the habit of figuring out the reasoning behind an opinion and the point of law is of incalculable value. Without a sense of the progression of legal thought, the legal concepts that our regulatory and management processes rely upon will be difficult to grasp. Legal concepts are fluid, varying with time, justices, and substantive areas.

Managers preparing new rules or planning to implement a program need to be able to predict, or at least to explain, judicial reactions to their behavior. By following judicial guidelines, managers may avoid problems. After the *Calvert Cliffs* decision (discussed in chapter 2), federal agency managers had no doubts about the requirements of the Environmental Impact Statement (EIS) provisions of the National Environmental Policy Act (NEPA). Understanding case law also helps managers interact with the attorneys in their agencies and in the private sector institutions with which they must deal. While the entire scope of environmental law is impossible for one person to master, the specific case law applying to any given agency's activities is accessible. Being able to distill the importance and impact of judicial decisions for themselves, and then to integrate their knowledge of recent cases with existing laws and agency regulations, puts managers in control of the law rather than at the mercy of others.

Briefing a Case

The first thing to understand about law school briefs is that they are short, hence the word *brief*. A formal brief starts out with the full name and legal citation of a case, including the year. (See Box 4.1, the sample brief of *Tennessee Valley Authority* [*TVA*] *v. Hill* [1978].) For administrators, the year a case is decided is very important, because the technology, social conditions, and political temper of the time the case was decided are critical to understanding how the case may be applied in current situations. The citation, or source, provides the volume number, the name of the series that reports the cases of the deciding court, and the page on which the court opinion begins. For example, in the *TVA* case, the opinion begins on page 153 of volume 437 of the *United States Reports* (the official government publication for Supreme Court decisions).

Second is the summary of the essential facts of the case. These are the behaviors and decisions that led to this particular case or controversy coming before the court. Was a species declared an "endangered species"? Was a cement plant constructed using the best available technology? Will individual members of the Sierra Club be affected when a recreational facility is built in Mineral King Valley? Only those facts necessary to understand the judicial reasoning in the opinion, concurrences, or dissents are included. This section also catalogs how the case comes before the court that wrote the opinion. Have administrative appeals been exhausted? Which court heard the case originally and how did those judges rule? What has been the history of the appeals process for this case?

Next, the issues of the case are stated in the form of a question or questions that can be answered "yes" or "no." For example, in the *Boyce* case, the question is: Are the ICC regulations governing transportation of hazardous material impermissibly vague? The judicial response to this particular question, which is the next piece of information in a brief, is "no." The court's response to each issue is followed by the action it ordered, if any.

A summary of the legal reasoning used by the judge writing the opinion follows. In a law school brief, only the reasoning that directly supports the opinion is included. Judicial excursions into interesting tangents are not put into a brief. The name of the judge writing the opinion is important because judges often develop a chain of reasoning over a series of cases or form temporary alliances with other judges. How the individual judge views an issue may be a key factor in anticipating later judicial decisions. Also, the opinions of some judges are more respected than others, so the prestige of the judge writing the opinion may give more weight to the decision.

Next are noted concurring and dissenting opinions, if any, and their reasoning. On courts in which more than one judge gives an opinion, a judge may agree with the outcome of the case but not agree with the reasoning by which it was reached; he may then write a *concurring opinion* in which he explains his own reasoning or changes the emphasis of the court's reasoning. A judge may disagree with the outcome and write an opinion in dissent. It is in concurring opinions and dissents that we sometimes find the clearest expressions of judicial opinions because judges are under no obligation to write either one, so their language is often more passionate and candid. In a court's majority opinion, the author is often fusing the decisions and rationales of more than one judge, but in a concurrence or dissent, the author is unfettered by such considerations. Since the manager needs to

BOX 4.1 EXAMPLE OF A LAW SCHOOL BRIEF

Tennessee Valley Authority v. Hiram Hill et al.

437 U.S. 153, 1978

FACTS

Construction began on Tellico Dam in 1967. August 1973: a new perch species (snail darter) was discovered in the river behind the dam site. December 1973: the Endangered Species Act (ESA) was passed. Congress continued to fund the dam after the ESA was enacted and had spent over $100 million on its construction. November 1975: the snail darter was listed as endangered. April 1976: seventeen miles of the Little Tennessee River behind the dam was declared critical habitat for the snail darter. February 1976: trying to save the snail darter, Hill brought suit in federal district court for an injunction to halt construction and was denied the injunction. On appeal, the Court of Appeals reversed the district court and ordered the injunction. TVA appealed to the United States Supreme Court.

ISSUES

1. Would TVA be in violation of the ESA if it completed and operated the Tellico Dam as planned? Yes.
2. If "yes," is an injunction the appropriate remedy? Yes. The decision of the Court of Appeals is affirmed.

REASONING

Justice Burger for the Court

The language of the ESA and the legislative history are clear. Congress intended to protect endangered species and their habitats without regard for cost. The ESA applies to all federal agencies, regardless of their primary missions. An injunction is the only appropriate remedy because it is the only way to halt activities that threaten the snail darter.

CONCUR

None

(continued)

4.1 EXAMPLE OF A LAW SCHOOL BRIEF (*continued*)

DISSENT

Justice Powell joined by Justice Blackmun: Congress has funded the Tellico Dam project for twelve years and continued this funding even after the ESA passed. There is no indication that the ESA was intended to be retroactive. While Congress will probably exempt the dam from the act, the Court should not force the congressional hand.

Justice Rehnquist: The District Court had the authority to issue an injunction to halt construction on the dam, but it was not required to do so even if it found a violation of the ESA.

SUMMARY

Barring explicit Congressional exemptions, the Endangered Species Act is a bar to any federal project that threatens the survival or habitat of a listed species.

---

understand the *reasoning* as a guide to his own behavior, it is important to understand all the legal motivations of the judges who are sufficiently concerned about an issue to write a concurrence or a dissent. Finally, the author of the brief should summarize the related principles and distinguish them, if necessary, from related cases.

It is critical that environmental managers do not carelessly assume that legal decisions and concepts from other policy areas also hold true for environmental policy. A good example of this is the concept of standing (discussed later). The criteria used to establish standing in environmental matters are not the same as the criteria in, for example, product liability cases

DUE PROCESS

Due process is at the heart of the administrative process; it is the set of rules that arbitrate between exercise of government power and rights of individuals. There are two forms of due process: *procedural* and *substantive*. Procedural due process is concerned with the forms and procedures followed by government when exercising its legitimate functions, while substantive due process is concerned with the legitimacy of government action in a particular sphere. Usually a reference to "due process" refers to *procedural* due process. Substantive due process is rarely invoked, although it is of more importance in environmental policy than in many other policy areas.

Procedural Due Process

Any government action that will affect a person's property requires some form of hearing before the action is taken.[2] Environmental management usually involves administrative hearings before government agencies rather than court proceedings; there are important differences between the two. In an administrative hearing there is no right to a trial by jury. Evidence is presented in a less formal manner than in court. The decisionmaker is not totally independent of the agency holding the hearing; unlike Article III judges (judges who derive their powers from Article III of the Constitution, the article establishing the federal judiciary), administrative law judges are civil servants and vulnerable to transfers, salary changes, and some political pressures. Usually the individual affected in an administrative hearing has the option to appeal the decision but he must first exhaust nonjudicial remedies before being allowed to take his case to the courts. Some statutes even forbid judicial review of agency decisions.

The case that lays the constitutional foundation for hearings in the administrative decision process is *Londoner v. Denver* (1908). The Colorado legislature had authorized the city of Denver to order street paving and to apportion costs to the adjoining property owners. The city did not allow a hearing for the property owners. The Supreme Court decided that when a tax is determined by a *subordinate body* (that is, an administrative agency acting under delegated legislative authority), constitutional due process guarantees the taxpayer the right to a hearing. Later cases restricted taxpayers' right to a hearing,[3] but the important point here is that when an administrative agency is acting under delegated legislative authority, its actions may constitutionally require a hearing.

The precise nature of the required hearing differs dramatically, depending on the legislative language, the nature of the issue, and the parties involved. A school child may be entitled to due process before being suspended from school, but her hearing can be a simple conference in the hall with the school principal. A food manufacturer challenging new FDA regulations will probably receive a full-scale, trial-like administrative hearing.

Substantive Due Process

Substantive due process is of particular interest in environmental administration because so much of environmental law deals with regulation and economic impact. At least in the early years of the republic, the courts were willing to argue that the legislative power did not include economic regulation.

For the judges who endorsed natural law as generating fundamental rights entitled to judicial protection from legislative interference, property was one of the three basic rights of individuals (along with life and liberty). In *Lochner v. NewYork* (1905), the Supreme Court invalidated a New York law regulating the hours of bakery workers on the grounds that it interfered with the right of contract between employers and employees. From 1905 to the mid-1930s, substantive due process provided justification for the courts to invalidate many state laws involving economic regulation, especially labor legislation, price regulation, and limitations on entry into business. By 1934, because of such actions, the court was on a collision path with President Franklin Roosevelt and the New Deal programs. Roosevelt prevailed; the first change occurred in 1934 when, in *Nebbia v. NewYork*, the Court refused to invalidate a New York law that fixed the selling price of milk. By 1941, the about-face was complete.[4] This posture has given both the federal and the state legislatures a freer hand in regulating businesses for environmental reasons. Business and industrial interests have tried unsuccessfully to claim that the legislatures lack the authority to regulate their enterprises, but proponents of environmental regulation have usually prevailed.

The "Due Process Explosion"

One of the greatest expansions in legal rights in the administrative state has come from the "due process explosion": the transformation of entitlements to property rights. The key case is *Goldberg v. Kelly* (1970), which established that welfare was a property right that could not be taken away without due process. Just when a government benefit becomes a right was spelled out in *Board of Regents v. Roth* (1972). In that case, the Court held that, in order for a due process hearing to be required, the interested person first must have more than a unilateral expectation of the benefit; he must also have a legitimate claim of entitlement. Moreover, this entitlement must originate in some independent source such as a law or already existing rules and regulations.

The expansion of entitlements to property rights is rarely an issue in environmental law. However, some states have established statutory rights to clean, safe environments; others have written such rights into their state constitutions. If these changes create entitlements for citizens, then state administrative agencies may be required to exercise due process safeguards when managing or regulating the environment. Usually constitutional safeguards are designed to protect citizens against government actions, but interpretations of the due process clause may create positive obligations to act:

> The courts have struggled with the issue of imposing liability for state inaction because they have failed to identify any workable Constitutional standard. But in fact the Supreme Court developed such a standard when it set forth the due process requirements for the withdrawal of statutory entitlements. Even assuming that a state has no obligation to provide protection in the first place, it may violate the due process clause when it assumes such an obligation and then fails to fulfill it.[5]

A special problem arises because of the general nature of environmental protection. Some government benefits, such as police protection, do not create property interests because there is no special class of citizen entitled to the benefits. However, one might argue that environmental protection is not analogous to police protection, which states must provide, but rather that the provision of environmental protection is voluntary and therefore creates rights. A supporting argument is found in a 1971 California case, *Marks v. Whitney*, in which one party sought to build a marina that would have limited the access of his neighbor to the ocean. The neighbor's standing—the right to bring suit—was challenged. The California Supreme Court held on appeal that the neighbor had standing because, if the plaintiff were allowed to build his marina, he would be "taking away from [his neighbor] rights to which he is entitled as a member of the general public."[6]

STANDING

Traditionally, standing is the right to have one's case heard before a tribunal, that is, the right to "stand" before the judge. To have this right at common law, one must have suffered an actual injury to a legally protected right. In federal cases, the requirement that a party bringing an action must have standing, or a sufficient stake or connection to the litigation, arises from the U.S. Constitution's "case or controversy" requirement (Article III, § 2).[7] The *Fontainebleau* case illustrates some of the common law considerations for standing. The Fontainebleau Hotel, built in 1954, was one of the grand hotels of Miami Beach. Its rival, the Eden Roc, was built next door in 1955. The owners of the Fontainebleau planned to add a fourteen-story addition that would shade the Eden Roc's beach, cabana, and pool after 2:00 p.m. The Eden Roc's owners obtained an injunction to stop the construction, and the Fontainebleau appealed. The appeals court supported the Fontainebleau because, under Florida law, the Eden Roc's owners had neither a statutory right nor a state or federal constitutional right to the sunshine.[8] They could not bring a suit because they had no standing: no legally protected right of the hotel owners had been infringed.

This venerable common law view of standing has changed as the administrative state has evolved. In 1946, the Administrative Procedure Act (APA), which is discussed in chapter 5, broadened access to judicial review of agency actions:

> A person suffering a legal wrong because of agency action, or adversely affected or aggrieved by agency action within the meaning of a relevant statute, is entitled to judicial review thereof. (5 U.S.C. § 702)

This section of the APA liberalized access to judicial review of agency actions. Standing is a very complex issue, and judicial interpretations of standing vary with the policy area being reviewed. Several United States Supreme Court decisions since 1970 illustrate the evolving standing doctrine in environmental law. The first of these is *Association of Data Processing Service Organizations v. Camp* (1970), in which the Association attempted to reverse an administrative decision allowing banks to provide data processing services to their clients. The question of the Association's standing to bring the suit was raised. In this case, the Supreme Court significantly altered the criteria for standing to two questions: (1) is the person bringing the suit "aggrieved in fact," and (2) is the interest to be protected "arguably within the zone of interests to be protected or regulated by the statute or constitutional guarantee in question?"[9] *Data Processing* thus effectively eliminated the more rigorous test of "legally protected right" in cases of judicial review of administrative action.[10]

A second case is the famous *Mineral King* case, *Sierra Club v. Morton* (1972). The Sierra Club tried to halt development of a $35 million recreation facility by Walt Disney Enterprises on national forest land in Mineral King Valley. The Sierra Club did not allege any actual injury to its members; instead it asserted a right to be heard because of its organizational interests in protecting the environment. The Supreme Court relied on *Data Processing* and refused to grant the Sierra Club standing because individual members were not shown to be "injured in fact." However, the Court spelled out how standing might be achieved: the Sierra Club only had to assert that some of its members would be unable to enjoy their usual outdoor recreational pursuits if the Disney resort were built. It is in this case that Justice Douglas wrote his famous dissent suggesting that even trees should have standing. He noted that American law already gave legal standing to some inanimate objects, such as ships, and even to some organizations, such as corporations, and he asserted that environmental objectives would be enhanced if litigators could sue on behalf of the trees or valleys or rivers.[11]

In 1973, the Court took its expanded notion of standing to new heights in *United States v. Students Challenging Regulatory Agency Procedures (SCRAP)*. Five Washington State students had formed an organization to challenge an ICC decision to allow across-the-board rate increases for the railroads.[12] The ICC already had in place a higher rate for recycled materials. The students argued that by increasing the rates, recycled materials would be even less profitable to ship, thus discouraging recycling and increasing the litter in the parks they enjoyed near their home city of Seattle. They also claimed that the lowered demand for recycled materials would cause an increase in logging and mining (to provide raw material for new products), thereby reducing their pleasure in the surrounding countryside. Improbably, the Supreme Court granted standing, although the challenge to the regulation was unsuccessful.

This decision to grant standing rested on reasoning that must have been a shock to the ICC. The Court said that SCRAP's argument was strengthened by the notion that many people would be affected, and that the rather minimal nature of each person's harm was not a relevant factor. This is opposite the argument that was accepted by the Court for years as an absolute bar to taxpayer's suits: there are so many taxpayers, and the individual harm done by one new tax to the economic status of any one taxpayer is so small, that taxpayer suits against the government are unacceptable.[13]

After *SCRAP*, the Court seemed to pull back from its liberal interpretation of standing in nonenvironmental cases. However, in environmental issues it continued to accept rather tenuous arguments for standing. *Duke Power Co. v. Carolina Environmental Study Group* (1978) challenged the Price-Anderson Act, which limited the liability for damages caused by nuclear power companies to $560 million for any one accident. The Carolina Environmental Study Group claimed that their damages from an accident would probably exceed the Price-Anderson limit, which meant that the statute was depriving them of property (their projected damages) without compensation. The nuclear power plants, they also contended, would never be built without the Price-Anderson protections, and the reactors were harming the environment. The Court granted standing and found that the Price-Anderson Act was an acceptable substitute for common law remedies for damages.

There are several reasons why the courts were initially more liberal in granting standing in environmental cases than in nonenvironmental ones. First, in the early 1970s, and following on the heels of NEPA and Earth Day, the courts were eager to give environmentalists a chance to be heard, although being allowed to bring the suit did not guarantee victory for environmentalists. The Sierra Club in *Mineral King* was denied standing at first, although the Court carefully pointed out what they needed to do to establish standing, and they immediately refiled. The students in *SCRAP* lost their challenge to the ICC regulations. And Duke Power continued to build its reactor. The courts are as sensitive as any other branch of government to public opinion (although they are less vulnerable to expressions of public ill-will), and in these cases they were willing to open the judicial doors for discussion of issues.

Second, during the early seventies, the Supreme Court had a number of liberal, activist justices; Justice Douglas was an ardent environmentalist and often brought his fellow justices along with him. Finally, in most cases the decisions required only statutory interpretation, and the judges were rarely asked to interpret (and perhaps to amend informally) the Constitution in their decisions. Thus one of their traditional barriers to review—a reluctance to reach constitutional issues—was almost certain to be avoided.

In recent years, as the Court has become more conservative, it has indicated that it might want to tighten the liberal standing requirements a bit, holding in *Lujan v. National Wildlife Federation* (1990) that vague allegations of a connection between the environmental group members and federal lands with which they were concerned was not sufficient to convey standing.[14] However, at present, to be granted standing persons must satisfy four general requirements.[15] First, they must be within the "zone of interest" covered by the statute. Second, they must establish that they have suffered an "injury in fact."[16] Third, they must show that the agency action is the cause of the harm. Finally, they must demonstrate a substantial likelihood that a judicial relief will reduce the injury.[17]

CASE DISCUSSION 4.1

Animal Watchers Abroad

The Endangered Species Act (ESA) was passed in 1973. Five years later, in 1978, the United States Fish and Wildlife Service (FWS) and National Marine Fisheries Service (NMFS) issued regulations stating that the ESA applied to actions of federal agencies abroad. (FWS is in the Department of Interior, and NMFS is in the Department of Commerce. The two agencies share ESA responsibilities because marine resources are managed under Commerce.) In 1986, a new joint regulation changed the agreement: now consultation with the relevant secretary was necessary only for federal agency actions in the United States or on the high seas.

Defenders of Wildlife challenged the new regulation. However, because the harm was alleged to occur outside the United States, they had a new set of barriers to overcome to be granted standing.

Two members of Defenders of Wildlife filed affidavits about their interests in international wildlife. Joyce Kelly claimed that American involvement in rehabilitation of the Aswan Dam in Egypt was contributing to loss of habitat for the endangered Nile crocodile; in 1986 she had traveled to Egypt to observe the crocodile and intended to do so again. Amy Skilbred made similar allegations about the U.S. Agency for International Development's funding for the Mahaweli project in Sri Lanka.

Defenders of Wildlife offered three other rationales for standing. The "ecosystem nexus" argued that any person who used part of a contiguous ecosystem has a legal interest in any federally funded activity that

(continued)

CASE DISCUSSION 4.1 (*continued*)

harms that ecosystem, no matter how far away the harm might be. The "animal nexus" suggested that anyone concerned about seeing or studying an endangered species anywhere in the world would have standing if federally funded activities were harming the species. The "vocational nexus" argued that anyone who worked professionally with a species (for example, a zookeeper) would have standing to intervene if that species were at risk from a federal agency action.

What are the arguments against these claims to standing? In particular, what are the problems with *redressability* for overseas projects that are funded in part by American money? Do you think the *Mineral King* court would have accepted any of these arguments?

(Source: *Lujan v. Defenders of Wildlife*, 504 U.S. 555 [1992])

COMMON LAW: NUISANCE, PROPERTY, AND PUBLIC TRUST

Allegations of environmental harm have always had remedies available at common law, and courts are inclined to follow this tradition. Although the circumstances of the environmental harm have changed, judges still have the common law and its precedents upon which to draw for remedies. One of the common law concepts that applies to environmental cases is that of nuisance.

Nuisance

The concept of nuisance has a distinguished pedigree in common law. Nuisance usually involves a suit by one neighbor against another, or by the public prosecutor suing on behalf of the public. The general rule for nuisance is that no one may act so as to unreasonably interfere with the property rights of another person. There are two kinds of nuisance: private nuisance and public nuisance. A private nuisance is the unreasonable interference with the use or enjoyment of one's land, but it does not include physical invasion or trespass, for example, throwing trash over the fence. Playing drums at dawn or keeping pigs in an urban setting would be private nuisances.[18]

A public nuisance is an activity that adversely affects the health, morals, safety, welfare, comfort, or convenience of the public in general. Large-scale air and water pollution may be considered public nuisances. It is sometimes difficult to distinguish trespass from nuisance; for example, air pollution technically involves particulate matter falling in inappropriate places and is therefore really trespass, but the law tends to treat it as a nuisance. This allows a governmental remedy rather than requiring individuals to sue for damages from trespass.

Whether or not an activity is a nuisance may depend on its location. Rural areas are typically more lenient in the kinds of undertakings they will permit. A hog farm in rural Vermont does not impair the neighbors' use of their property, but transported to Boston, the same hog farm would be cast out. Residential areas tend to be the most restrictive, and even when the "nuisance" was in place first, often the residential use may have priority, as illustrated in the following case of *Spur Industries v. Del Webb Development* (1972).

In 1954, a suburban development catering to retirees was established west of Phoenix, Arizona. Two years later, in 1956, a feed lot, later sold to Spur Industries, was started about two miles south of the development. In May of 1959, Del Webb began to develop Sun City, building south from the first retirement community. As Sun City grew, so did the feedlot, and by December of 1976, the two were only five hundred feet apart. Although Webb had chosen to develop south, and at least in the early years did not consider Spur to be a problem, by 1967 he was having trouble selling residential lots near Spur. Not even Sun City could tolerate 30,000 head of cattle and a million tons of wet manure per day, baking in the Arizona heat. Webb sued to close Spur, alleging that Spur was both a private and a public nuisance.

Spur contested the action with the defense of "coming to the nuisance": Spur Industries had preceded Del Webb into west Phoenix, and Webb had known all along that the feedlot was there.

The court was sympathetic to the interests of the people living in Sun City and found that Spur constituted a nuisance. The court ordered Spur to move but also ordered Webb to pay for the costs of the move. The court reasoned that in the interests of public health and enjoyment of property, Spur must move, but since Webb had put himself and his home buyers in the predicament, he must pay to extricate them.

Not all such cases end so satisfactorily for both parties. Usually when an activity is economically beneficial and yet still a nuisance, the courts find themselves using the "balancing of hardships" or "balancing of the equities" doctrine. The Boomer case is a classic example of this doctrine. As is often the case with common law remedies, the exigencies of the situation may confound our ideas of equitable settlement. The benefits of allowing a nuisance to continue must be balanced with the costs of the nuisance. Who is to blame for the problem? What are the relative hardships for each of the parties? Are there third parties or the public involved?

CASE DISCUSSION 4.2

Shake, Rattle, and . . . Boom

In 1962, Atlantic Cement Company began operating a large cement plant in the Hudson Valley near the houses of Oscar Boomer and his neighbors. The plant spewed dirt and smoke into the air, which settled on the houses and property of the nearby landowners, and the vibration from the plant disturbed them. Common law is quite clear that these activities were a nuisance; the remedy at common law for a nuisance is an injunction to stop.

The plant cost $45 million to build and employed over 300 people. The plant used all available technology to reduce the smoke, dirt, and vibrations; any improvements that might be possible in the future would require research and development, most likely by the cement industry in general rather than by a single company. Such research would take years.

Should the plant be forced to close because it is a nuisance? If not, what remedies would you suggest?

(Source: *Boomer v. Atlantic Cement Company*, 26 N.Y. 2d 219 [1970])

The next section deals with property, a concept dear to the heart of Americans; we place it in the pantheon of national values, side by side with life and liberty.[19]

Property

The concept of property is rooted in English common law. Although the notion of property has expanded since the 1960s to include entitlements such as welfare, this section focuses on real property—land and the economic issues related to land.

The first section, Origins of Land Use Control, looks at the changes in land tenure systems from feudal days to the Industrial Revolution in the United States. Next is the discussion of eminent domain, the ancient right of the sovereign to take private property for public use. In American law, this right is constrained by our notions of due process, both procedural and substantive. Zoning, the regulation of private property uses, is the topic of the third section; some argue that this is really a taking or exercise of eminent domain. A discussion of regulation versus taking (which requires compensation) concludes the section on property.

Origins of Land Use Control

The concept of land use controls or regulations is not a phenomenon of the twentieth century, despite the resistance to zoning and other forms of regulation in rural areas. The regulation of land extends through Anglo-Saxon common law to ancient times; the earliest code of Roman law, dating to 451–450 BC, provided for setbacks in housing construction.

Land use law is not constant; as social and economic conditions change, the law must adapt to protect new arrangements of land use and ownership and to encourage the policies preferred by the authorities. In the eleventh and twelfth centuries, English villages were largely feudal and had "common" land for the villages to use for grazing their livestock. Our modern-day notions of *common* as a public right does not accurately describe the medieval commons.[20] In the commons system, either by common law right as a freehold tenant or through usage and grants, a villager was entitled to pasture limited numbers of specific animals on the land not otherwise used by the feudal lord. The villager also had rights to cut wood, to fish, and to cut peat or turf for fuel. Even from the beginning, the use of the common was restricted and subject to communal control.[21] Villages determined what kinds of animals and how many might be put on the common, the time of year they could be set loose, how long they might graze, and when they must be removed.

Although the commons system lasted for centuries, abuses of the system by the wealthier landholders were frequent. Problems of the sixteenth, seventeenth, and eighteenth centuries sound familiar:

> the poor owning rights may largely be kept out of their rights by the action of large farmers who exceed their rights. . . . Again, jobbers would hire cottages in order to obtain, as it were, a right of entry to the common and then proceed to eat up the common; or new cottages would spring up near the common, and though legally without rights, would encroach in practice on those to whom the common really belonged.[22]

The unfortunate poor tenant was denied his remedy at law for the illegal abuses of the more powerful landowners. The ultimate conclusion was the enclosure of the common land, mostly between 1720 and 1880.[23] Political demands for land reform were frequently no more than a sophisticated land-grab, justified in part by the admittedly striking increase in productivity of enclosed common land.[24]

While the system of communal land control was changing in rural areas, the urban landscape was also under examination. Urban crowding reached previously unthinkable heights, and in London, the Great Fire recorded by Samuel Pepys in the seventeenth century produced building codes and land use restrictions.

The American colonists had brought with them an acceptance of land use controls, but they found such regulations were not necessary in the New World. Land was plentiful, and only when the Census of 1890 declared the American frontier officially closed did Americans really begin to come to grips with the need for land reform and regulation.

Conflicts over land use were at first easy to settle. Usually the common law remedy of nuisance was sufficient to settle private disputes. Initially, the strength of the concept of property rights (and the Lockean notion that if a person had worked for something, and paid for it, it was his to do with as he wished) overrode any suspicion that the public might be better served if some activities were prohibited or restricted. However, as the American cities grew, public controls became necessary. Cities began to pass ordinances restricting certain kinds of activities (such as tanneries, or candle makers, or slaughterhouses with their attendant odors and refuse) to particular parts of town. The source of the power to regulate such activities is the *police power.* Although the term is not specifically mentioned in the federal Constitution, it refers to the inherent power of a state (subject to constitutional limitations and due process) to promote order, public health, safety, morals, and general welfare. Early objections to the exercise of the police power generally rested on the notion of "taking" (the government was taking an individual's property for public use), but in the nineteenth century, charges of taking only meant the actual physical seizure of property. (This notion of "taking" is discussed more thoroughly later.)

Most controls on land use come from government regulation, but some arise at common law. One is the concept of nuisance, discussed earlier. Another is the notion of *waste*, which can arise when people share interests and rights in a resource. Waste is committing acts upon the land that are harmful to the rights of the party not in possession. A tenant who cut down all the trees in his landlord's yard would be guilty of waste. Waste can be affirmative (cutting down the trees) or permissive (allowing a roof to deteriorate so that rain damages the interior of the house). The remedy for waste can be money damages, an injunction to stop the conduct that is causing the harm, or some combination of the two.

Land use may also be controlled by private law or contractual devices such as easements and covenants. An easement is the legal right to use or traverse someone else's land and must be transferred when the property is transferred. Often utility companies have easements across private property for power lines or telephone wires or water pipes. Covenants are restrictions that "run with the land." Unlike easements, which in effect allow a physical trespass on the owner's property, covenants restrict the uses to which the land may be put. These covenants are voluntary, in the sense that buyers don't have to buy if they don't like them, but they are usually binding and also transfer with the property. Examples of covenants include prohibitions on children in retirement communities, restrictions on the types and heights of fences that may be erected around property, and minimum house sizes. Covenants that are discriminatory, such as banning racial or religious groups from owning property in a neighborhood, are not legal.

Eminent Domain

The right of the state to take private property is ancient. In English law, all property at one time belonged to the Crown, and in England today this is still technically true. When the sovereign took his subject's property, he was simply reclaiming property that already belonged to him. The sovereign was not required to use due process, nor was he required to pay compensation. In the United States, the Fifth Amendment to the Constitution imposes an obligation on the national government to exercise due process of law in taking private property, as well as an obligation to pay for it:

> No person shall . . . be deprived of life, liberty, or property, without due process of law; *nor shall private property be taken for public use, without just compensation.* (Emphasis added.)

From an analytic perspective, there are several critical factors in interpreting the Fifth Amendment. First, the amendment protects *persons* and not just *citizens*; some sections of the Constitution (for example, the Eleventh Amendment) apply only to citizens. Second, the amendment does permit persons to be deprived of life, liberty, or property; the restriction is that such persons must have "due process of law." What is "due process"? Due process embodies society's fundamental concepts of legal fairness. At a minimum, due process includes the right to a hearing. The government does in fact deprive persons of life (capital punishment), liberty (imprisonment), and property (taxes). There is, however, a restriction on taking real property; the last part of the amendment states that private property may not be taken for public use without just compensation; in other words, if the federal government wants a person's farm for a military base, it may take the farm but must pay a reasonable price for it. The power to do this is known as the power of eminent domain. It is not, however, essential for the exercise of eminent domain that the government be taking property for actual use by the government; "public use" can mean either actual use by the public (beaches, new military bases) or use for public advantage (for example, easements for electric power lines).[25] In the nineteenth century, the federal government even gave the power of eminent domain to the railroads as an incentive for them to build a transcontinental line.

CASE DISCUSSION 4.3

Playing Chicken

In May 1942, the federal government leased an airport near Greensboro, North Carolina, for use as a military airfield. The Causbys owned a chicken farm about one half-mile from the end of the runway. The glide path for the airplanes went directly over the property. Airplanes cleared the house by 67 feet, the barn by 63 feet, and the highest trees by a mere 18 feet, occasionally passing close enough to blow old leaves off the trees. These heights met Civil Aeronautics Authority standards. Bombers, cargo planes, and fighters took off frequently, often in great numbers, and during both daylight and nighttime hours. The chickens were terrified; many died of fright, and production fell. The farm could no longer be used as a commercial operation. The family was unable to sleep, and several airplane accidents near their property had made them reluctant to stay in so dangerous a place.

- The United States has "complete and exclusive national sovereignty in the air space" above U.S. territory. 49 U.S.C. §176(a)
- "Navigable air space" is "airspace above the minimum safe altitudes of flight prescribed by the Civil Aeronautics Authority." 49 U.S.C. 180
- The minimum safe altitudes for flight were 500 feet (day) and 1,000 feet (night) for air carriers and 300/1000 for other aircraft. (Civil Air Regulations)
- Under North Carolina law, the state has airspace sovereignty "except where granted to and assumed by the United States." Overflights are lawful "unless at such a low altitude as to interfere with the then existing use. . . or unless . . . imminently dangerous. . . ." Otherwise, "ownership of the space above the lands and waters of this state is . . . vested in the several owners of the surface beneath." North Carolina General Statute's 1943, 63–11

Has the federal government "taken" Causby's land? If so, is this a permanent taking or an easement? Is Causby entitled to damages?

Regardless of the legal ruling, do you think Causby should be compensated?

(Source: *United States v. Causby*, 328 U.S. 256 [1946])

The Fifth Amendment is found in the federal Constitution and until the end of the nineteenth century was held to apply only to the actions of the federal government. Although many states had similar clauses in their state constitutions, in 1868 when the Fourteenth Amendment passed, five states still lacked the requirement for just compensation when the state seized private property. The Fourteenth Amendment reads in part:

> No State shall make or enforce any law which shall abridge the privileges or immunities of citizens of the United States; nor shall any State deprive any person of life, liberty, or property, without due process of law; nor deny to any person within its jurisdiction the equal protection of the laws. (§ 1)

Through a long series of Supreme Court cases that do not concern us here, the Supreme Court has held that the Fourteenth Amendment incorporates virtually all of the Bill of Rights, that the protections the citizens have from the federal government apply as well to state government actions. While this has been of interest primarily in criminal cases, in environmental law the application of due process rights can be critical. Through the nationalization of the Bill of Rights, the national constitutional protections for property also apply to the states. This has important ramifications for issues of zoning and other forms of land use regulation; states must use due process when taking property, and owners whose property is taken by eminent domain must receive just compensation.

Just compensation is usually determined by fair market value: what a willing buyer would pay a willing seller to put the land to its highest and best use. If only part of the property is taken, and the value of the remainder is changed, compensation is adjusted to include the loss or increase of value. A simpler calculus that is sometimes employed is to pay the difference between the value before the taking and the value after. There are other kinds of property rights that must be compensated; people other than the owner may have vested rights in the property. For example, some states still have dower rights that give the wife a certain percentage of the value of all of her husband's real property, regardless of when or how he acquired it. When this property is taken, the dower rights must also be compensated. A lessee may need compensation, as may a person holding an easement across the property, or someone with other rights such as mineral rights. Who is entitled to compensation and how that entitlement is calculated is a complex issue that varies widely among political jurisdictions.

Not all governmental actions that affect property require compensation. Land use regulation through zoning, which rarely involves compensation, has been used for well over a century.

Zoning

The first comprehensive zoning plan in the United States was passed by New York City in 1916.[26] Since then the validity of zoning has repeatedly been upheld by the courts as a legitimate use of the police power. Zoning is invalid only if it is unreasonable or arbitrary and capricious—the usual standards against which administrative action is judged—or if it deprives the owner of all or practically all of the use of his property. The general rule is that to be valid, zoning must be authorized by enabling statutes; comprehensive zoning is usually governed by statute and therefore is better able to withstand judicial challenge than incremental or piecemeal zoning.

The landmark case for comprehensive zoning is *Euclid v. Ambler Realty Company* (1926). This was the first case in which the U.S. Supreme Court directly addressed the constitutionality of zoning. Ambler Realty owned property abutting an industrial area. When the property was zoned residential, its value was cut by two-thirds. Ambler sued the city on the grounds that the zoning restriction was an unconstitutional taking without either due process or compensation. The Supreme Court upheld the use of the state's governmental police power.

Why would this case rest on an exercise of *state* power when it was the village of Euclid that had enacted the zoning ordinance? The reason rests on a peculiarity of American land use law. Counties and cities have no sovereign status.[27] The powers that they have are given to them by the states, and so the exercise of land regulation is indirectly an exercise of a state power. The basis for many zoning challenges is that the localities exceeded the authority given to them by their state governments. However, because the zoning process is based on state legislative authority, a local zoning ordinance will usually not be overturned unless it is found to be arbitrary or capricious.

Regulation versus Taking

A big quandary in land use law is distinguishing between *regulation* (a permissible use of the police power to regulate land use for the general welfare) and *taking* (government action that takes a person's property and requires compensation). Land use regulation often affects the value of property; for example, a setback requirement may interfere with plans for a home addition. This sort of regulation does not usually require compensation. However, if the regulation effectively removes any possibility of an economic return on the property, even if the government does not actually take legal possession of the property, it is likely to be ruled a taking. Determining the status of cases between these two scenarios has occupied the courts for decades. The original distinction was between public protection and public benefit: if the government action that diminished use or value of the property was to protect the public health, safety, or welfare (for example, installing sewer lines, requiring yards to be trimmed for rodent control, segregating housing from industry), it was regulatory and did not require compensation. If the government action was to provide a public benefit (wider roads, new schools, easements for power cables), it was a taking and did require compensation. It was a neat distinction but it did not help in complex cases.[28]

In 1978, the Supreme Court provided some clarification. It decided in *Pennsylvania Central Transportation Co. v. New York* that "taking" must meet a three part test. First, a taking probably exists if there has been a physical invasion of the property, for example, running a power line. Second, a taking may exist if the restriction on the property does not produce widespread public benefit or it is not applied to all property in similar situations. Finally, the third test examines the extent to which the property owner is restricted from earning a reasonable rate of return on his investment in the property.

Cases in the late 1980s brought into sharper focus the concerns of municipal and state planning authorities over the exercise of their land use powers. In *First English Evangelical Lutheran Church of Glendale v. City of Los Angeles* (1987), the Supreme Court gave damages to the landowner for income lost as the result of land use regulations. Also in 1987, the Court ruled in *Nollan v. California Coastal Commission* that the Coastal Commission requirement for public access to the beach over Nollan's property was a taking.

In the early 1990s, the federal courts continued to restrict the power of government to regulate private property if its economic value is reduced. In *Lucas v. South Carolina Coastal Council* (1992), the Court held that the state's Beachfront Management Act, enacted to increase the protection of coastal areas after the devastation of Hurricane Hugo, rendered Lucas's housing lots valueless and therefore constituted a taking. In effect, a regulation that eliminates all economic value of a property now entitles the owner to compensation. In *Dolan v. City of Tigard* (1994), the Court held that requiring a public easement as a condition for a building permit was a taking, and unlike the *Nollan* case, the Court placed the burden of proof on the government rather than the land owner.

CASE DISCUSSION 4.4

Redistributing Paradise

Under original Hawaiian law, all land was controlled by the high chief: there was no private ownership of land. Despite attempts by political leaders and settlers to redistribute land, by the 1960s very few people owned land in Hawaii. Public lands comprised 49 percent of the state, with 47 percent of the remaining land owned by only 72 individuals. Eighteen landowners with properties of 21,000 acres or more owned almost half of the private property; on Oahu, ownership was even more concentrated, with 22 people owning 72.5 percent of the private land. The Hawaii legislature decided this led to inflated land prices and was harmful to public welfare.

Landowners claimed they had been reluctant to sell any land because of federal tax liabilities. In 1967, Hawaii passed the Land Reform Act, which allowed the state to condemn leased residential tracts and then to transfer them to the current lessees. The condemnation process avoided some federal tax liability. The Hawaii Housing Authority managed the transactions with safeguards in place to avoid any new concentrations of ownership.

- ". . . nor shall private property be taken for public use without just compensation." (U.S. Constitution, Amendment V)
- The 1945 District of Columbia Redevelopment Act allowed condemnation of private lands (slums) and possible transfers to private interests. This was a "public use" because slum clearance is a proper use of the police power. *Berman v. Parker*, 348 U.S. 26 (1954)

(continued)

CASE DISCUSSION 4.4 (*continued*)

- Legislatures may decide what is a "public use" unless their decision is completely unreasonable. (*United States v. Gettysburg Electric Railway Company*, 160 U.S. 668 [1896])
- "Public use" does not require the general public to use or to have access to the property. (*Rindge Co. v. Los Angeles County*, 262 U.S. 700 [1923])

Is such a massive redistribution of private land a legitimate "public use"?

(Source: *Hawaii Housing Authority v. Midkiff*, 467 U.S. 229 [1984])

The law on takings versus legitimate regulation remains unclear. The most recent judicial pronouncements on this problem have come in two major cases, *Tahoe-Sierra Preservation Council v. Tahoe Regional Planning Agency* (2002),[29] and *Kelo et al. v. City of New London et al.* (2005).[30] In Tahoe, the local planning authority imposed two moratoria on development while they were formulating a comprehensive land use plan. Some landowners, following *Lucas*, claimed a taking. Relying on the *Penn Central* test, the Supreme Court ruled that a temporary ban necessitated for planning that affected all property owners equally was not a taking and therefore did not require compensation. The Court refused to announce an absolute rule on takings because such decisions must rest on the particular circumstances of each case. Justice Stevens, writing for the Court, wrote:

> A rule that required compensation for every delay in the use of property would render routine government processes prohibitively expensive or encourage hasty decision-making. Such an important change in the law should be the product of legislative rulemaking rather than adjudication.[31] (Notes omitted.)

In 2000, New London, Connecticut, approved a downtown and waterfront revitalization project coordinated by a nonprofit organization, the New London Development Corporation (NLDC). Susette Kelo and nine of her neighbors refused to sell their properties to the city, and the city began condemnation proceedings. The city planned to convey the condemned properties to the NLDC for development. Kelo argued that the city could not authorize the condemnation because their property was not going for "public use." The Supreme Court disagreed five to four, holding that because a Connecticut state statute specifically authorizes the use of eminent domain for economic development, and the city made a reasonable determination that economic rejuvenation was appropriate, the Court deferred to the city's decision. In a stinging dissent, Justice O'Connor wrote:

> Under the banner of economic development, all private property is now vulnerable to being taken and transferred to another private owner, so long as it might be upgraded—i.e., given to an owner who will use it in a way that the legislature deems more beneficial to the public—in the process.[32]

Later she makes the point again: "Nothing is to prevent the state from replacing any Motel 6 with a Ritz-Carlton, any home with a shopping mall, or any farm with a factory."[33]

The backlash that followed the Kelo decision was substantial. The U.S. House of Representatives passed a resolution deploring the result in a 365–33 vote.[34] Several states have passed or initiated legislation to limit the power of eminent domain.[35] One response was directed at a member of the Court. Freestar Media LLC proposed using eminent domain to seize land in New Hampshire owned by Justice Souter. They would then build the Lost Liberty Hotel; the hotel restaurant would be called the Just Desserts Café.[36]

Public Trust Doctrine

In American law, the notion of the public trust dates to *Martin v. Waddell* (1842) (see chapter 1) and is based on the common law doctrine that navigable rivers and waterfronts are held by the sovereign for the use of all the people.[37] Traditionally the public trust applied only to tidelands and waters used in navigation, water-related commerce, and fisheries; under the original English common law, inland resources were the property of the Crown and were not within the public trust.[38] The public trust doctrine in the

United States has, however, been expanded to include national parks, inland lakes, and wildlife.

The landmark case in public trust is *Illinois Central Railroad Company v. Illinois* (1892). In 1869, the state of Illinois had granted some submerged Chicago shorefront lands in Lake Michigan to the Illinois Central Railroad. Four years later, repenting of its gift, the state repealed the grant. The state then filed suit to "quiet the title" so the chain of ownership would be clearly recorded. Understandably, the railroad objected: the state retaking title to land that was privately owned seemed to raise the constitutional question of a violation of due process. However, the Supreme Court cleverly avoided the constitutional question by finding the original grant of land to be invalid because it violated the public trust obligations of Illinois.[39] This case established the central tenet in public trust litigation:

> When a state holds a resource which is available for the free use of the general public, a court will look with considerable skepticism upon *any* governmental conduct which is calculated *either* to reallocate that resource to more restricted uses *or* to subject public uses to the self interest of private parties.[40] (Emphasis added.)

The public trust doctrine has been used in three basic legal settings: *resource defense* (human activities threaten trust assets); *alienation* (relinquishing publicly owned resources into private hands); and *diversion* (government attempts to use trust resources in inappropriate ways).[41] The public trust doctrine is rarely invoked unless a violation of the public trust is alleged.[42] *National Audubon Society v. Department of Water and Power of the City of Los Angeles (Mono Lake)* (1983), in which the trust doctrine was invoked to halt the city of Los Angeles from drawing municipal water from Mono Lake, is an example of resource defense. *Illinois Central* (discussed earlier) is the classic alienation case; another alienation case frequently cited is *Gould v. Greylock Reservation Commission* (1966), in which the Commonwealth of Massachusetts tried to lease part of a public park to a private corporation for ski development.[43] *Paepke v. Building Commission* (1970) illustrates diversion; in this case, the city of Chicago was sued unsuccessfully to stop public school construction in a public park.[44]

The public trust includes "an affirmative protective duty of government—a fiduciary obligation—in dealing with certain properties held publicly."[45] Some authorities go even further: one said that resource managers "have to view the [public trust] as the Bank of America trust officer would for a trust you set up for your children—strict adherence to trust principles."[46] Public trust resources

> are protected by the trust against unfair dealing and dissipation, which is classical trust language suggesting the necessity for procedural correctness and substantive care. . . . The public trust doctrine demands fair procedures, decisions that are justified, and results that are consistent with protection and perpetuation of the resources.[47]

At least one state court has found that the public trust in natural resources is an active trust. In 1927, the Wisconsin state Supreme Court ruled that:

> The trust reposed in the state is not a passive trust; it is governmental, active, and administrative. . . . [T]he trust, being both active and administrative, requires the lawmaking body to act in all cases where action is necessary, not only to preserve the trust, but to promote it. . . . A failure so to act, in our opinion, would have amounted to gross negligence and a misconception of its proper duties and obligations in the premises.[48]

SUGGESTED READING

Bean, Michael J., and Melanie Rowland. *The Evolution of National Wildlife Law*. 3rd ed. New York: Praeger, 1997. This is the only comprehensive book that I know of on this topic; fortunately for us all, it is a clear, complete, and well-written treatise.

Cooper, Phillip. *Public Law and Public Administration*. 3rd ed. Itasca, IL: Peacock, 2000. This is *not* a casebook, which makes it a rarity among books on administrative law. I think it is the best administrative law book available; a fourth edition is rumored to be forthcoming.

Friedman, Lawrence M. *A History of American Law*. 3rd ed. New York: Touchstone, 2005. The widely praised and definitive introduction to the topic.

Schuck, Peter. *Foundations of Administrative Law*. Oxford, UK: Oxford University Press, 1994. An invaluable collection of classic articles in the field of administrative law.

NOTES

1. A case I find particularly frustrating is *Shaughnessy v. United States* ex rel. *Mezei*, 345 U.S. 206 (1953). Mezei was an alien resident who remained abroad for nineteen months and, upon attempting to return to the United States, was excluded for overstaying. He had gone to Europe to visit his sick mother and been caught by World War II. No other country would receive him, on the logical grounds that if the United States wouldn't let him in, there must be a good reason, and he was confined to Ellis Island for twenty-one months. I have been unable to find out what happened to poor Mezei. Was he ever allowed to return to his home of twenty-five years? Did he return to Europe?

2. Although an agency may be required to provide a hearing, the adversely affected person is not required to take advantage of the offer. In fact, the right to a hearing may be waived and often is.

3. Notably *Bi-Metallic Investment Co. v. State Board of Equalization*, 239 U.S. 441 (1915), in which the city had increased the valuation of all taxable property without affording individual property owners the right to a hearing. The Court ruled that when a taxing action applied to all taxpayers (rather than a definite subset as in *Londoner*), no hearing was required. This is not a surprising decision in light of the absolute bar to taxpayer suits that was the rule until *Flast* (see note 13).

4. William B. Lockhart, Yale Kamisar, and Jesse Choper, *The American Constitution: Cases–Comments–Questions* (St. Paul, MN: West, 1970), 332.

5. Lisa Heinzerling, "Action Inaction: Section 1983 Liability for Failure to Act," *University of Chicago Law Review* 53 (Summer 1986): 1063.

6. *Marks v. Whitney*, 6 Cal. 3d 251, 491 P. 2d 374, 98 Cal. Rptr. 790 at 797 (1971), quoted in David B. Hunter, "An Ecological Perspective on Property: A Call for Judicial Protection of the Public's Interest in Environmentally Critical Resources," *Harvard Environmental Law Review* 12 (1988): 372, n. 288. Although this is a public trust case, the neighbor is granted positive rights as an individual.

7. Some environmental statutes grant citizens the right to bring suit without needing to demonstrate an actual physical or substantial economic injury. Among the acts providing for citizen suits are Toxic Substances Control Act; Endangered Species Act; Marine Protection, Research, and Sanctuaries Act of 1972; Federal Water Pollution Control Act Amendments of 1972; Deepwater Port Act of 1974; Safe Drinking Water Act; Clean Air Amendments of 1970; Noise Control Act of 1972; Energy Policy and Conservation Act; and Resource Conservation and Recovery Act of 1976. Most of these acts permit citizen suits only when the agency actions are not discretionary, but there are some exceptions: for example, the Endangered Species Act of 1973 allows a citizen to sue the Secretary of the Interior "to compel application of prohibitions against the taking of resident endangered species or threatened species." 16 U.S.C.A. 1540 (g)(1)(B).

8. The Eden Roc tried to establish a right, arguing that one existed at common law and invoking the doctrine of "ancient lights." The court rejected both arguments. There was, they said, no common law easement given to the Eden Roc, and the hotel had not been built long enough to claim an automatic easement from length of usage. The ancient lights doctrine, which states that after twenty years, the windows of a building may not be shadowed, has never been an accepted doctrine in American law. Thus, while common sense would argue that no beachfront hotel should be allowed to build a shadow over its competitor's pool, the common law did not agree.

9. *Association of Data Processing Service Organizations v. Camp*, 397 U.S. 150 at 153 (1970).

10. This holding would not have affected *Fontainebleau* because in that case there was no question of an improper administrative action. The old standard was still good because it was a civil action between two private parties, not between an aggrieved party and the government.

11. Responding to Douglas's dissent was John Naff:

> If Justice Douglas has his way—
>   O Come not that dreadful day—
> We'll be sued by lakes and hills
>   Seeking a redress of ills.
> Great mountain peaks of name prestigious
>   Will suddenly become litigious.

> Our brooks will babble in the courts,
>   Seeking damages for torts.
> How can I rest beneath a tree
>   If it may soon be suing me?
> Or enjoy the playful porpoise
>   While it's seeking habeas corpus?
> Every beast within his paws
>   Will clutch an order to show cause.
> The courts, besieged on every hand,
>   Will crowd with suits by chunks of land.
> Ah! But vengeance will be sweet
>   Since this must be a two-way street.
> I'll promptly sue my neighbor's tree
>   for shedding all its leaves on me.

John Naff, *Journal of the American Bar Association* 58 (1972): 820, reprinted in Christopher Stone, *Earth and Other Ethics* (New York: Harper & Row, 1987), 5.

12. I can't locate a source for the story that this case began as a law school class assignment, but true or not, it's a lovely story. The *Tennessee Valley Authority v. Hiram Hill et al.* case (see Box 4.1) was brought by a student "who discovered the potential for this endangered species litigation while writing an environmental law term paper" (Zygmunt Plater, Robert Abrams, William Goldfarb, and Robert Graham, *Environmental Law and Policy: Nature, Law, and Society*, 2nd ed. [St. Paul, MN: West Group, 1998], 685, n. 11). Plater should know: he was the lead attorney for Hill.

13. The Court had liberalized the absolute bar against taxpayer suits in *Flast v. Cohen*, 392 U.S. 83 (1968), but replaced the bar with a stringent test of a constitutional link between the taxpayer's harm and the government action. *Flast* challenged the 1965 Elementary and Secondary Education Act providing public funds to religious schools, alleging that the act violated the constitutionally mandated separation of church and state.

14. In *Lujan v. Defenders of Wildlife* (1992), the court refused to accept that potential injuries to wildlife in other countries caused in part by U.S. funding were a sufficient "injury in fact" to grant standing. In a famous phrase, Justice Blackmun (joined by Justice O'Connor) dissented: "I cannot join the Court on what amounts to a slash-and-burn expedition through the law of environmental standing." 504 U.S. 555 at 606.

15. Jeffrey M. Gaba, *Environmental Law* (Black Letter Series) (St. Paul, MN: West, 1994), 38–39.

16. *Mineral King* established that environmental groups whose individual members have suffered an injury may bring suit, although in *Lujan v. Defenders of Wildlife* (1992), the environmental group was not granted standing to challenge changes to

FWS and National Marine Fisheries Service regulations applying the Endangered Species Act to the actions of federal agencies taken overseas. Defenders of Wildlife argued that two of its members with established records of overseas travel justified the suit, but the Court disagreed, noting that if one of the members had been a scientist working on a foreign endangered species, or if they had even had tickets to travel, the outcome would have been different. An interesting sidebar to this case was the "ecosystem nexus" argument that maintains that the use of any part of a contiguous ecosystem justifies a defendable right in the entire ecosystem. Justices Black and O'Connor were the only justices to accept this argument.

17. Although it is not an environmental law case, the best example I know of these last two requirements is found in *Simon v. Eastern Kentucky Welfare Rights Organization* (1976). The Internal Revenue Service had changed its regulations, reducing the amount of free care a hospital had to provide in order to have a tax-exempt status. The welfare rights organization and several individuals sought judicial review on the grounds that their members and the individuals were denied free medical care. The Court denied standing because it was not clear that they would have received free care even if the rule were still in place (lack of causality), and even if the IRS were forced to reinstate the rule, there was no guarantee that the hospitals would continue to seek a tax-exempt status (no clear judicial relief).

18. In England, where the rights to fish a particular stream are property rights that may be bought and sold, the doctrine of nuisance has been used to force upstream industrial polluters to stop their activities. Since the anglers' associations have a property right in the fishing, the pollution that impairs the fishing is actionable for monetary damages, and the prospect of reimbursing a group of trout fishermen often leads to prompt remedial action by the polluters.

19. Unless otherwise noted, the discussion on property is from Robert R. Wright and Susan Webber Wright, *Land Use in a Nutshell* (St. Paul, MN: West, 1985).

20. See Susan Jane Buck Cox, "No Tragedy on the Commons," *Environmental Ethics* 7 (Spring 1985): 49–61, for a more detailed discussion of the medieval commons and the causes of the success of enclosure.

21. W. O. Ault, *Open-Field Farming in Medieval England* (London: Allen and Unwin, 1972), 17.

22. E. C. K. Gonner, *Common Land and Inclosure*, 2nd ed. (London: Cass, 1966), 306.

23. Elimination of the feudal commons system is often cited as an example of the inevitable failure of community control of resources. The famous article by Garrett Hardin, "The Tragedy of the Commons," (*Science* 162: 1243–1248) is based on just such erroneous analysis. In the past twenty years, a large, empirically based literature on common property management has demonstrated the utility of community management of common pool resources (see, for example, Elinor

Ostrom, *Governing the Commons* [Cambridge, UK: Cambridge University Press, 1990] and Elinor Ostrom, *Understanding Institutional Diversity* [Ewing, NJ: Princeton University Press, 2005]). This is not to say that Hardin's "tragedy" never occurred, but it is not the dominant model and in fact did not occur on medieval English commons.

24. The increased productivity was often touted by land reformers—wealthy or otherwise—as proof of the evils of the commons system. However, the change was the result of many factors and not just of enclosure. Some of the increase would probably have occurred without enclosure, but enclosure hastened the process. The common land was not the best land. The lord's waste was often reclaimed land, cultivated from forest and marsh. Enclosure took the better land and subjected it to the new and improved methods of agriculture that had been all but impossible under the common system, for the management of the common could not be changed unless all commoners agreed and, just as important, remained agreed. Improved roads and transportation facilities made marketing easier, and of course, the land had fewer people to support. Economies of scale made it profitable to use improved stock. In 1760, Robert Bakewell, the founder of modern methods of livestock improvement, began selective breeding of farm animals. Previously forbidden by ecclesiastical authorities as incest, inbreeding of animals with desirable qualities soon led to dramatic improvements in stock. Planting the enclosure with nitrogen-fixing crops such as clover improved the soil; drainage improved livestock health. Animals were disturbed less by driving to and from pasture land. All of these factors combined to improve the productivity of the formerly common land. Economic pressures from abroad encouraged enclosure, and by the end of the eighteenth century, the commons system was effectively gone.

25. It is vital to realize that the right to property is not a single right; it is a bundle of rights. For example, a farmer may use his land to grow any crop—as long as it is a legal plant. A homeowner may fence her property—as long as the fence height and location do not conflict with any covenants or local building ordinances. A renter has some of the rights of the property owner (for example, he can sue a neighbor for nuisance), but he cannot sell the property and may not be able to sublease it. We own our cars, but we are restricted on speeds, window tints, and fuel emissions, and we must pay annual taxes (in some states) and license fees to operate it on public roads.

26. Unless otherwise noted, the discussion of zoning is drawn from Robert Wright and Morton Gitelman, *Land Use in a Nutshell*, 4th ed. (St. Paul, MN: West, 2000), esp. chapter 7.

27. Although in many states the cities are subordinate to counties, in some, such as Virginia, the cities are governments independent of the counties in which they are found.

28. Those who wish to read the early developments in the judicial attempt to strike a balance between regulation and taking should look at the following cases: *Pennsylvania Coal Co. v. Mahon*, 1928 (Pennsylvania law forbidding mining that causes subsidence of residential property is a taking of the coal company's subsurface mining rights), the original landmark case for this policy area; *Miller v. Schoene*, 1928 (requirement that a grove of ornamental trees be removed to protect apple trees from disease is legitimate regulation to protect the public from economic harm), which vindicated Justice Brandeis's dissent in *Pennsylvania Coal*; *Morris County Land Improvement Company v. Township of Parsippany-Troy Hills*, 1963 (regulations restricting the use of filled land constitute a taking); *Just v. Marinette County*, 1972 (ordinance requiring permit to fill wetlands is valid exercise of public trust and police power); *Pennsylvania Central Transportation Company v. New York*, 1978 (restrictions on designated historic landmarks do not constitute a taking, sets three-part test for takings).

29. *Tahoe-Sierra Preservation Council v. Tahoe Regional Planning Agency*, 535 U.S. 302 (2002). This case is also notable because John Roberts Jr. argued this case for the respondents. As this is written, he is the nominee for Chief Justice of the United States.

30. *Kelo v. City of New London et al.*, 125 S. Ct. 2655 at 2671. At the time this is written, the Supreme Court has not published the official opinion. It is available on both LexisNexis and Findlaw.

31. 535 U.S. 302 at 335. See note 29.

32. 125 S. Ct. 2655 at 2671. See note 30.

33. 125 S. Ct. 2655 at 2676. See note 30. One of the cases on which *Kelo* rests is *Hawaii Housing Authority et al. v. Midkiff et al.*, 467 U.S. 229 (1984).

34. Kenneth Harney, "Eminent Domain Ruling Has Strong Repercussions," *Washington Post*, 23 July 2005, F1.

35. Michael Corkery and Ryan Chittum, "Eminent-Domain Uproar Imperils Projects," *Wall Street Journal*, 3 August 2005, B1.

36. Harney, "Eminent Domain," F1.

37. Unless otherwise noted, this discussion is drawn from William H. Rodgers, *Handbook on Environmental Law* (St. Paul, MN: West, 1977), 170–186.

38. Charles Wilkinson, "Public Trust Doctrine in Public Land Law," in *The Public Trust Doctrine in Natural Resources Law and Management*, edited by Harrison Dunning (Davis, CA: University of California, 1981), 169.

39. Plater et al. assert that the state court used the public trust doctrine to avoid being forced to reveal the true reason for the original sale: political corruption. Plater et al., *Environmental Law and Policy*, 91.

40. Joseph Sax, "Public Trust Doctrine in Natural Resource Law: Effective Judicial Intervention," *Michigan Law Review* 68 (3) (January 1970): 490.

41. Plater et al., *Environmental Law and Policy*, 92–93.

42. There is no traditional use of the doctrine to compel agency activity. The Superfund Amendment and Reauthorization Act (1986) provided for states to designate a state natural resource trustee, but this provision was not emphasized and few states have taken advantage of it. See Susan J. Buck and Edward Hathaway, "Designating State Natural Resource Trustees under SARA," in *Regulatory Federalism, Natural Resources and Environmental Management*, edited by Michael Hamilton (Washington, DC: ASPA, 1990), 83–94.

43. 350 Mass. 410, 215 N.E. 2d 114 (1966).

44. 46 Ill. 2d 330, 263 N.E. 2d 11(1970).

45. Joseph Sax, "Introductory Perspectives," in Dunning, *The Public Trust Doctrine*, 6.

46. James Trout, "A Land Manager's Commentary on the Public Trust Doctrine," in Dunning, *The Public Trust Doctrine*, 57. At the time of this statement, Mr. Trout was the Assistant Executive Officer for the California State Lands Commission.

47. Rodgers, *Handbook on Environmental Law*, 172.

48. *City of Milwaukee v. State*, 193 Wis. 423, 214 N.W. 820 (1927) at 830, quoted in Helen Althaus, *Public Trust Rights* (Washington, DC: GPO, November 1978), 157.

CHAPTER FIVE

Pollution Control
and Hazardous
and Toxic Substances

Regulating the production, use, and disposal of harmful substances is a responsibility shared by the national government and the states. This chapter presents the administrative framework for such regulations. The chapter begins with a discussion of the Administrative Procedure Act (APA). Although APA does not deal directly with environmental matters, it is the basic legislation that governs all federal agencies. Most states have similar legislation, so to understand the framework that informs environmental legislation, it is necessary first to grasp the basic points of APA. Within this section are discussions of rulemaking, benefit–cost analysis of regulations, and judicial review. The second section presents the basic legislation aimed at controlling air and water pollution. The third section focuses on hazardous and toxic wastes and outlines regulation of pesticides (FIFRA), solid and hazardous waste (RCRA), the Toxic Substances Control Act (TSCA), and Superfund and the Superfund Amendment and Reauthorization Act (SARA).

THE ADMINISTRATIVE PROCEDURE ACT

The Administrative Procedure Act, passed in 1946, was the culmination of years of anxious debate among government officials, legal scholars, and the business community. Although the administrative state had been growing since the late nineteenth century, the New Deal led to a proliferation of both independent agencies and the overall bureaucracy. Some lawyers were especially concerned as power shifted from the courts to the executive agencies. They were being closed out of the decision process by Roosevelt's bright young men in the agencies.

In 1934, the second year of the New Deal, the American Bar Association (ABA) formed an administrative law committee that issued annual reports stressing the reduced power of the judicial branch. Joining these critical voices were the conservatives who used complaints about fairness, due process, and conformity to common law to cloak their opposition to Roosevelt's economic and social policies. Some of the critics, however, were genuinely concerned about what they perceived as threats from the administrative process to traditionally protected rights. Their basic question was how the political system could maintain justice and the constitutionally mandated separation of powers if one person or agency acted as legislature (making rules), prosecutor (investigating infractions), judge (conducting hearings), and enforcing agent. Concerns about the substantive law increased as it became increasingly clear that the agencies were involved in *making* policy as well as interpreting legislation.[1]

The Special Committee on Administrative Law of the ABA had managed, in 1935, to engineer the passage of the Federal Register Act. For the first time, the *Federal Register* provided a daily record of the administrative activities of the executive branch; it contains texts of executive orders and proposed and final rules. Encouraged by this success, the Special Committee lobbied successfully for an administrative procedures bill, which was passed by Congress in December 1940.

Although the bill passed Congress, President Roosevelt vetoed it. Opponents of the bill charged that the act was nothing more than a blatant attempt to wrest control of the administration from the president. In his veto message, Roosevelt singled out for opprobrium two particular groups: lawyers and large business interests: "The bill that is now before me is one of the repeated efforts by a combination of lawyers who desire to have all processes of government conducted through lawsuits and of interests that desire to escape regulation."[2]

Roosevelt had another reason for his veto. The Final Report of the Attorney General's Committee on Administrative Procedure was almost complete. The work of this Committee was unique; instead of merely taking testimony and generating a report, it conducted primary investigations and produced legislation. For the first time, the administrative process was studied on the basis of knowledge rather than of hypothesis or preconceived ideas. . . . [The Committee] studied the administrative establishment from the inside, thoroughly and dispassionately. Its acute discussion of the characteristics of the administrative process, its conclusions as to defects existing in the process, and its proposals to remedy them all sprang from and were buttressed by facts laboriously ascertained and carefully weighed.[3]

The Attorney General's Report affirmed the necessity for and value of the administrative process. It found that agencies were an inevitable development essential to the effective management of modern, industrial government. The majority felt that the substantive issues dealt with by the various agencies were so complex and idiosyncratic that no uniform code could govern them all; the minority disagreed, and it is their recommendations that actually provided the basis for the APA.

Although extensive hearings were held in the summer of 1941 on the proposed Administrative Procedure Act, America's entry into World War II delayed further consideration. Close to the end of the war, the ABA began again to agitate for legislation, and in 1946, the Administrative Procedure Act was passed.

The major impact of the act was that it codified existing practice and law; in other words, it found a common ground among the agencies. The APA has six major portions, all of which have relevance to environmental administration and law: definitions of terms used in the act; the rules for fair information practices; guidelines for rulemaking; procedures for adjudication; creation of administrative law judges; and provisions for judicial review of agency actions.

One sign of the amazing success of the APA is how little it has been amended since 1946. Section 552 contains most of the amendments, and they are primarily grafts to the basic APA rather than changes to the law's essential structure. Section 552 is the Freedom of Information Act; section 552(a) is the Privacy Act of 1974, and 552(b) is the Government in the Sunshine Act. Sections 561–569 are the Negotiated Rulemaking Act, and sections 601–612 (Regulatory Flexibility Act) protect the interests of smaller organizations when new rules are adopted.

Rulemaking

The third section of the APA is perhaps the most important. It provides the guidelines for the federal rulemaking procedures.[4] The definition of "rule" is quite detailed:

[R]ule is the whole or a part of an agency statement of general or particular applicability and future effect designed to implement, interpret, or prescribe law or policy or describing the organization, procedure, or practice requirements of an agency and includes the approval or prescription for the future of rates, wages, corporate or financial structures or reorganization thereof, prices, facilities, appliances, services or allowances therefore or of valuations, costs, or accounting, or practices bearing on any of the foregoing. (5 U.S.C. §551[4])

It is important to distinguish between rulemaking and adjudication. Rulemaking is the administrative equivalent of legislation: it is sometimes called "secondary legislation." Rulemaking establishes *future* standards of *general* applicability. Rules cover a class of people or actions and are not particularized. Adjudication is the administrative parallel to the judicial process: it deals with particular cases. Adjudication takes place after some activity has occurred; rulemaking prescribes the activity before it happens. Agencies can make policy through either rulemaking or adjudication; courts prefer them to use rulemaking because rules announce guidelines for individual behavior, and persons subject to rules have a better basis for decision making. Agencies can also make policy by informal actions, such as the suspension action taken by EPA in 1979 when it banned 2,4,5-T (dioxin) on an emergency basis just before the spring crop spraying season.[5]

The courts are more likely to review rules on procedural due process grounds than substantive due process. Regulations and rules must stay within the statutory authority given to the agency by the legislature, but this authority is often vague and leaves a great deal to the agency's discretion. The rules must have a reasonable basis; that is, they may not be arbitrary, capricious, or involve an abuse of discretion, and they must be promulgated in accordance with the APA and with the restrictions laid down in their own enabling or organic act.

Types of Rules

There are three types of rules: substantive (legislative), procedural, and interpretive. Substantive rules implement or prescribe law or policy, for example, safety requirements for nuclear power plants. They are legally binding and can be enforced in court as though they were primary legislation. The amount of authority that an agency has to promulgate rules varies with the enabling legislation. Some agencies have very broad authority; for example, NEPA states:

> The Administrator is authorized to allow appropriate use of special Environmental Protection Agency research and test facilities by outside groups of individuals and to receive reimbursement or fees for costs incurred thereby when he finds this to be *in the public interest.* (42 U.S.C §4379, emphasis added.)

Since "in the public interest" is not defined in the statute, the administrator has been given very broad powers. Other agencies find their authority quite restricted; for example, the Endangered Species Act of 1973 requires that:

> [T]he Secretary shall make a finding as to whether the petition presents substantial scientific or commercial information indicating that the petitioned action may be warranted. If such a petition is found to present such information, the Secretary *shall* promptly commence a review of the status of the species concerned. The Secretary *shall promptly* publish each finding made under this subparagraph in the *Federal Register.* (16 U.S.C §1533[b][3][A], emphasis added.)

Here the statute requires action if certain conditions are met; the secretary has no discretion. The courts have the final word on whether a substantive rule is legitimate.

Procedural rules "describe the organization, procedure or practice requirements of an agency." For example, they may define who is allowed to intervene in an agency adjudication and under what circumstances. The APA does not apply to procedural rulemaking, and indeed, an agency is allowed to go beyond APA and its own organic act in restricting the procedures under which it operates. However, an agency is required to honor these rules once they have been issued. For example, during the Watergate investigation, U.S. Attorney General Elliot Richardson appointed Archibald Cox as Special Prosecutor and at the same time issued a procedural rule giving the Special Prosecutor the authority to contest claims of executive privilege. When Cox tried to get President Nixon's tapes and rejected Nixon's claims of executive privilege, Nixon ordered him fired. The first two attorneys general that he ordered to fire Cox refused; the third was Robert Bork, who complied with Nixon's order.[6] The DC District Court invalidated the firing on the grounds that the procedural rule was binding.

Interpretive rules are "statements issued by agencies that present the agency's understanding of the meaning of the language in its regulations or the statutes it administers."[7] They are exempt from APA requirements but must be published in the *Federal Register*. They do not add or subtract any information from existing law; they simply give the public a more detailed idea of how the agency intends to act. In this sense they are the administrative equivalent of advisory opinions. It is not clear how binding an interpretative rule is on the agency. On occasion the courts have judged that an interpretive rule was actually substantive and held the agency to it. The safest approach is for the agency to assume that a court will find the rule binding but for the affected party to assume it is not. Why would an agency bother with such an ambiguous process? It allows the administrative agency to make small adjustments to policy without going through the cumbersome rulemaking procedures.

Rulemaking Procedures

There are three basic procedures for making rules: informal rulemaking, formal rulemaking, and hybrid rulemaking.

Informal rulemaking is informal only in contrast to formal rulemaking. It is also called Notice and Comment Rulemaking and is governed by section 553 of APA. This section exempts from the act all military and foreign affairs functions (since these are committed to the executive by the Constitution), agency management and personnel actions, and "public property, loans, grants, benefits, or contracts."

The informal rulemaking procedure requires the agency to publish a notice of the proposed rule in the *Federal Register*. An exception is allowed if everyone subject to the proposed rule is individually notified, but this exception is rarely used. There are several necessary components of the notice. It must give the time, place, and nature of the rulemaking proceedings and refer to the legal authority under which the rule is made. The notice either provides the term or substance of the proposed rule or gives a description of the subjects and issues involved. Finally, the notice includes an opportunity for written or oral (and sometimes both) comment by interested parties.

Once the agency has fixed upon the rule, it must publish the text of the rule, and a general statement of its basis and purpose, in the *Federal Register* at least thirty days before the effective date to allow affected parties to come into compliance. Even then, interested persons have the right to ask for an "issuance, amendment, or repeal" of the rule.

This sort of rulemaking is relatively simple and informal. There is no formal hearing in which evidence and testimony about the rule is heard. The time period is short; a rule might complete the process in less than sixty days if it is simple and noncontroversial. There is no record required: the agency merely announces its intention, receives comments, and issues the rule. In contrast, formal rulemaking is much more complex.

The distinguishing characteristic of formal rulemaking is the administrative hearing that is required. Several statutes require full hearings as part of the rulemaking process, and a hearing must be held only if the statute explicitly requires one. There is, however, nothing to prohibit an agency from having one voluntarily. Administrative hearings are conducted under the regulations spelled out in sections 556 and 557 of the APA. An administrative law judge presides over these hearings, and his opinion is conveyed to the administrator charged with making the final rule. His opinion must be considered, although it is not binding. Any final rule must be based on the "substantial evidence" criterion: the agency must demonstrate that its position is upheld by "reliable, probative, and substantial evidence" (§556[d]).

There are many arguments that favor the formal process over the informal. The formal record that is generated by the hearing process provides a pedigree for the development of the new regulation. There is full opportunity for public participation and, because there are rules of evidence (although not the same rules of evidence as apply in a criminal trial), all information can be verified. The burden of proof rests with the agency, and the formal hearing provides a record for the interested parties to be sure that the weight of the evidence is sufficient to support the rule.

There are also many counterarguments. Formal rulemaking is costly in terms of both money and time. Flexibility of the administrators is reduced—an evil that the administrative process is designed to avoid. And the process itself, resembling a court trial, is increasingly judicialized. For example, the original APA created independent "hearing examiners" who had specialized knowledge in their own regulatory fields. These hearing examiners have metamorphosed into "administrative law judges" who are attorneys with at least seven years experience presenting cases before federal courts or agencies.

Hybrid rulemaking uses a combination of informal and formal procedures; the impetus for hybrid rulemaking came from the judiciary. Federal courts prefer administrative agencies to use their rulemaking powers to make policy rather than to use case-by-case adjudicatory powers, because judicial review is simplified when a rule is the basis of the administrative decision. However, the informal process does not require establishment of a reviewable record. The lack of a formal record complicates the judge's task when reviewing agency action. As the administrative agencies continued to utilize their rulemaking powers, and as the need for regulation increased, in part because of increased environmental regulation, the courts found their job increasingly complex. Deference to administrative expertise was a nice concept, but a court had difficulty judging the "substantial" basis of a rule that was technically complex and lacked a formal record.

Partly in self-defense, the agencies began to generate records of the informal rulemaking processes, and the courts, followed by the Congress, applauded. The keystone of the hybrid process is the record before the administrator. The record allows not only judicial review; it also allows peer preview, legislative oversight, and public criticism. Surprisingly, it also increases administrative flexibility because it simplifies changing rules to meet changing circumstances.

Congress has followed the judicial lead, and most rulemaking legislation in the past thirty years has included hybrid rulemaking requirements. For example, the Toxic Substance Control Act of 1976 requires hybrid rulemaking:

> Any rule under subparagraph (A), and any substantive amendment or repeal of such a rule, shall be promulgated pursuant to the procedures specified in section 553 of [APA], except that (i) the Administrator shall give interested persons an opportunity for the oral presentation of data, views, or arguments, in addition to an opportunity to make written submissions, (ii) a transcript shall be kept of any oral presentation, and (iii) the Administrator shall make and publish with the rule the finding described in subparagraph (A). (15 U.S.C. § 2604[b])

Generally, hybrid rulemaking follows informal rulemaking procedures with several additions on the record: the basis and purpose of the rule, with supporting documentation; evidence that adequate notice was given or made available to all interested parties; sufficient time for comments and alternative interpretations; evidence that the agency did consider and respond to comments; and the reasoning followed by the administrator.

A recent refinement in federal rulemaking is *negotiated* rulemaking. To reduce the likelihood of lengthy challenges to a rule, stakeholders negotiate the language of the rule before the proposed rule reaches the *Federal Register*. Although the negotiation process is announced in the *Federal Register*, the process is often criticized as limiting public participation and creating expectations among stakeholders of particular results before the rule is open for public notice and comment, Use of this method of formulating rules is encouraged by the Negotiated Rulemaking Act of 1990.[8]

Benefit–Cost Analysis

Substantial presidential efforts have been made to take control of the regulatory process, particularly as industry frequently complains that the cost of regulations are not properly considered when new regulations are issued.[9] President Carter created the Regulatory Analysis and Review Group (RARG), replaced by Reagan's Executive Order 12291 (and later Executive Order 12498), which required agencies to conduct a benefit–cost analysis of all proposed rules and to choose the least costly alternative. George H. W. Bush "found the contention [over Executive Order 12291] too politically costly and quietly backed away from Reagan's aggressive enforcement policies."[10] In 1993, President Clinton issued Executive Order 12866, revoking Reagan's Executive Order 12291. His order required consultation with state, local, and tribal agencies and required agencies to impose the "least burden on society" in promulgating regulations. During Clinton's administration, both Democratic and Republican congresses passed stiffer benefit-cost analysis requirements.[11] The use of benefit–cost analysis for regulatory rulemaking is now routine, except in those few areas such as the Clean Air Act where the law prohibits consideration of economic effects.

Administrative Adjudication

The fourth section of the Administrative Procedure Act deals with adjudication. The specific kind of adjudicatory procedure required in agency processes varies from relatively informal, oral hearings to very structured procedures that resemble formal civil trials. Some statutes require hearings, and it is only these statutes that automatically trigger the full hearing described in the APA. In some circumstances, the courts have mandated adjudicatory hearings based on constitutional requirements. Finally, the agencies themselves may have rules independent of their enabling legislation or court decisions that require them to hold hearings. The necessity for hearings originates in the due process clause of the Constitution, discussed in chapter 4. When an administrative agency affects a citizen's property rights, the citizen is entitled to a hearing.

There are five central components of any administrative hearing: notice of the hearing given to all interested parties; the opportunity to be heard by an impartial examiner, to present evidence and to challenge opposing evidence; to receive a reasoned decision based on a written record; and to have the right of appeal. These requirements are spelled out in sections 554 and 557 of the APA, although the precise nature of a hearing varies with the enabling statute, previous judicial interpretations, and agency regulations.

Judicial Review

The sixth section of the APA deals with judicial review of agency actions.[12] Judicial review is the "power of a court to determine the legality and constitutionality of an action of a government official, agency, or legislative body."[13] Some agency actions are not subject to review. The Supreme Court does not have jurisdiction over all agency actions because the Congress has the power to exempt some activities:

> In all the other Cases before mentioned, the Supreme Court shall have appellate Jurisdiction, both as to Law and Fact, *with such Exceptions, and under such Regulations as the Congress shall make.*" (U.S. Constitution, Article III, §2[2], emphasis added.)

Section 701 of APA, which defines the application of judicial review of agency actions, exempts actions where the "statutes preclude judicial review" or that have been "committed to agency discretion by law." However, section 706 (2)(A) of the act forbids arbitrary and capricious action and abuses of discretion. The reviewing courts must determine when an action is committed to agency discretion and when these actions are reviewable under section 706. The overall effect of these two seemingly contradictory sections is to encourage agencies to maintain records of their actions and interactions.

Courts do not have an unlimited license to oversee agency activities. The scope of judicial review for administrative actions is defined in section 706:

> To the extent necessary to decision and when presented, the review-ing court shall decide all relevant questions of law, interpret constitu-tional and statutory provisions, and determine the meaning or appli-cability of the terms of an agency action.

The court may "compel agency action unlawfully withheld or unreasonably delayed" as well as "hold unlawful and set aside agency action, findings, and conclusions" that are arbitrary, capricious, abuses of discretion, violations of constitutional rights, exceed statutory authority, violate due process, or are unsupported by substantial evidence.

For adjudicatory decisions, the primary judicial question is whether the agency position is supported by substantial evidence. Since most adjudica-tory hearings are adversarial and therefore may produce conflicting evi-dence, a court often has a difficult time determining which evidence is applicable. In formal rulemaking, the scope of review also rests on substan-tial evidence, while review of informal rulemaking is limited to the "arbi-trary and capricious" standard. In hybrid rulemaking, the scope of review is determined by the authorizing statute. For example, the Toxic Substances Control Act cited earlier gives as part of the standard of review:

> Section 706 of [APA] shall apply to review of a rule under this section, except that, (i) in the case of review of a rule under [several sections of the Act] of this title, the standard for review prescribed by paragraph (2)(E) of such section 706 shall not apply and the court shall hold unlawful and set aside such rule *if the court finds that the rule is not sup-ported by substantial evidence in the rulemaking record.* (15 U.S.C. § 2618 [c][1][B], emphasis added.)

Some agencies have a great deal of discretion conferred by their enabling statutes. Since 1984, the Chevron doctrine has provided some protection from judicial review of discretionary action. In *Chevron U.S.A., Inc. v. Natural Resources Defense Council* (1984), the court was examining EPA's interpretation of "stationary source" in applying the Clean Air Act. The Court articulated a two-part test: if the statutory language or the intent of Congress are clear, the agency must follow them. If not, the agency's interpretation need only be *reasonable* (not subject to the test of "arbitrary, capricious, or an abuse of discretion") to pass judicial muster.

The preceding sections have shown the importance of the Administrative Procedure Act as a framework for understanding the administrative process in environmental administration. The following sections summarize the current status of air and water pollution regulation.

AIR POLLUTION

Aaron Wildavsky defined pollution as *matter out of place*, and this is particularly true of air pollution. An air pollutant develops "when the concentration of a normal component of air or of a new chemical added to or formed in the air builds up to the point of causing harm to humans, other animals, vegetation, or materials such as metals and stone."[14] According to one study, the major sources of air pollution are transportation (49 percent), industrial processes (13 percent), fuel combustion in stationary sources (28 percent), solid waste disposal (3 percent), and miscellaneous (7 percent).[15] Some pollutants are harmful as soon as they enter the atmosphere; these *primary air pollutants* contribute the majority of air pollution in the United States. *Secondary air pollutants* are formed from the chemical reaction of several air components; for example, sulfur dioxide combines with oxygen to form sulfur trioxide, which then combines with water vapor to produce acid rain.

The dangers of air pollution and its dramatic consequences have been known for centuries. In 1273, the King of England tried to reduce air pollution by banning the burning of coal. In 1911, over 1,000 Londoners died from coal smoke. London was known as "the Smoke" for good reason, and Sherlock Holmes' romantic "pea-soup" fogs were deadly; in 1952 the infamous Killer Smog killed over 4,000 Londoners in one long weekend.[16] While this was sufficient to trigger English air pollution control laws, the United States waited through several disasters (in 1963 there were 200 deaths in New York City) before passing the Clean Air Act in 1970.

The first national attempt to control air pollution was the Air Pollution Act of 1955. The main impact of this law was to require federal research on the detrimental effects of air pollution. In 1963, the Clean Air Act set emission standards for major stationary air pollution sources. Subsequent amendments expanded the act's mandate: the Motor Vehicle Pollution Control Act (1965); the 1966 amendments, which expanded *state* programs;

and the Air Quality Act (1967). The 1970 Clean Air Act was a major turn-
ing point.[17]

In 1970, amendments to the Clean Air Act of 1955 provided the basic
structure for the current shape of air pollution control. The 1970 amendments required the national government to set air quality standards that
would be achieved through State Implementation Plans (SIPs). The Clean
Air Act Amendments of 1977 reinforced federal authority over air quality
standards. EPA was required to establish National Ambient Air Quality
Standards (NAAQSs) for seven major pollutants: suspended particulate
matter (SPM), sulfur oxides, carbon monoxide, nitrogen oxides, ozone,
volatile organic compounds, and lead. The cost of meeting the standards
was not supposed to be a criterion in setting the standards. EPA had to set
two types of NAAQSs: the *primary ambient air quality standards* were
designed to protect human health and to provide a margin of safety for the
most vulnerable populations such as infants and the elderly, while the *secondary ambient air quality standards* targeted visibility and crops, buildings,
and water supplies.

To implement the Clean Air Act, EPA divided the nation into 247 air
quality control regions, each of which was supposed to meet the primary
standards by 1982. Areas that did not achieve primary standards by 1982, or
within whatever deadline extensions were granted, were labeled *nonattain-
ment regions*, with restrictions on new plant construction and old plant
expansions until emission standards were met.

Of course, some areas of the county were already cleaner than the
NAAQSs required, and EPA sought to protect these through a policy of *prevention of significant deterioration* (PSD). Three classes of existing air quality
were established. Class I areas, which had the highest existing air quality,
were protected from virtually any deterioration. Class II and Class III areas
were allowed progressively more pollution, with the NAAQSs being the
absolute limit of permissible pollution. Each state was responsible for developing SIPs to meet federal standards by the late 1980s.

Under the Reagan administration, industry and the executive branch
cooperated to ease federal auto emission standards, to extend EPA deadlines, and in general to relax expansion and enforcement of existing air
pollution regulations. The conservatives asserted that the economic cost
of clean air was too high and accepted levels of pollution were too low.
They charged the regulating agencies with inflexibility. Environmentalists
were also critical of EPA, and the chaos in EPA during the first Reagan

administration seemed to justify their complaints. Enforcement of existing regulations was problematic, and new regulations were halted or delayed under executive orders requiring benefit–cost analysis and other evaluations not always in agreement with legislative intentions. All this changed in November 1990, when President George H. W. Bush signed the Clean Air Act Amendments, "the most important, and imaginative, regulatory reform in more than a decade."[18] It was the environmental high point of his administration.

BUYING THE RIGHT TO POLLUTE

Three approaches to controlling pollution are available to managers: common law remedies, such as nuisance suits discussed in chapter 4; the command-and-control regulatory approaches used in Clean Air and Clean Water acts; and economic incentives. Unlike most regulatory plans that constrain the private sector, forcing it to utilize and to develop technologies, economic incentives can promote environmental protection by using the market.

Two economic factors that distort the operation of a free market are externalities and free-riders. Simply put, externalities are spillover effects that have an impact on individuals or groups that have not contributed to the project. For example, a factory may dump pollutants into the air, harming the health of local residents. The factory saves the cost of pollution control, but these costs are then borne by others who are external to the factory (both figuratively and literally). Thus the costs of polluting activities are not borne by those who reap the benefits, and polluters have no economic incentives to reduce pollution.

Free-riders are individuals who participate in the benefits of an activity without contributing to the activity's cost and are a special case of externalities; for example, nonresidents who use a tax-supported public park are free-riders. Air pollution provides a good example of the relationship between pollution, externalities, and free riders:

(continued)

BUYING THE RIGHT TO POLLUTE (*continued*)

There may be many agents who produce the pollution. It can come from automobiles, factories, electrical power plants, and so on. Also, large numbers of individuals "consume" the pollution by breathing air filled with particulates, sulfur dioxide, and oxides of nitrogen. Producers of the externality can also be consumers of air pollution. Anyone who drives a car and lives in an area of low air quality is both a producer and consumer. The reason this public externality arises is simple: Air is an open access resource. Because no property rights to air exist, those who generate air pollution are free to use the air as a waste dump without paying any fees. Once air pollution is generated, large numbers of individuals (animals, vegetation, and property) are affected. Each person affected might be willing to pay something to reduces the pollution, but if he or she did so, others who did not pay would also benefit.[1]

First proposed by Dales in 1968,[2] pollution permits provide transferable property rights for the disposal of waste. The government chooses the level of pollution it is willing to tolerate by issuing Pollution Rights equal to that amount. The rights then become marketable commodities. This strategy is less effective with multiple-source pollution (such as automobiles) and nonpoint pollution (such as agricultural runoff). However, as a substantial proportion of both air and water pollution is generated by single-source industrial polluters, Dales's scheme had great appeal to those with market inclinations. Air pollution was especially amenable to market solutions because the existing regulatory mechanisms were easy to adapt Title IV of the Clean Air Act Amendments of 1990 applied these strategies to air pollution.

This sort of rights scheme has many advantages. Many businesses would be more environmentally responsible if their internal affairs and their relations with EPA were modified. While some obstacles to waste reduction are internal to business, others are imposed externally by the government emphasis on emissions control rather than source reduction. In addition to reducing administrative costs, pollution rights

(continued)

BUYING THE RIGHT TO POLLUTE (*continued*)

schemes encourage business to find alternative ways to reduce emissions and other wastes. They might allow business to focus on waste production, to revamp internal accounting systems to charge pollution to operations and thus encourage improved production technologies, and to improve their internal information management systems.[3]

NOTES

1. John Hartwick and Nancy Olewiler, *The Economics of Natural Resource Use* (New York: Harper & Row, 1986), 387 (notes omitted).
2. J. H. Dales, *Pollution, Property & Prices: An Essay in Policy-Making and Economics* (Toronto: University of Toronto Press, 1968).
3. Hartwick and Olewiler, *Economics of Natural Resource Use*, 443–445.

The 1990 Clean Air Act Amendments strengthened existing legislation and added three major new areas to federal regulatory control: acid deposition, reduction of chlorofluorocarbons (CFCs), and increased control of toxic substances in the air. A national permitting program was established under Title V, and enforcement was strengthened. The amendments also initiated an emissions trading system that applied market-based strategies to the problems of air pollution.

In Title I, the amendments set precise goals for national air quality standards for ozone, carbon monoxide, and particulates. Areas falling under the new standards had to satisfy the requirements within firm deadlines. In 1997, EPA issued new standards for ozone and particulates over strenuous congressional objections. The process was mired in lawsuits from northeastern states wanting restrictions on the Midwest and the regulated utilities.[19] Regulation of particulates was also problematic as scientific findings indicated more serious concerns with small (less than 2.5 microns) particles. The particulates standards issued in 1997 by EPA were the third set of standards since 1987, prompting industry complaints about the costs of complying with frequently changing regulations.[20] In Title II, the amendments set more and stronger emission standards for cars, trucks, urban buses, and off-road vehicles.

Title III of the 1990 amendments set standards for hazardous air pollutants. This title was prompted by the information generated from the "community right-to-know" provision (Title III) of SARA. The discovery that over 2.7 billions pounds of toxic air pollutants were released annually was a powerful trigger for increasing regulation of air toxics. In a radical departure from previous programs, the new act was technology-based rather than emissions-focused, and 189 substances were regulated (as opposed to the eight controlled under the old legislation). The act contains an extensive list of hazardous pollutants and provisions for revision of the list.[21] Once a standard is promulgated by EPA, all new sources must adhere to the standard. Rather than enforce emission standards, EPA may "issue regulations controlling design, equipment, work practices, or operations."[22]

To meet the act's Title IV acid deposition requirements, industries had to achieve a permanent 10-million ton reduction from 1980 levels in sulfur dioxide emissions during a two-phase implementation process to be fully effective on 1 January 2000. This title established the innovative emissions trading program: each major coal-fired plant was allocated a set amount of permissible sulfur dioxide emissions that may be traded, bought, or sold.[23]

Title VI addressed the problem of stratospheric ozone and global climate protection. The act used the economic incentives and requirements established by EPA under the 1977 amendments to phase out CFCs and halons according to the schedules established in the Montreal Protocol (discussed in chapter 7). This involved complete elimination of CFCs and carbon tetrachloride by 2000 and methyl chloroform by 2002. On 1 January 1994, a total ban on aerosols, with exemptions for flammability and safety, went into effect.

The enforcement provisions of the 1990 amendments were very important and new in clean air legislation.[24] Four provisions were especially noteworthy: the field citation program, the inclusion of endangerment crimes from releases, compliance certification, and the citizen suit provisions. Under the field citation program, inspectors would visit plants to perform inspections of the plants and the plant records and were authorized to issue citations immediately with fines up to $5,000. The act established civil and criminal liability for releases that endanger the public: "knowingly endangering" the public through a deliberate, illegal release may result in prison terms up to fifteen years and fines to $250,000 for individuals and $500,000 for corporations. Regulated industries are required to certify their compliance with the permit conditions on a regular basis and to provide monitoring and other forms of evidence to support their compliance record. The citizen suit provisions are stronger under the new law; citizen suits may be used to enforce the permits. Citizens may now sue corporations for past violations if the violation is continuing, and penalties may be imposed to require mitigation of harmful effects.

Despite the substantial changes mandated by the 1990 CAA Amendments, some pollutants have proved resistant to regulation.[25] Auto emissions controls have substantially reduced emissions from new cars but have been avoided on light trucks and sport utility vehicles. Although air quality has improved over the past twenty-five years,[26] a majority of Americans live in areas out of compliance with Clean Air Act Standards.[27]

CASE DISCUSSION 5.1

Blowing Smoke

The Clean Air Act distinguishes between *stationary* sources of pollution and mobile sources. Major new stationary sources usually require a permit. In Boston, MA, which exceeds national carbon monoxide standards, major new stationary sources must have a permit that demonstrates the sources have the lowest feasible emission rates for carbon monoxide.

In the design plans for a new highway tunnel, six buildings would collect air and motor vehicle emissions from the tunnel and exhaust them through stacks that ranged from 90 to 225 feet in height. In March 1991, the Sierra Club sued state and federal officials to define the ventilation buildings as "major stationary sources" that required special permits. Presumably in anticipation of the Sierra Club suit, the Massachusetts Department of Environmental Protection had proposed an amendment to the state implementation plan that would have classified tunnel ventilation buildings as "indirect sources" under the Clean Air Act. Indirect sources did not require permits.

(continued)

CASE DISCUSSION 5.1 (*continued*)

Here are the statutory definitions.

- "Stationary source": The statute is amazingly unhelpful. Apparently Congress thought the term was self-evident and never considered the possibility of ventilation buildings. A "major stationary source" is a stationary source or facility that emits a minimum level of a particular range of pollutants. (One narrow section of the act defines "stationary sources" as "any building, structure, facility, or installation which emits or may emit any air pollutant," but that definition is limited to performance standards, not air quality standards.)
- "Indirect source": "a facility, building, structure, installation, real property, road, or highway which attracts, or may attract, mobile sources of pollution. Such term includes parking lots, parking garages, and other facilities subject to any measure for management of parking supply. . . ." 42 U.S.C § 7410(a)(5)

While we might think that there is some overlap between these "stationary sources" and "indirect sources" (after all, parking garages are not usually mobile), Congress imposed a different legal regime—permit versus nonpermit—on indirect sources. This indicates that Congress perceived them as different, although it is hard to know if the difference was technical or political. EPA weighed in on the debate in 1992 when it approved the Massachusetts amendment: "Tunnel ventilation systems, which do not generate their own emissions but rather simply funnel emissions from mobile sources, are not stationary sources within the meaning of the Clean Air Act." 57 Fed. Reg. 46310, 46311 (1992)

What are the environmental consequences of ruling that ventilation buildings are not stationary sources?

What would be your preferred outcome if you were governor of Massachusetts? Mayor of Boston? Secretary of Transportation? Commissioner of the Boston Department of Public Works? A resident near the ventilation buildings? A commuter?

What would your decision have been? Why?

(Source: *Sierra Club v. Larson*, 2 F. 3d 462 [1st Cir. 1993])

In George W. Bush's administration, a hotly contested issue has been new-source performance standards. The 1970 Clean Air Act grandfathered in existing pollution sources; businesses were not required to retrofit old plants with pollution control devices. Not surprisingly, the older plants chose to modify existing plants rather than to build new ones that would be required to comply with more expensive technologies. In 1977, the amendments had required compliance for a "major modification." The result was years of legal wrangling over compliance. During the Clinton administration, lawsuits were filed by the energy industry to continue protection for older plants; when George W. Bush took office, the plaintiffs were environmentalists fighting to impose stricter standards. Bush's Clear Skies Initiative in 2002 failed to pass Congress, but Bush used his power of executive order to try to implement some of its provisions, including rules relaxing new-source review requirements. The rules failed to withstand a court challenge.[28]

WATER POLLUTION

Water pollution poses an immediate threat to public health, and, because it is usually dispersed over an identified area, water pollution may be more amenable to control than air pollution. Water pollution is "any physical or chemical change in surface water or groundwater that can adversely affect living organisms."[29] The levels of pollution that are acceptable in any water supply depend in part on the use to which the water is put. A waterway used primarily for large ships can tolerate a higher level of pollution than one that provides drinking water, and water for industrial needs does not have to meet swimming water criteria. Environmentalists like to point out that water *could* be used for industrial needs if it met swimming water criteria: the cleaner, the better. Economists talk instead about "beneficent degradation," the desirable level of pollution in a body of water.

Pollution is usually classified as either *point source* pollution, that is, pollution with a readily isolated egress point, such as a sewer treatment plant or oil tankers, or *nonpoint source* pollution, which is more difficult to control because it is spread over a large area. The pollution caused by agricultural pesticides in rainwater runoff, for example, is difficult to measure or to identify. Best Management Practices (BMPs) may reduce the incidence of behavior that causes agricultural nonpoint source pollution, but urban nonpoint source pollution is more difficult to control.

CASE DISCUSSION 5.2

Moving Violations

Concerned Area Residents for the Environment (CARE) were landowners living near Southview Farms, one of the largest dairy farms in New York. In 1991, Southview Farms raised crops on 1,000 acres and owned 2,190 dairy cows (1,290 mature dairy cows and 900 young ones). Southview cows were not pastured; instead they were kept in barns. Their manure was collected in five storage lagoons, each with a capacity of six to eight million gallons of liquid manure from which solids had been removed.

Southview spreads liquid manure on crop fields by a combination of central pivot sprayers, rigid hoses, and spreaders pulled by tractors.

CARE sued Southview for violations of the Clean Water Act. They alleged three specific violations. First, on 13 July 1989, two members of CARE saw liquid manure run through a swale (natural ditch) into a drainage pipe and from there into a stream that feeds the Genesee River. Second, on 12 July and 22 August 1989, two members saw heavy liquid manure being spread on the same field but did not observe any runoff. Third, on 26 September 1990 and 15 April 1991, CARE members observed that rain caused liquid manure to run into the swale and drainage pipe from the fields that had previously been heavily soaked with liquid manure.

- Under the Clean Water Act, "the discharge of any pollutant by any person shall be unlawful" unless he holds a permit or is excused under some other specific statutory limitation. 33 U.S.C. § 1311(a)
- Pollutants include "solid waste, . . . sewage, . . . biological materials, . . . and agricultural waste discharged into water." 33 U.S.C. § 1362 (6)
- A "discharge" is "any addition of any pollutant to navigable waters from any point source." 33 U.S.C. § 1362 (12)
- "Point source" includes "any discernible, confined and discrete conveyance [vehicle], including but not limited to any . . . concentrated animal feeding operation. . . . This term does not include agricultural stormwater discharges and return flows from irrigated agriculture."

(continued)

CASE DISCUSSION 5.2 (*continued*)

(33 U.S.C. § 1362 [14]) In other words, a concentrated animal feeding operation is, by definition, a point source, as is its manure-spreading equipment.

- A concentrated animal-feeding operation (CAFO) is any animal-feeding operation with more than 700 mature dairy cattle. 40 C.F.R. 122.23(b)
- The only occasion on which runoff from an animal feeding operation with more than 700 animals is not regulated as a CAFO is when "a discharge of pollutants into navigable waters occurs . . . during a 25 year, 24-hour rainfall event." 41 Fed. Reg. 11458

Does the runoff through the swale and pipe into the Genesee River qualify as point source pollution?

Was the runoff in September 1990 and April 1991 exempted because it was an "agricultural stormwater discharge"? (Clearly it is necessary to distinguish between a stormwater discharge and an average rainy day. Which would apply here?) If those events were not a stormwater discharge, would the CAFO exception have protected Southview?

(Source: *Concerned Area Residents for the Environment v. Southview Farm*, 34 F. 3d 114 [1994])

Water supplies are classified as surface water and groundwater. Surface waters, such as lakes, rivers, and oceans, are to some extent self-cleansing, although some pollutants are so deadly even in small concentrations that neither dilution nor dispersal are helpful. These surface water systems are easily overloaded, but they are at least accessible. Groundwater is much more vulnerable to pollution and harder to restore. Almost half of the American population and virtually all of the rural population obtain their drinking water from groundwater sources,[30] and over 80 percent of municipal water systems rely on groundwater.[31]

Although only a small percentage of the nation's groundwater is polluted, the proximity of these contaminated aquifers to population centers means that five to ten million Americans have polluted water sources. This problem may be more severe than reported since many chemicals found in groundwater are not subject to federal standards or testing, and no testing at all is required for private wells. One EPA survey found almost half of municipal water systems contaminated with synthetic organic chemicals; a different survey found two-thirds of private wells unsafe for drinking.[32]

There are eight major types of water pollution: disease-causing agents such as bacteria; oxygen-demanding wastes such as manure; water-soluble inorganic chemicals; inorganic plant nutrients; organic chemicals, sediment, or suspended matter; radioactive substances; and thermal pollution.[33]

The centerpiece of U.S. water pollution-control strategies is the Clean Water Act. This law began as the Federal Water Pollution Control Act of 1948 and was substantially amended in 1972, 1977, 1981, and 1987. Although it has passed through a number of popular names, it is generally referred to as the Clean Water Act (CWA). Implementation is based on technology-forcing: requiring such high standards that new technologies must be developed and installed for affected industries and municipalities to comply.

Prior to 1974, there were no uniform water quality standards for drinking water among the states. The federal Safe Drinking Water Act (SDWA) imposed federal safety standards on the states. The act requires EPA to set standards for drinking water for pollutants with potentially adverse effects on human health. The scope of the act is broad: it applies to all water systems with at least fifteen service connections or that regularly serve a minimum of twenty-five people for sixty days each year. Although a "margin of safety" is also mandated, EPA must take technical feasibility and cost into account as well. In 1986, substantial amendments to the Safe Drinking Water Act required EPA to set standards for sixty-one new contaminants by 1989 and for an additional twenty-five by 1991; by 2005, only seventy-two contaminants had been included. In 1996, Congress passed amendments to the SDWA. For the first time under this law, Congress required assessment and protection of drinking water sources, an issue that was not being addressed adequately under the Clean Water Act.[34] Congress also mandated regular reports for users of community drinking water systems and federal aid for system upgrades. Unfortunately, some dangerous pollutants are not removed by conventional water treatment systems; one of the most insidious is the increasing level of environmental hormone disruptors.[35]

Municipal wastewater is a significant source of water pollution. To help municipalities come into compliance, between 1972 and 1986 almost $45 billion was provided to them by the federal government (supplemented by $15 billion of state and local government funds) to upgrade or to construct municipal wastewater treatment facilities. By 1986, two-thirds of American municipalities had completed construction of their effluent control systems, but of these, 12 percent were still not in compliance. The failure of the remaining one-third to complete construction on schedule is "attributed to fraud, over-building, bureaucratic and construction delays, and a 37% cut in federal funding for water pollution control between 1981 and 1986 by the Reagan administration."[36] The federal government no longer provides financial assistance to local governments for upgrading treatment facilities.

By 2002, the goal of the 1972 Act to have "fishable and swimmable waters" was not even close to attainment, although improvement has been made. In 1972, the estimate was that a mere 36 percent of rivers, lakes, and estuaries were fishable and swimmable.[37] In 2000, EPA reported water quality results based on limited state surveys of surface waters: 61 percent of rivers and streams and 55 percent of lakes, ponds, and reservoirs met minimum national criteria.[38] This was accomplished largely by adding new standards based on actual harm (Water Quality-Based Effluent Standards or WQBELs) to the old technology-forcing standards. This dual focus has given an estimated 90 percent reduction in point-source pollution.[39]

Unfortunately, nonpoint source pollution is more difficult to curtail. Urban and agricultural runoff are prime nonpoint offenders. A few federal statutes address agricultural runoff; for example, the 1985 Farm Bill required farmers to use Best Management Practices (BMPs) for soil conservation to be eligible for crop subsidies. However, water pollution programs are implemented by the states rather than by the federal government, and state governments and agencies are more vulnerable to political pressures from major industrial and agricultural interests.

Whether water pollution control programs are viewed as partial successes or partial failures, the reasons for their effects are found in the political climate of implementation. By assigning the major implementation strategies to the states, the process was opened to the vagaries of state economics and politics. While the overt intention behind state implementation was to respect the differences between the states, the effect was to blunt the effectiveness of the legislation. In addition, the early action-forcing provisions left EPA vulnerable to claims of technological impossibility, and the immediate stew of litigation that arose from enforcement efforts hampered successful implementation. Finally, because water pollution control is protective regulatory policy, the policy actors include the White House and senior members of the Congress; their high visibility and the conflicts between them also reduced the effectiveness of implementation efforts.

Toxic and hazardous substances pose qualitatively different problems from the problems of air and water pollutants. Separate regulatory programs to deal with these substances have been established; these are discussed in the next section.

HAZARDOUS AND TOXIC SUBSTANCES

The problems associated with the production, use, and disposal of hazardous wastes and chemicals are the result of the high standard of living associated with our industrialized society. Large scale production of synthetic chemicals did not begin until after the Second World War. Before that, pesticides were the predominant hazardous chemical, and these were under the control of the U.S. Department of Agriculture (USDA) and the Food and Drug Administration (FDA). Today EPA "has over 48,000 chemicals on its inventory of toxic substances and no information on the toxic effects of 79 percent of them."[40]

Public awareness of the chemical problem was aroused in 1962 by Rachel Carson's book *Silent Spring*, but the more salient issues of air and water pollution dominated environmental action throughout the sixties. Congress was not fully informed about the dangers of accumulating chemicals until 1971, when the Council on Environmental Quality (CEQ) reported on the dangers of toxic chemicals.

Prior to 1976, chemicals and hazardous wastes were controlled and regulated on an individual basis. There was no coordinated attempt to deal with the problem. Chemicals or wastes found in water supplies were regulated under the Federal Water Pollution Control Act of 1972. Chemicals or wastes emitted into the air were controlled by the Air Quality Act of 1967 and the 1970 amendments. Agricultural chemicals and wastes were controlled by the strong 1972 amendments to the Federal Insecticide, Fungicide, and Rodenticide Act of 1947 (FIFRA). If the substance was a residue on food, then it was the responsibility of the FDA.

In 1976, five years after the CEQ report on chemical dangers, Congress enacted two pieces of legislation designed specifically to deal with the problems associated with chemicals and hazardous wastes. The Toxic Substances Control

Act of 1976 (TSCA) was designed to identify and to evaluate the environmental and health effects of existing chemicals and any new substance entering the United States market. The Resource Conservation and Recovery Act (RCRA) was designed to control solid waste-management practices that could endanger public health or the environment. Both of these laws were implemented slowly due to the underestimation of the chemical and waste problem and the low priority given the issue by the executive branch. Few rules and regulations had been promulgated by the late 1970s and early 1980s. There was also a failure to resolve the problem of leaking and abandoned dumps that presented a threat to human health or the environment. This problem was aggravated because usually no Potentially Responsible Parties (PRPs) could be found to bear the cleanup costs.

The most important acts governing toxic and hazardous substances are the Federal Insecticide, Fungicide and Rodenticide Act of 1947 (FIFRA); the Resource Conservation and Recovery Act of 1976 (RCRA); the Toxic Substances Control Act of 1976 (TSCA); and the Comprehensive Environmental Response, Compensation, and Liability Act of 1980 (CERCLA or Superfund) and its 1986 amendments (Superfund Amendment and Reauthorization Act or SARA).[41]

Federal Insecticide, Fungicide and Rodenticide Act of 1947

Although the publicity surrounding pesticide control might lead us to suspect that controlling toxic substances is a relatively new government activity, the federal government has been regulating pesticides since the first labeling act, the Insecticide Act of 1910, was passed. This was repealed in 1947 when the comprehensive Federal Insecticide, Fungicide, and Rodenticide Act (FIFRA) was passed. Like the 1910 act, FIFRA focused on labeling.[42] Originally the Department of Agriculture (USDA) enforced FIFRA, but in 1970, EPA assumed responsibility for administering the Act. FIFRA was amended in 1972, 1975, 1978, and 1988. It requires a benefit-cost analysis on regulatory controls; this standard "is unusual among federal environmental statutes: others employ risk-based standards softened only by the availability of control technologies."[43] Persons wishing to sell or to distribute a pesticide must register the pesticide with EPA; the burden of proof of the chemical's efficacy and safety rests with the manufacturer or distributor. "Safety" is predicated on the legal concept of "unreasonable risk" to people or the environment, which is an unfortunately fluid phrase. Pesticides that pose a substantial risk but are the only option to control a dangerous or expensive pest might pass the "unreasonable" test. Canceling registration can be expensive and time-consuming, although in extreme cases EPA can issue an emergency suspension, as it did for dioxin.

CASE DISCUSSION 5.3

Birds and Birdies

Ciba-Geigy Corporation manufactured pesticide products containing diazinon. The administrator of the U.S. Environmental Protection Agency (EPA) cancelled the registration of diazinon for use on sod farms and golf courses because of dangers to birds.

- The Federal Insecticide, Fungicide and Rodenticide Act authorizes the administrator to cancel registration of a pesticide if "when used in accordance with widespread and commonly recognized practice, [it] *generally* causes *unreasonable* adverse effects on the environment." 7 U.S.C. § 136d(b), emphasis added.
- "Unreasonable adverse effects on the environment" is defined in the statute as "any unreasonable risk to man or the environment, taking into account . . . costs and benefits." 7 U.S.C. § 136 (bb)

Ciba-Geigy argued that, to have a registration revoked, the unreasonable adverse effects needed to occur most of the time. It also argued that the benefits of using the products outweighed the costs and that the administrator had to show that the overall populations of the bird species were endangered by pesticide-related deaths.

Does the word "generally" imply that the adverse effect must occur frequently? More than 50 percent of the time? What if birds died in very large numbers on some golf courses using the products but rarely on others?

How should the administrator define "unreasonable"?

(continued)

CASE DISCUSSION 5.3 (*continued*)

Must the administrator consider population effects? Is the administrator required to continue the registration if he cannot show that costs outweigh benefits?

(Source: *Ciba-Geigy Corporation v. United States Environmental Protection Agency*, 874 F. 2d 277 [1989])

Resource Conservation and Recovery Act (1976)

The Resource Conservation and Recovery Act (RCRA) is focused primarily on solid and hazardous *waste*, and it is notable for its tracking system of hazardous materials from "cradle to grave," that is, from production to final disposal.[44] This system has standards for generators, transporters, and disposal sites. Generators must keep detailed records and must meet reporting, labeling, and packaging requirements. Transporters are also required to meet labeling and records standards and must track materials through a permitted manifest system. The final stage, disposal, includes issues such as location, construction, recordkeeping, and operation of disposal sites.

Enforcement is implemented through the permitting system set out in section 3005 of RCRA. EPA may inspect and can bring both civil and criminal actions for violations.[45] States may assume responsibility for hazardous waste control, and while they may exceed federal standards, they must at least meet federal requirements in their controlling systems.

CASE DISCUSSION 5.4

The Foolish Trucker

Waste Conversion owned and operated a hazardous and residual waste treatment, storage, and disposal facility in Pennsylvania. Waste Conversion hired Wills Trucking Company of Ohio to transport

(continued)

CASE DISCUSSION 5.4 (*continued*)

processed waste to disposal facilities. In turn, Wills Trucking hired Al Cullenen, an independent trucker, to transport the waste to Michigan.

With Cullenen's knowledge, Waste Conversion employees over-loaded Cullenen's truck by 3,500 pounds. To avoid a weigh station, Cullenen took to the back roads. Faced with a steep hill that his poorly loaded truck could not negotiate, he tried to redistribute his load by raising the truck bed. A substantial amount of waste slid to the road.

Waste Conversion, Wills, and Cullenen were charged with violating the 1980 Pennsylvania Solid Waste Management Act. Waste Conversion claimed, among other things, that Cullenen's actions were so far beyond its control that its due process rights were violated by charging Waste Conversion with Cullenen's spill.

- "It shall be unlawful for any person . . . to consign, assign, sell, entrust, give or in any way transfer residual or hazardous waste which is at any time subsequently . . . dumped or deposited . . . unless a permit . . . has first been obtained." Pennsylvania Solid Waste Management Act, § 610(8)(I)
- A tavern owner cannot be held criminally liable for liquor code violations of an employee committed without his personal knowledge, participation, or presence. *Commonwealth [PA] v. Koczwara*, 155 A. 2d 825 (1959)

Is it reasonable to hold Waste Conversion responsible for acts caused by an independent trucker who apparently lacks common sense and was not hired by Waste Conversion? What are the public policy advantages to holding Waste Conversion accountable?

(Source: *Waste Conversion Inc. v. Commonwealth of Pennsylvania*, 568 A. 2d 738 [1990])

Toxic Substances Control Act (1976)

The intent of the Toxic Substances Control Act (TSCA) was to fill the gaps between the federal environmental protections statutes that had been enacted between 1970 and 1976; under TSCA, EPA was empowered to regulate new toxic substances, removal of asbestos from schools, radon, and the disposal of polychlorinated biphenyls (PCBs).[46] TSCA gave EPA "broad authority to control chemical risks that could not be dealt with under other environmental statutes."[47]

The main purpose of TSCA is to ensure that manufacturers test the chemicals they market and to allow EPA to regulate the use of chemicals that present unreasonable risks. TSCA emphasizes three policies: data collection, primarily by the industries involved; government authority to prevent risks—especially imminent ones—to public health or the environment; and consideration of economic impacts. Compared to other federal laws, such as those governing air and water, TSCA has not been utilized extensively by EPA, in part because EPA has been overwhelmed with legislative mandates and deadlines.[48]

Superfund (1980) and SARA (1986)

In 1978, Love Canal, a housing development near Niagara, New York, was declared to be in a state of emergency because long-buried chemicals were seeping into the basements of the public school and several houses. A high incidence of health problems triggered an investigation that unveiled the presence of 21,900 tons of chemical wastes buried in fifty-five gallon drums.[49] The publicity surrounding Love Canal led to the discovery of thousands of other similar dump sites around the country.

In direct response to the public outcry over Love Canal, the Comprehensive Environmental Response, Compensation, and Liability Act of 1980 (CERCLA or Superfund) was enacted. Superfund is an unusual environmental statute because it does not regulate industry activities. Instead it gives the president the power to compel cleanup of hazardous substances and to recover the costs of cleanups. The president has delegated his enforcement authority to the EPA by executive order.

Superfund was developed to assure financial responsibility for the long-term maintenance of waste disposal facilities and to provide for the cleanup of old and abandoned hazardous waste-disposal sites that were leaking or that otherwise endangered the public health. This law was designed to close the gap between TSCA and RCRA concerning closed dumps. Superfund also had provisions to respond to emergency spills of hazardous wastes. A National Priorities List (NPL) of all uncontrolled hazardous waste sites was established. Two types of government action were possible under Superfund. First, a removal action (primarily emergency response) had a time limit of six months and a cost limit of one million dollars; second, a remedial action could be undertaken to clean up sites that were not considered an immediate threat to human health but were listed on the National Priorities List. Remedial actions were to follow recommendations of the remedial investigations and feasibility studies (RI/FS) and be performed in accordance with the National Contingency Plan (NCP). The NCP under Superfund was an expanded version of the original NCP created in the Federal Water Pollution Control Act of 1972. It included the hazardous substance response plan that established procedures and standards for responding to releases of hazardous substances, pollutants, and contaminants. It specified procedures, techniques, materials, equipment, and methods to be employed in identifying, removing, or remedying releases of hazardous substances to minimize the damages of the releases.

Superfund was allocated a trust fund of $1.6 billion over five years for cleanup, financed primarily by a feedstock tax on certain chemicals and on petroleum plus a congressional appropriation. The main accomplishment of Superfund was to develop an understanding of the magnitude of the problem. An early Office of Technology Assessment report on Superfund estimated that as much as $100 billion and fifty years could be needed to clean up the estimated 10,000 sites. By 2004, 1,600 sites were listed on the National Priorities List; 11,500 sites await listing. About 800 have been cleaned up.[50] This is not an impressive record, especially as EPA estimates 50,000 additional sites are eligible.[51]

Superfund expired in 1985 and, in 1986, Congress passed the Superfund Amendments and Reauthorization Act of 1986 (SARA). SARA expanded the funding of Superfund to $9 billion. This funding included not only an increase in the feedstock tax, but it also added an environmental tax on corporate income over $2 million dollars.[52] SARA set performance deadlines and achievement standards for EPA. Section 206 gave citizens standing to file suit for any violation of CERCLA or SARA, subject to some restrictions.[53] SARA also allocated $500 million to the leaking underground storage tank (UST)[54] problem. In retrospect, one of the most important provisions of SARA was Title III, the Emergency Planning and Community Right-to-know Act (EPCRA). In some communities, this led to a reduction in chemical storage and releases, and it has certainly provided vital information to local emergency responders.

Superfund was ill-designed from the beginning. In retrospect, one of the worst provisions was joint-and-several liability, which led to a ludicrous and almost infinite regression of attempts to pass cleanup costs on to minor parties. Conflict rages over how clean or remediated a site must be, and who is responsible. The litigation burden is almost insurmountable; the costs of losing a contested Superfund cleanup fight are so high that almost any legal fee is preferable. During the Clinton administration, EPA aggressively pursued cleanups. Unfortunately, taxes to replenish the trust fund have not been reauthorized by Congress since 1995,[55] and repayments by Potentially Responsible Parties (PRPs), when they could be identified, were lagging far behind expenditures. By 2004, the program was running out of funds, and funding has shifted to general appropriations, always a risky position in Washington's money-driven politics.

CASE DISCUSSION 5.5

Dead Batteries

Sapp Battery Salvage recycled lead-acid batteries in Cottondale, Florida, from 1970 to January 1980. At the height of its operations, it processed about 5,000 batteries per day. The lead was recovered for resale, but the contaminated plastic casings were shredded and buried on site. The acid was drained into a swamp on the property. In 1982, the Sapp Battery Salvage site was placed on the Superfund National Priorities list. Under the joint and several liability provisions of Superfund, 57 companies consented to financing the cleanup. In turn, they sued 36 more companies to share the costs.

The defendants argued they were not "disposing of" or "treating" the batteries; they were selling a valuable commodity for profit. Charles Cleveland, one of the defendants, owned Carolina Waste & Salvage in South Carolina. During 1978, he sold batteries to Sapp at least five times. Each time, Sapp made the initial contact and sent a truck to pick up the batteries; the batteries were paid for when they were collected. Sapp's checks and trucks were marked "Sapp Batteries," but on most of the sales receipts, the batteries were invoiced as "junk batteries." In

(continued)

CASE DISCUSSION 5.5 (*continued*)

addition, Sapp paid per pound rather than per battery. Cleveland said he thought the batteries would be refurbished.

- "Any person who by contract, agreement, or otherwise arranged for disposal or treatment, or arranged with a transporter for disposal or treatment, of hazardous substances owned or possessed by such person, by any other party or entity, at a facility or incinerator vessel owned or operated by another party or entity and containing such hazardous substances" is liable for cleanup costs. 42 U.S.C.A. § 9697 (a)(3)

Should Cleveland be held liable for part of the Superfund cleanup costs for Sapp Battery Salvage?

(Source: *Chatham Steel Corporation et al. v. Sapp et al.*, 858 F. Supp. 1130 [1994])

An unanticipated consequence of Superfund was the development of the brownfields program. Understandably, investors and developers are reluctant to become involved with former industrial sites lest a Superfund action fall on them. To encourage development, the Department of Housing and Urban Development (HUD) and EPA have provided grants for brownfields development, new tax laws allow special breaks for brownfields developers, and EPA offers protective agreements for those willing to take a chance on an otherwise dicey site.[56]

THE FUTURE

In an assessment of environmental progress since the first Earth Day in 1970, William Stevens of the *New York Times* noted in 1995 that while substantial progress has been made in some areas such as toxic chemicals and CFC releases, the problems that remained were larger and more complex, and their solutions required dramatic changes in the ways ordinary people live.[57] This is still true. The developed nations live well but at a high environmental cost; the less developed nations face exploding populations, poor health, and environmental degradation.

The antiregulatory posture of the Congress in the mid-1990s led some environmentalists to predict environmental disaster. This was an overreaction, although the policies of George W. Bush's administration to increase energy production and use of the nation's natural resources are sparking similar concerns in the first decade of the new century. First, the shift in the regulatory agencies away from command-and-control toward cooperative, market-driven control strategies seems to be effective; losing regulatory power may be just the incentive needed to push the agencies toward more creative programs. Second, even if every environmental regulatory program were dismantled immediately, pollution levels would not explode. Control technology is still in place, accounting procedures have been institutionalized, new markets for greener products have been established. The laws of physics tell us that bodies in motion tend to remain in motion; similarly, the laws of public policy tell us that established policies tend to remain established. Finally, it is not clear that American business would choose to go on an environmental rampage if its regulatory bonds were loosened.

SUGGESTED READING

Bryner, Gary. *Blue Skies, Green Politics: The Clean Air Act of 1990*, rev. ed. Washington, DC: CQ, 1995. A clear and thorough analysis of the evolution of clean air policy in the United States, with a detailed account of the passage of the 1990 Clean Air Act Amendments.

Colbern, Theo, Dianne Dumanoski, and John Myers. *Our Stolen Future*. New York: Dutton, 1996. The frightening best-seller about the dangers of hormone disruptors to humans and the rest of the natural world.

Dales, J. H. *Pollution, Property & Prices*. Toronto: University of Toronto Press, 1968. The classic and very readable essay that sets out the concept of pollution rights. He is persuasive, even if you're not an economist.

Rosenbaum, Walter A. *Environmental Politics and Policy*. 6th ed. Washington, DC: Congressional Quarterly, 2005. Primarily an undergraduate text, this furnishes an excellent overview of several areas of environmental policy: air pollution, water supply and pollution, toxic and hazardous wastes, energy, and public lands. The discussions on the relationships between science and politics alone make the book worthwhile.

NOTES

1. This debate is still current. See, for example, Martin Nie, "Administrative Rule-making and Public Lands Conflict: The Forest Service's Roadless Rule," *Natural Resources Journal* 44 (Summer 2004): 687–742.

2. H.R. 986, p. 3.

3. Charles K. Woltz, preface to *Administrative Procedure in Government Agencies* (Attorney General's Committee Report) (Charlottesville, VA: University Press of Virginia, 1968). This is a facsimile edition of Senate Document No. 8, 77th Congress, 1st Session, 1941.

4. Unless otherwise noted, this material is from Phillip Cooper, *Public Law and Public Administration*, 3rd ed. (Itasca, Ill: Peacock, 2000), esp. chapter 5.

5. Zygmunt Plater, Robert Abrams, William Goldfarb, and Robert Graham, *Environmental Law and Policy: Nature, Law, and Society*, 2nd ed. (St Paul, MN: West, 1998), 2.

6. This action is one reason Bork was not confirmed as Associate Justice of the Supreme Court, leading to a new verb in Washington political parlance: "getting borked."

7. Cooper, *Public Law and Public Administration*, 145.

8. See Cooper, *Public Law and Public Administration*, 158–161.

9. Unless otherwise noted, this material is from Walter A. Rosenbaum, *Environmental Politics and Policy*, 6th ed. (Washington, DC: CQ Press, 2005), 140–155.

10. Rosenbaum, *Environmental Politics and Policy*, 6th ed., 143.

11. For a full discussion of the case for and against benefit-cost analysis, see Rosenbaum, *Environmental Politics and Policy*, 6th ed., 144–152.

12. Unless otherwise noted, this discussion is from Florence Heffron and Neil McFeeley, *The Administrative Regulatory Process* (New York: Longman, 1983), chapter 11.

13. Heffron and McFeeley, *The Administrative Regulatory Process*, 293.

14. G. Tyler Miller Jr., *Living in the Environment*, 5th ed. (Belmont, CA: Wadsworth, 1988), 423.

15. Miller, *Living in the Environment*, 424.

16. Scott Brennan and Jay Withgott, *Environment: The Science behind the Stories* (San Francisco: Pearson/Benjamin Cummings, 2004), 325.

17. See Paul Rogers, "The Clean Air Act of 1970," *EPA Journal* (January–February 1990), www.epa.gov/history/topics/caa70/11.htm (accessed 22 December 2005). Rogers was the long-term chair of the House Subcommittee on Health and the Environment.

18. Rosenbaum, *Environmental Politics and Policy*, 6th ed., 184.

19. Rosenbaum, *Environmental Politics and Policy*, 6th ed., 186–187.

20. Rosenbaum, *Environmental Politics and Policy*, 6th ed., 188–189.

21. 42 U.S.C.A. 7412 (b).

22. Roger Findley and Daniel Farber, *Cases and Materials on Environmental Law*, 4th ed. (St. Paul, MN: West, 1995), 137.

23. The first government sponsored auction of the rights took place in March 1993. The major purchaser was the Carolina Power and Light Company, which bought the rights to emit over 85,000 tons of sulfur dioxide; this represented 57 percent of the permits sold at the auction and cost $11.5 million. The company planned to use the emission rights to delay installation of expensive "scrubbers" at its plants ("Carolina Power Is Top Buyer," *New York Times*, 31 March 1993, C2; "CP&L Spends Big to Delay Buying Air 'Scrubbers,'" *Greensboro* [North Carolina] *News and Record*, 31 March 1993, B8.). A delightful contrast occurred in March 1995, when students from seven law schools pooled their resources to buy the rights to 18 tons of sulfur dioxide emissions. The students' plan was ingenious: they intend to let the permits expire, unused, thus reducing pollution and simultaneously driving up the price of other permits. ("Law Students Buy and Hold Pollution Rights," *New York Times*, 31 March 1995, B13.) Students from law schools at the University of Maryland, City University of New York, Detroit, Duke, Hamline, and New England spent $3,256. The project was organized by Robert Percival, an environmental law professor at the University of Maryland. This market-based approach was, for many, a welcome relief from the old command-and-control system of the federal regulatory agencies.

24. This information is drawn from panel remarks by Kathy Bailey, Assistant General Counsel for the Chemical Manufacturers Association, during the *Legal Winds of Change* video-conference.

25. This discussion is drawn from Rosenbaum, *Environmental Politics and Policy*, 6th ed., 185–192.

26. EPA estimates a 51 percent reduction in the criteria pollutants despite population and economic growth. U.S. Environmental Protection Agency, *Air Emissions Trends–Continued Progress through 2003* (Washington DC: EPA, January 2005), www.epa.gov/airtrends/aqtrnd04/emissions.html (accessed 4 September 2005).

27. U.S. Environmental Protection Agency, *National Air Quality and Emissions Trends Report, 2003*, (Washington, DC: EPA, September 2003), www.epa.gov/airtrends/reports.html (accessed 4 September 2005).

28. Norman Vig, "Presidential Leadership and the Environment," in *Environmental Policy: New Directions for the Twenty-First Century*, 6th ed., edited by Norman Vig and Michael Kraft (Washington, DC: CQ Press, 2006), 115–116.

29. Miller, *Living in the Environment*, 455.

30. Walter A. Rosenbaum, *Environmental Politics and Policy*, 3rd ed. (Washington, DC: CQ Press, 1995), 53.

31. Rosenbaum, *Environmental Politics and Policy* 6th ed., 208.

32. Miller, *Living in the Environment*, 475.

33. Miller, *Living in the Environment*, 456.

34. Nancy Kubasek and Gary Silverman, *Environmental Law*, 5th ed. (Upper Saddle River, NJ: Pearson, 2005), 242. An additional concern for safe drinking water was addressed in the Public Health Security and Bioterrorism Preparedness and Response Act of 2002. See Kubasek and Silverman, 244–245.

35. For a full discussion of this issue, see Theo Colborn, Dianne Dumanoski, and John Myers, *Our Stolen Future* (New York: Dutton, 1996).

36. Miller, *Living in the Environment*, 484.

37. Plater et al., *Environmental Law and Policy*, 503.

38. Michael Kraft and Norman Vig, "Environmental Policy from the 1970s to the Twenty-First Century," in *Environmental Policy: New Directions for the Twenty-First Century*, 6th ed., edited by Norman Vig and Michael Kraft (Washington, DC: CQ Press, 2006), 22–23. (What they actually wrote was that 39 percent of the rivers and streams and 45 percent of lakes, pond, and reservoirs were *not* in compliance, and I did the math.)

39. Plater et al., *Environmental Law and Policy*, 503.

40. Kubasek and Silverman, *Environmental Law*, 260.

41. In addition to the listed legislation, both the Clean Air Act and the Clean Water Act have provisions for dealing with hazardous waste. The Clean Air Act provisions are in Title III; the Clean Water Act used Best Available Technologies (BATs) to determine effluent limitations. Other acts with hazardous substance provisions include the Safe Drinking Water Act, Occupational Health and Safety Act, and the Food, Drug, and Cosmetic Act.

42. Over 20,000 pesticides are registered under FIFRA. Kubasek and Silverman, *Environmental Law*, 263. Also, an excellent, more detailed introduction to FIFRA is in Kubasek and Silverman, 262–270.

43. Findley and Farber, *Cases and Materials on Environmental Law*, 438.

44. By focusing on end-of-pipe controls, federal regulators fail to provide some incentives for manufacturers to improve their production processes. Most companies are divided into function-based divisions with separate financial reporting requirements. If production and sales numbers reflected the true costs of waste disposal, companies would have internal motivation to reduce their waste.

45. These may be substantial. In 1998, the owner of a salvage ship received a forty-year sentence for, among other crimes, illegally disposing of hazardous waste. Kubasek and Silverman, *Environmental Law*, 20.

46. Ray Vaughn, *Essentials of Environmental Law* (Rockville, MD: Government Institutes, 1994), 30–31.

47. Bureau of National Affairs, *U.S. Environmental Laws*, 1988 ed. (Washington, DC: Bureau of National Affairs, 1988), 145.

48. See Rosenbaum, *Environmental Politics and Policy,* 6th ed., 238–239.

49. U.S. Environmental Protection Agency, *Environmental Monitoring at Love Canal* (Washington, DC: USEPA, 1982).

50. Rosenbaum, *Environmental Politics and Policy*, 6th ed., 240.

51. See Jonathan Lash, Katherine Gillman, and David Sheridan, *A Season of Spoils: The Reagan Administration's Attack on the Environment* (New York: Pantheon, 1984), especially chapter 2. See also Steven Cohen, "Defusing the Toxic Time Bomb: Federal Hazardous Waste Programs," in *Environmental Policy in the 1980's: Reagan's New Agenda*, edited by Norman Vig and Michael Kraft (Washington, DC: Congressional Quarterly, 1984), 273–291.

52. This represented a major deviation from the past theory that "polluter pays."

53. For example, citizen suits are not allowed within sixty-days of the notification of the potentially responsible parties of the site violation. Citizen suits are also prohibited if the president is diligently prosecuting the case under CERCLA or RCRA.

54. The acronym was originally LUST but was changed for obvious, silly reasons. I've heard that it was because President Reagan refused to have a LUST program in his government, but I've never seen that story in writing.

55. Norman Vig and Michael Kraft, "Toward Sustainable Development?" in *Environmental Policy: New Directions for the Twenty-First Century*, 6th ed., edited by Norman Vig and Michael Kraft (Washington, DC: CQ Press, 2006), 380.

56. James Salzman and Barton H. Thompson Jr., *Environmental Law and Policy* (New York: Foundation Press, 2003), 208–209; Kubasek and Silverman, *Environmental Law*, 314–316.

57. William K. Stevens, "The 25th Anniversary of Earth Day: How Has the Environment Fared?" *New York Times*, 18 April 1995, B5.

CHAPTER SIX

Managing Wildlife and Public Lands

Management of wildlife and public lands are related issues that generate complex webs of statutes, regulations, and even international treaties. As in the preceding chapter, it would be impossible to discuss or even to mention every law that affects public lands and wildlife. The purpose of this discussion is not to present the individual provisions of each and every act but rather to acquaint readers with the political context of various policy areas and the general intent behind the major acts and their subsequent implementation and revision.

The chapter is divided into three major sections. Federal-state cooperative wildlife management is discussed in the first section. The central topics are the state ownership doctrine, the Federal Aid in Wildlife Restoration Act, the Federal Aid in Sport Fish Restoration Act, and a brief discussion of other federal-state programs. The second major section addresses federal wildlife management, including regulation of taking wildlife, commerce in wildlife, conservation of endangered species, and marine mammals. The final section discusses six periods of federal land history: acquisition, disposal, reservation, custodial management, intensive management, and consultation and confrontation.

FEDERAL-STATE COOPERATIVE WILDLIFE MANAGEMENT

Until the late nineteenth century, wildlife management was essentially *game* management, and conservation was practiced to restore and to protect game animals. The responsibility for game rested with state governments because they were the legal owners of the wildlife. Although partially discredited today, the state ownership doctrine has had a great impact on international, federal, and state wildlife law.[1]

The Rise and Fall of the State Ownership Doctrine

In *Martin v. Waddell* (1842), Chief Justice Taney found that the rights to the navigable waters, submerged lands, fish, and wildlife were a public trust (see chapter 1). Technically this decision applied only to the original thirteen states. However, in 1845, a question arose about the status of wildlife in new states. In *Pollard's Lessee v. Hagan* (1845), the Court applied the ruling to newly admitted states as well, citing the legislative convention that new states are admitted on an equal footing with previously existing states.

The state ownership doctrine was challenged again in 1855 in *Smith v. Maryland*. The case involved a ship owner who had been taking oysters with a scoop or drag in defiance of Maryland law. Smith's vessel was licensed by the federal government, and he contended that the state law was an unconstitutional interference with the federal power to regulate interstate commerce. The Supreme Court held that because Maryland owned the soil in which the oysters were located, Maryland was allowed to regulate the oyster fisheries. Maryland's claim of state ownership in this case overrode the Commerce Clause. The Court carefully protected its own prerogatives on future related questions:

> Whether this liberty [to take oysters] belongs exclusively to the citizens of the State of Maryland, or may lawfully be enjoyed in common by all citizens of the United States; whether this public use may be restricted by the States to its own citizens, or a part of them, or by force of the Constitution must remain common to all citizens of the United States; whether the national government, by a treaty or act of congress, can grant to foreigners the right to participate therein; or what, in general, are the limits of the trust upon which the State holds this soil, or its power to define and control that trust, are matters wholly without the scope of this case, and upon which we give no opinion.[2]

Of course, the Court was not allowed to leave so many loose ends forever. *McCready v. Virginia* (1876) gave Virginia ownership of not only the tidewaters but also the fish and oysters in those waters. At issue was a Virginia statute that forbade non-Virginia residents from planting oysters in the Virginia tidal waters. The Court held that the state was only regulating the common property of the people it represented. This was a substantial expansion of the earlier decisions in *Martin* and *Smith*. However, in 1891, the Court decided that the commonwealth of Massachusetts could regulate fishing in Buzzards Bay, not because it owned the fish but because, absent any conflicting federal regulation, the state probably had the right to regulate within its territorial waters.[3] This represented a change from the strong endorsement of state ownership laid out in *McCready*. The Court was growing cautious, and it seemed to distinguish *McCready* on the basis that *McCready* dealt with shellfish (stationary and imbedded in soil) rather than finfish, which move through waters that are under federal as well as state jurisdiction.

In 1896, *Geer v. Connecticut* indicated a return to the notion that the states owned their wildlife and were independent of federal interference in the management of the wildlife. Geer was prohibited under Connecticut law from exporting lawfully killed game birds, and the Court offered three separate arguments to support the state law. First, since the state owned the game, "commerce" within the meaning of the Constitution was—perhaps—not created when the game was killed. Second, even if commerce were created, it was at the most *intra*state commerce, because the Connecticut statute prohibited the export of the game. Finally, even if interstate commerce were occurring, and the statute was then an interference with interstate commerce, the right of the state to exercise the police power and to preserve a food supply for its citizens overrode any federal interest in such a small amount of interstate commerce. Although the Court in *Geer* recognized that some states' rights in wildlife were transferred by the Constitution to the federal government, the case was still a stunning affirmation of the state ownership doctrine.

At the turn of the nineteenth century, the conservation movement was part of the larger Progressive movement. Disgusted with the excesses of big business, monopolistic control of industry, and machine politics, reformers struggled to protect the rights of the people to the natural resources of the land, not in a spirit of preservation but rather to ensure that the opportunities and benefits held in reserve in these resources were accessible to the general public. The conservation movement was partly a response to the drive for rational and efficient organization of time and resources imposed on many facets of American life during this era. The precepts of scientific management in business overflowed into the public sector; government regulation of businesses such as the railroads and passage of pure food and drug laws were motivated as much by goals of efficiency as by the public interest. The conservation movement also reflected a concern of the American people that the frontier was truly gone; the 1890 Census had formally declared the closing of the American frontier. With the disappearance of the frontier, Americans could no longer accept wasteful exploitation of resources, and the movement to preserve some of the natural world that had partially defined the American experience gained wider acceptance.

In 1900, Teddy Roosevelt's conservation movement was in full cry. The Sierra Club was eight years old, the federal government had passed the Forest Management Act (1897), and the Rivers and Harbors Act (1899) had established a legal basis for controlling some forms of pollution on navigable waterways.[4] The passage in 1900 of the Lacey Act provided federal assistance to state efforts to regulate their wildlife. The Lacey Act prohibits interstate transportation of any game killed in violation of state law. In addition, it expanded the holding in *Geer*, which allowed states to prohibit the export of lawfully killed game; the Lacey Act allows them to prohibit the import of lawfully killed game.

In 1912, the Court confirmed the expansion of the state power to regulate the taking of wildlife. Justice White, author of the *Geer* opinion, found in *The Abbey Dodge* (1912) that the state ownership doctrine preempted federal wildlife law.[5] This extreme position did not hold for long: in 1926, *Foster-Fountain Packing Company v. Haydel* softened *Geer* by holding that once wildlife (in this case, Louisiana shrimp) enters the stream of commerce, the state lost absolute control over that wildlife.

Geer was the high water mark for state regulation of wildlife. Since then, various Supreme Court decisions have established three constitutional bases for federal regulation of wildlife: the federal treaty-making power, the federal property power, and the federal commerce power.

Treaty Power

In 1913, Congress passed the Migratory Bird Act, which declared all migratory game and insectivorous birds to be under federal protection and regulation. Promptly challenged in two federal district courts in different circuits, the act was found unconstitutional.[6] While the federal appeal was pending, the government concluded a treaty with Great Britain to protect migratory birds, and in 1918, Congress passed the Migratory Bird Treaty Act to implement the treaty. The Supreme Court never ruled on the appeals from the Migratory Bird Act cases.

The states moved quickly to challenge the Migratory Bird Treaty Act in court, but use of the federal treaty power complicated their arguments considerably. The landmark case that eventually decided the issue and established the supremacy of the treaty power over the reserved rights of the states is *Missouri v. Holland* (1920).[7] This case arose in federal district court against federal game warden Ray P. Holland, whose enforcement of the Migratory Bird Treaty Act in Missouri was interfering with the amount of state revenues generated by hunting. The district judge found that the treaty-making power of the United States is supreme over state authority, and therefore the Migratory Bird Treaty Act was constitutional. Missouri appealed to the Supreme Court, but the Court upheld the lower court decision. The Migratory Bird Treaty Act was indeed constitutional; the erosion of the state ownership doctrine confirmed in *Geer* had begun.

Federal Property Power

Although the federal power to regulate wildlife through the treaty provisions of the Constitution had been established, the federal power to hunt or to manage wildlife on federal lands within state borders was not so clearly established. The federal government as landowner within state boundaries was viewed by the states as simply another property owner subject to state wildlife regulations. However, in *Kleppe v. New Mexico* (1976), the Supreme Court ruled that the federal government had power to regulate and to protect wildlife living on federal land.

Commerce Clause

Until 1977, there was no Supreme Court decision that specified the reach of the commerce clause in federal wildlife regulation. In that year, *Douglas v. Seacoast Products, Inc.* determined that a Virginia residency requirement for menhaden fishing was preempted by the federal licenses held by the fishing vessels. In *Douglas* the Court clearly rejected the state ownership doctrine:

> A State does not stand in the same position as the owner of a private game preserve and it is pure fantasy to talk of 'owning' wild fish, birds, or animals. Neither the States nor the Federal Government, any more than a hopeful fisherman or hunter, has title to these creatures until they are reduced to possession by skillful capture.[8]

The primacy of the state ownership doctrine was finally laid to rest in the *Tangier Sound* controversy, discussed in chapter 1, which granted fishing rights in Virginia waters to Maryland fishermen.

Federal assumption of control over wildlife was part of a larger effort to centralize national power. Virtually all congressional debates over the Migratory Bird Act and the Migratory Bird Treaty Act focused on the constitutional issues of the proper relationship between the state and federal governments. It is clear from the congressional debates and judicial opinions that everyone agreed that game in general, and migratory birds in particular, needed protection. They also agreed that the federal acts would provide protection, yet they argued bitterly over the legislation. For the most part, the arguments were not on scientific or administrative grounds but rather on constitutional grounds. Even those who favored the policy ends were driven to object to the policy means.

Using a popular policy agenda to achieve a hidden agenda is an ancient political ploy. Certainly environmental policy is often used to camouflage less respectable goals, partly because environmental issues have such high social appeal. For example, in California, regulation of the state shrimp fishery was as much an attempt to force the Chinese out of business as it was scientific regulation of a natural resource.[9] Similarly, early English game laws were instituted in part to restrict the use of weapons by potential dissidents or criminals.[10]

CASE DISCUSSION 6.1

The Price of Hunting Elk

In 1975, elk hunting was big business in Montana. The state hunting license fee structure made a sharp distinction between nonresident licenses for elk ($151) and resident licenses ($4). The nonresident fee also allowed two deer, but there was no elk-only license for nonresidents. Non-resident license sales had increased by 530 percent between 1960 and 1970; in the same period residential license sales increased 67 percent. For the 1975 license year, 43,500 nonresident elk and deer licenses were issued for a total license revenue of $6,568,500.

(continued)

CASE DISCUSSION 6.1 (*continued*)

Each nonresident hunter spent an estimated $1,250 while in the state, for an economic boost of $54,375,000. That's a total of $60,943,500 for the year from nonresident hunters.

In 1976, the fee structure changed. A resident elk license was now $9, but the nonresident combination license, which covered more game and fish than the 1975 license, was now $225. For a resident to have access to all the opportunities of the nonresident license, the total fee would have been $30.

Most states charge higher hunting license fees for nonresidents; however, Baldwin (a Montana outfitter and hunting guide) and four Minnesota residents who had hunted in Montana challenged the fee differential as excessive. They based their claim on two constitutional protections:

- "The Citizens of each State shall be entitled to all Privileges and Immunities of Citizens in the several States." (U.S. Constitution, Article IV, § 2[1]; and
- "No State shall make or enforce any law which shall abridge the privileges or immunities of citizens of the United States, nor shall any State . . . deny to any person within its jurisdiction the equal protection of the laws." (U.S. Constitution, Amendment XIV)

Montana justified its fee structure by contrasting the residential hunters' desire to provide meat for the table with the nonresidents' desires for trophies. In addition, Montana ranchers often fed elk during the harsh winter months. Montana Fish and Game Commission personnel spent more time on elk management than any other game species. The state argued that their costs in maintaining elk herds and policing hunters, the limited supply of elk, and the residents' interest in preserving a food supply all justified the differential fee.

Should Montana be allowed to charge such comparatively high fees? If not, how would you determine how high nonresident fees could be?

(Source: *Baldwin v. Montana Fish and Game Commission*, 436 U.S. 371 [1978])

Having flexed its muscles over migratory birds, the federal government allowed the states to retain some control over wildlife.[11] Throughout much of the twentieth century, the states were given considerable autonomy in choosing how and to what extent they complied with federal guidelines, subject of course to the silken chains of federal money through such programs such as the Pittman-Robertson Act (1937), which redistributes a federal tax on ammunition and firearms sales to the states for wildlife restoration, and the Dingell-Johnson Act (1950), which uses a similar strategy to support state sport fisheries.

Federal Aid in Wildlife Restoration (Pittman-Robertson) Act

The Pittman-Robertson Act is a federal-state cooperative endeavor that drew together the same interests that supported efforts to protect migratory birds.[12] Passed in 1937, the bill was unique. It is funded by an excise tax on hunting equipment and supplies; the money is then redistributed to the states under a formula based on, among other things, the number of hunting licenses issued and the size of the state.[13] As a condition of eligibility for federal funds, states are prohibited from diverting hunting license fees collected by the states from state fish and game department administration.[14] Thus state fish and game departments that participate in Pittman-Robertson also have a steady source of license revenue; this deceptively simple section of the law has been the basis for one of the most successful environmental laws in the country. Pittman-Robertson was signed by Franklin Roosevelt on 2 September 1937; within the first year, forty-three of the forty-eight states had passed legislation to become eligible for funding.[15]

Although Pittman-Robertson as originally drafted had enormous potential for federal influence on state wildlife management decisions, subsequent amendments have broadened the powers of the state decisionmakers. In 1946, an amendment allowed up to one-fourth of the state's allocation of federal aid funds to be used to maintain completed projects.[16] Although the states were quick to comply with Pittman-Robertson requirements, Congress was slow to appropriate the full amount of the excise tax due to the Pittman-Robertson program. In the FY1951 Appropriations Act, Congress finally gave Pittman-Robertson funds a "permanent-indefinite" appropriations status that automatically transferred the excise tax to the Fish and Wildlife Service.[17] In 1955,

Congress passed an amendment that permitted grant funds to be used for straightforward wildlife management (rather than discrete projects). Then in 1970, the law was amended in two important areas. First, the federal excise tax on handguns was added to the Pittman-Robertson supply with half of these revenues apportioned for hunter safety programs. Second, the 1970 amendment allowed the states to substitute a "comprehensive fish and wildlife resource management" plan for individual project proposals. Finally, in 1972, sales of archery equipment were included in the tax.

Pittman-Robertson is unusual in its reliance on a tax that is supported enthusiastically by those subject to the tax. In the 1930s, excise taxes in general were being phased out, but the wildlife interests pushed for retention of the excise tax on arms and ammunition.[18] In 1950, manufacturers, sportsmen, conservation groups, and state agencies joined forces once again to defeat the repeal of the federal excise tax on arms and ammunition.[19]

The mechanics of Pittman-Robertson are fairly straightforward.[20] Federal excise taxes are collected on firearms, ammunition, and archery equipment (11 percent), and on handguns (10 percent) at the manufacturer or wholesale level. The full amount of the excise tax receipts are automatically appropriated to FWS in the fiscal year following their collection. FWS then makes the funds available to the states through an equitable formula: one-half of the fund is distributed based on the ratio of the land area of the state to the total area of the country, while the second half is distributed based on the ratio of the number of paid hunting license holder per state to license holders nationwide.[21] State grants are limited to a maximum of 5 percent and minimum of 0.5 percent of any one year's total appropriation. The federal-state match for Pittman-Robertson is 75–25 for each project. Any state allocation that is not used within two years automatically reverts to the Migratory Bird Conservation Fund.

By most measures, Pittman-Robertson has been a success.[22] Since 1937, over 4 million acres of land have been purchased for wildlife restoration and another 40 million acres are managed under cooperative agreements. Many species, such as elk, wild turkey, wood duck, white-tailed deer, and pronghorn antelope, have been restored; some have been brought back from the brink of extinction.[23] Between 1939 and 2004, revenues to the wildlife restoration account totaled $4,557,081,106;[24] in FY2005, the states received $235,455,853.[25]

Federal Aid in Sport Fish Restoration (Dingell-Johnson) Act

Passed in 1950, the Dingell-Johnson Act is modeled on the Pittman-Robertson Act.[26] The act provides federal grants to the states for sport fish restoration and management. In 1984, the Wallop-Breaux Amendment established the Aquatic Resources Trust Fund and gave states the option of using the funds for recreational boating facilities and public education projects.[27]

Dingell-Johnson has two funding sources. First, paralleling the funding mechanism for Pittman-Robertson, the federal government assesses a 10 percent federal excise tax on sport fishing equipment, yachts, pleasure boats, and imported fishing equipment. Second, a portion of the tax on gasoline purchased for motorboats is allocated to the Dingell-Johnson program. The funds are distributed according to a formula based on geographical area and the proportion of state fishing licenses sold relative to national license sales. Apportioned funds not spent by the states revert to the federal government after two years to be used for sport fisheries research. Between 1952 and 2004, sport fish restoration account receipts totaled $4,456,291,917;[28] in FY2005, the states received $294,691,282.[29]

Other Federal-State Programs

A third law analogous to the Pittman-Robertson Act and the Dingell-Johnson Act is the Fish and Wildlife Conservation (Forsythe-Chafee or Nongame) Act of 1980. Forsythe-Chafee is focused on nongame wildlife and fish and has never received an appropriation. However, the planning provisions of the act have been integrated with Pittman-Robertson and Dingell-Johnson programs by FWS.

Many natural resource agencies in the federal government have programs with a state component. For example, some national parks allow hunting, fishing, or trapping, and these activities are generally regulated either by the states in which the park is located or according to state regulations. The Forest Service has a State and Private Forestry Program that works with state forestry agencies, private landowners, and forest product industries to improve forest quality; some wildlife habitat is also developed, primarily in the South and Northeast.[30] The Bureau of Land Management (BLM) makes payments to the states and counties as partial reimbursement for economic activities on BLM lands and to compensate the counties for lost property tax revenues.[31]

FEDERAL WILDLIFE PROGRAMS

Federal wildlife law is distinguished by its dispersal among many federal agencies. The federal agencies with major responsibility for wildlife are the Fish and Wildlife Service (FWS; Department of the Interior) and the National Marine Fisheries Service in the National Oceanic and Atmospheric Administration (NOAA; Commerce Department). The National Park Service, the Forest Service, and BLM also have strong roles in this policy area. Because of the interagency activity, the discussions of wildlife management and law are divided into topic areas rather than by agency: regulating the taking of wildlife; regulating commerce in wildlife; conservation of endangered species; protection of marine mammals; and acquisition and management of wildlife habitat.

Regulating the Taking of Wildlife

Although regulation of routine game laws, such as hunting seasons and limits, are state activities, the federal government has the responsibility for species protection. The most important acts dealing with the "taking" of wildlife are the laws protecting migratory birds (for example, the Migratory Bird Treaty Act, the Migratory Bird Conservation Act, and the Migratory Bird Hunting Stamp Act); the Bald Eagle Protection Act; the Wild Free-Roaming Horses and Burros Act; the Marine Mammal Protection Act; and the Endangered Species Act.

Migratory Bird Legislation

The Migratory Bird Treaty Act was passed in 1918 to implement a treaty made with Great Britain on behalf of Canada, providing federal protection through the Secretary of Agriculture for all migratory game birds and insectivorous birds. It also restricted shipping birds across state lines if such actions violated the laws of the states in which the birds were taken. The act withstood a court challenge by the states (see earlier discussion), and with that issue settled, the national government proceeded to sign similar treaties with Mexico (1936), Japan (1972), and the Soviet Union (1976).

It was soon clear that simply protecting the birds from hunters was not sufficient to guarantee the supply of birds. Habitat protection was also necessary, and in 1929 the Migratory Bird Conservation Act was passed to create a national system of bird refuges. Few refuges were actually purchased until the Migratory Bird Hunting Stamp Act passed in 1934 and provided funds for habitat protection. Amendments to this act (also known as the Duck Stamp Act) have varied the percentages of revenue allocated for refuge purchase and for management. Some amendments, and additional statutes such as the National Wildlife Refuge System Administration Act (1966), have given the Secretary of Agriculture authority to permit hunting on refuges. At the same time as the Duck Stamp Act was passed, Congress enacted the Fish and Wildlife Coordination Act to authorize the Bureau of Biological Survey (precursor to the FWS) to coordinate wildlife refuges on federal water impoundments. These refuges were under the control of the Secretary of the Interior.

The obverse of protecting migratory birds is minimizing damage that migrating birds may do to unharvested crops. The 1916 treaty allowed killing birds that endangered agricultural interests, and the Fish and Wildlife Coordination Act was amended in 1946 to permit the Secretary of the Interior to work with other agencies to minimize bird damage. The legislative solution was to provide alternative sources of feed for these birds. In 1948, the Lea Act authorized renting or purchasing land for feeding areas, and two other acts (the Waterfowl Depredations Control Act of 1956 and the Surplus Grain for Wildlife Act of 1961) provided the authority for federal feeding of migrating birds and resident game birds.

The agency with primary responsibility for regulating hunting and commerce of migratory bird species is the Fish and Wildlife Service (FWS). Through duck stamp revenues and congressional appropriations, FWS is able to purchase land and easements to protect habitat for migrating species. FWS is consulted by the Department of Agriculture and all federal water resource agencies to ensure that water projects affecting wetlands will not unduly harm the migratory species or their habitat. FWS may authorize killing of birds (as opposed to routine hunting) if agricultural crops or human health are threatened by the birds' activities.[32]

Bald and Golden Eagle Protection Act

This act was passed in 1940 to protect the national symbol of the United States. In addition to protecting the lives and nests of the birds, the Bald

Eagle Protection Act prohibits the sale, possession, or transport of bald eagles or of any part of an eagle (such as feathers). After 1959, Alaskan bald eagles were protected by the act, and in 1962, golden eagles were also covered, although state governors may authorize the shooting of golden eagles to protect livestock. Golden eagles were added to the act because immature bald eagles are difficult to distinguish from young golden eagles. The act was also amended in 1972 to prohibit "taking" birds by poison. Penalties for violation of the act are severe: criminal penalties up to $10,000 and two years in jail and civil penalties of up to $5,000 per violation. However, changes in federal sentencing laws have increased these fines. In 2005, a Florida developer paid $356,000 for cutting down a tree in which a bald eagle was nesting.[33] The civil penalties were also increased in 1972 by the automatic revocation of federal grazing privileges, while at the same time a "citizen bounty" of half of any fine (up to $2,500) was authorized for anyone giving information that leads to a conviction.

CASE DISCUSSION 6.2

High Wire Act

Moon Lake Electric Association is a rural electric cooperative at the northernmost juncture of Utah and Colorado. Moon Lake supplies electricity to an oil field near Rangely, Colorado, on lines spread over 3,096 utility poles. Moon Lake did not install bird protective equipment on the poles. This equipment is inexpensive and commonly used throughout the power industry. A number of protected birds (bald eagles, golden eagles, ferruginous hawks, great horned owls, and others) nest in the area. Because there are few trees, these birds use the power poles for perching, roosting, and hunting. Between January 1996 and June 1998, seventeen protected birds of prey died from electrocution on the poles; twenty-one more birds were injured.

(continued)

CASE DISCUSSION 6.2 *(continued)*

- Migratory Bird Treaty Act: "[I]t shall be unlawful at any time, by any means or in any manner, to pursue, hunt, take, capture, kill, attempt to take, capture or kill, possess, offer for sale . . . any migratory bird" (16 U.S.C. § 703). Under the Migratory Bird Treaty Act, "take" is defined as "pursue, hunt, shoot, wound, kill, trap, capture, or collect." (50 C.F.R. § 10.12 [1997])
- Bald and Golden Eagle Protection Act: "Whoever . . . shall knowingly, or with wanton disregard for the consequences of his act take, possess, sell, purchase, barter, offer to sell, purchase or barter . . . any bald eagle, or any golden eagle . . . shall be fined not more than $5,000 or imprisoned not more that one year or both" (16 U.S.C § 668). Under this law, "take" also means "pursue, shoot, shoot at, poison, wound, kill, capture, trap, collect, molest or disturb. . . ." (16 U.S.C § 668c)

Moon Lake was charged under both laws for the deaths of the birds. Its defense was that the laws did not apply to accidental behavior that would not be customary for hunters and poachers. They had no interest in the birds, nor any desire to kill them, nor any intention of keeping any part of the birds.

Should Moon Lake have been liable under both laws? Does it matter that the Bald Eagle Act says "knowingly, or with wanton disregard for the consequences of his act"? Should simply erecting a standard utility pole be considered an "act" under this law? Does it matter that the penalties under the Bald Eagle Act are criminal (imprisonment) and not just civil?

Suppose Moon Lake had retrofitted the poles with plastic insulators. If a bird were electrocuted with the insulators in place, should Moon Lake be liable?

(Source: *United States v. Moon Lake Electric Association*, 45 F. Supp. 2d 1070 [1999])

After the 1916 Migratory Bird Treaty between Great Britain and the United States was amended in 1972, the Migratory Bird Conservation Act was also changed to protect bald eagles and other raptors. The Endangered Species Act (discussed later in this section) also affords some protection for the bald eagle.

Wild Free-Roaming Horses and Burros Act

Just as the Bald Eagle Protection Act was passed to protect a national symbol, the Wild Free-Roaming Horses and Burros Act of 1971 had a great deal of popular sentiment behind it. The brutal slaughter of wild horses was publicized by the efforts of a few westerners, and the romantic attachment of Americans to horses in general and to symbols of the Old West in particular persuaded Congress to protect the animals on federal lands. Subsequent complications over animals wandering onto private property and the problems for legitimate owners of unbranded animals straying onto federally managed land have been resolved through the courts.

CASE DISCUSSION 6.3

Who Owns the Burros?

In 1971, Congress enacted the Wild, Free-Roaming Horses and Burros Act. "All unbranded and unclaimed horses and burros on the public lands of the United States" are protected from "capture, branding, harassment, or death" (16 U.S.C.§ 1332 (b) and § 1331). If protected animals stray onto private lands, "the owners of such land may inform the nearest federal marshal or agent of the Secretary [of Interior], who shall arrange to have the animals removed" (16 U.S.C. § 1334). The landowner may choose to let the animals stay on his property. The law also allows cooperative management agreements with state agencies.

In 1973, the federal government made such an agreement with the New Mexico Livestock Board, but three months later, the Livestock Board withdrew from the agreement. They claimed not only that wild horses and burros on federal, state, or private lands were under the

(continued)

CASE DISCUSSION 6.3 (*continued*)

jurisdiction of the Board but also that the federal government had no jurisdiction unless the animals were in interstate commerce (they weren't) or damaging public lands (not happening).

Kelly Stephenson was a New Mexico rancher who had a grazing permit for 8,000 acres that included a well he used to water cattle. On 1 February 1974, the Bureau of Land Management (BLM) notified him that several wild burros were near the well and that BLM was not going to remove them. Stephenson complained to the Livestock Board, which then captured and removed nineteen unbranded, unclaimed burros and sold them at public auction. BLM then demanded the Board recover the animals and restore them to federal land. The Board filed suit in federal district court, charging that the Wild, Free-Roaming Horses and Burros Act was unconstitutional.

- "The Congress shall have Power to dispose of and make all needful Rules and Regulations respecting the Territory or other Property belonging to the United States. . . ." U.S. Constitution, Article IV, § 3(2)
- The act declares that wild horses and burros are "an integral part of the natural system of the public lands" (16 U.S.C. § 1331), and their management should achieve "an ecological balance on the public lands." 16 U.S.C. § 1333(a)

. . . but

- The federal government can kill deer that are damaging foliage on public lands *because* they are damaging federal property. *Hunt v. United States*, 278 U.S. 96 (1928)

Were the burros on public land in a legal sense? After all, Stephenson had paid for a permit to graze his cattle there. (A private landlord relinquishes some of his rights when he rents property.)

The act says the federal government "shall arrange to have the animals removed." Does that mean the government must do so?

(continued)

CASE DISCUSSION 6.3 (*continued*)

Is a law passed by Congress to protect wild animals on federal land a violation of states' rights to manage their wildlife?

What happens if wild burros wander off federal land onto state or private land? Are they still protected?

What if Stephenson had used bait to lure the burros onto his private land? Would the act still protect them?

(Source: *Kleppe v. New Mexico et al.*, 426 U.S. 529 [1976])

Programs to manage wild horses and burros are administered primarily by BLM, although the Forest Service also has a program.[34] Since the beginning, these programs have been the focus of intense controversy between passionate animal advocates and ranchers who see horses as competition for grazing. A 1997 Congressional Research Service report on "Wild Horse and Burro Management" was remarkably inconclusive about BLM's estimates of carrying capacity and horse and burro impacts.[35] In the 1990s, accusations were leveled that some BLM employees were adopting horses for the sole purpose of resale for slaughter.[36]

The BLM has brought some of these problems on itself. Its estimations of the number of horses and burros on public land and the carrying capacity of the range are inconsistent. In March 2005, a BLM press release claimed 37,000 wild horses and burros were free on public lands; this was a surplus of 9,000 animals over BLM's desired management level of 28,000.[37] (Animal advocates point out that in 1960, the suggested management level was 60,000 animals.)[38] In August 2005, BLM claimed only 32,000 wild horses and burros were running free; however, its new plan was to remove 10,000 animals, which would put the population well below the optimum of 28,000 suggested just five months earlier.[39] It is easy to see why the wild horse lobby, unable to rely on BLM data, accuses the agency of pandering to ranching interests.

Public interest in this issue has always been high, partly because of the national affinity for horses in general, and a romanticized view of the Old West (cowboys and mustangs) in particular. On 18 November 2004, the United States Senate passed Resolution 452 designating December 13th the "National Day of the Horse."[40] That same month, Congress passed a new law directing BLM to sell "without limitation" any "excess" wild horse or burro, defined as any animal over the age of ten or that had been "offered unsuccessfully for adoption at least 3 times."[41] This effectively freed those animals for sale for slaughter. Despite BLM's public preference for finding permanent homes for the excess horses and burros, some did go to slaughter, and the resulting publicity caused a temporary halt in sales, which have now resumed. A small reprieve was granted for some horses in September 2005, when Congress passed an Agricultural Appropriations amendment prohibiting slaughtering horses or exporting horses for slaughter for *human* consumption. A permanent bill is expected to be introduced in 2006.[42]

Regulating Commerce in Wildlife

The issue of commerce in wildlife was discussed in some detail at the beginning of this chapter. The key legislation is the Lacey Act, passed in 1900. It had two purposes: "to strengthen and supplement state wildlife conservation laws . . . [and] to promote the interests of agriculture and horticulture by prohibiting the importation of certain types of wildlife determined to be injurious to those interests."[43] Although there is nothing in the language of the Lacey Act to exclude fish, the act was generally considered only in relation to game birds and furbearing mammals. In 1926, Congress passed the Black Bass Act to extend similar protections to black bass, an important game fish. Subsequent amendments to these acts have extended the Lacey Act to include "wild animals, birds, and parts or eggs thereof, captured or killed contrary to federal law or the laws of any foreign country."[44]

These acts had important implications for protecting wildlife in foreign countries. In 1930, the Tariff Act supplemented the Lacey Act by requiring that, if the laws of the exporting country protected an animal, the United States consul at the place of export must certify any such animal or any products derived from it before they could be brought in to the United States. Products or animals lacking the certification could be seized. Responsibility for the Lacey Act rests with the Commerce Department, and the Tariff Act is administered by the Department of the Interior.

Substantial changes were made in these acts in 1981 and 1988. The Lacey Act Amendments incorporated the Black Bass Act and drastically revised the original Lacey Act. The enforcement provisions were enhanced and the general scope of the laws expanded. Now the act extends to all wild animals, including animals bred and raised in captivity, and to some plant species. Criminal penalties were also increased: the maximum fine is $20,000 and jail terms range from one to five years. Under the 1981 amendments, these penalties no longer require that the violator "knowingly and willfully" violated the act, so that the government does not bear the burden of proof that the violator intended to break the law.[45]

Conservation of Endangered Species

Since 1969, the federal government has enacted three statutes aimed directly at the protection of endangered species, and the United States has become party to the Convention on International Trade in Endangered Species of Wild Fauna and Flora (CITES).

The first statute was the Endangered Species Preservation Act of 1966. The strongest provision of this act was habitat protection. Beyond this, it was primarily a statement of good intentions. The most notable limitation was that it did not provide any restrictions on the taking of wildlife, leaving such regulations to the states.

In 1969, Congress enacted the Endangered Species Conservation Act. For the first time, the Secretary of the Interior was authorized to list wildlife "threatened with worldwide extinction" and generally to prohibit importing threatened wildlife into the United States.[46] Unfortunately, the 1969 act fell short of providing the kind of legislation that could offer timely protection of endangered species. The Secretary of the Interior only listed species in imminent danger of extinction and provided no protection for species approaching the danger point. However, the act did call for an international meeting on endangered species. Held in 1973, the meeting produced the Convention on International Trade in Endangered Species of Wild Fauna and Flora (CITES), and this in turn provided incentive to pass the 1973 Endangered Species Act (ESA).

Almost immediately Congress realized that the federal endangered species program was not sufficient. Apart from the Marine Mammal

Protection Act, there were no restrictions on taking endangered species, and the constraints on federal activities that might harm species were narrow and embellished with many loopholes. The magnitude of the problem of vanishing species was all too apparent. In 1973, Congress voted almost unanimously to pass the Endangered Species Act.

Implementation for the Endangered Species Act is the responsibility of the Secretary of the Interior for terrestrial species and the Secretary of Commerce for marine species. The actual work is conducted by the Fish and Wildlife Service (Interior) and National Marine Fisheries Service (Commerce). Four key sections of the act provide its basic structure. Section 4 provides the formal listing process used to identify threatened and endangered species; this process allows increased access by interest groups in the protection process. It also provides protection for critical habitats, a departure from previous federal regulatory efforts, and requires the drafting of recovery plans for each listed species. The 1978 amendments elaborated on species recovery, defined by both FWS and the NMFS as "improvement in the status of listed species to the point at which listing is no longer appropriate under the criteria set out" in the ESA.[47] This has often meant reintroduction, a policy that has raised a firestorm of controversy and generated fascinating case law. Probably the most contentious of the recovery plans has been the gray wolf plan, which has been under almost constant legal attack since it was first proposed in 1987.[48]

Section 7 mandates that every federal agency consult with the appropriate Secretary before taking any action that might affect a listed species. The Endangered Species Committee (also known as the "God Squad" and one of the more interesting amendments to a federal statute) was added to Section 7 in 1978.[49] This provision established a cabinet-level committee to review cases in which species protection was in direct conflict with other, compelling federal policy goals. It was first used in the snail darter–Tellico dam controversy (*TVA v. Hill*, the case used in chapter 4 to illustrate law school briefs); the committee ruled in favor of the fish but was later overruled by Congress.[50] The God Squad is rarely convened; by early in 1994, it had only reviewed three proposed exemptions.[51]

CASE DISCUSSION 6.4

Don't Feed the Bears

In 1988–1989, nearly 10,000 tons of corn were spilled in northwestern Montana when three Burlington Northern Railroad (BN) trains derailed. The corn attracted grizzly bears to the site, and in the next year, seven bears were killed by BN trains; five were in the immediate spill area.

Grizzly bears are protected under the Endangered Species Act (ESA). The National Wildlife Federation claimed that the deaths were a taking under ESA and that the railroad activities were harassing the bears and harming their habitat. The National Wildlife Federation suit requested the Montana federal district court to require BN to reduce its speed in the area to 15 mph, to investigate installing bear protective devices on trains (one suggestion was airbags), and to require BN to get an incidental take permit.

This case is not quite as silly as it seems at first glance. However, by the time it came to trial, there had been no bear deaths in the area by train for three years, the habitat had been cleaned up (cost: $500,000), and the track upgraded (cost: $9,640,800).

Why would the National Wildlife Federation spend the time, money, and legal resources not only to bring this case to trial but also to appeal it to the Circuit Court?

(Source: *National Wildlife Federation v. Burlington Northern Railroad*, 23 F. 3d 1508 [1994])

Section 9 is the third major section, prohibiting both the taking of listed species and damage to their habitats; Section 11 provides the penalties for violations of the act.

In 1982, responding to Reagan's requirements that FWS consider the economic consequences of listing endangered and threatened species, Congress amended the act to clarify congressional intent that only scientific factors are to be used to assess the endangered or threatened status of species; the only place in the ESA for economic factors is in the designation of critical habitat. Additional amendments were passed in 1984, 1986, and 1988.

Following the 1994 midterm elections that returned a Republican majority to the Congress, and the uproar caused by *Babbitt v. Sweet Home Chapter of Communities for a Greater Oregon* (1995), which announced that the ESA applied to habitat on private lands, Secretary of the Interior Babbitt instituted several modifications to ESA habitat provisions. Habitat conservation plans (HCPs) allow developers to trade habitat set-asides and mitigations for "incidental take" permits. "Safe harbors" and "no surprises" policies protect landowners who have made good-faith efforts to comply with ESA provisions.

Even with congressional and public support, progress under the ESA has been marginal. As of 25 September 2005, 993 American species were listed as endangered (394 animals, 599 plants) and 275 were threatened (129 animals, 146 plants).[52] However, thousands of species are in the queue for review. Despite some highly publicized species recoveries, such as the California condor, the sea otter, and the bald eagle, the overall recovery rate is poor. On an international scale, the lack of success is even more alarming. The International Union for Conservation of Nature and Natural Resources (IUCN) lists 15,503 threatened species; this includes 23 percent of mammals, 12 percent of birds, and 31 percent of amphibians.[53]

The Endangered Species Act has been a frequent target for a wide spectrum of critics. Environmentalists bewail the slow pace of species listing and designation of critical habitat. Although economic factors are not legally considered in the listing process, they are allowed in habitat designation which makes the Fish and Wildlife Service (FWS) and the National Marine Fisheries Service (NMFS) vulnerable to political pressures; less than 2 percent of listed species have critical habitat designations.[54]

Budget cuts in both Democratic and Republican administrations have limited the ability of agencies to list species; the process is frequently driven by court orders. And of course, private landowners who fear government interference with their land use plans object in court or else resort to "shoot, shovel, and shut up" to avoid problems before they arise. All of these issues have made the ESA ripe for change, and in September 2005, the House of Representatives passed an ESA reform bill, optimistically called the Threatened and Endangered Species Recovery Act of 2005. "Critical habitat" would be replaced by "species recovery plans," and private landowners who unwillingly provide habitat for endangered species would be entitled to compensation. In addition, political appointees would be given some responsibility for scientific determinations.[55]

In December 2005, a companion bill was introduced in the Senate. This "Collaboration and Recovery of Endangered Species Act" was even less acceptable to environmental groups. As this is written, Senator Lincoln Chaffee (R–RI), a long-time advocate of wildlife protection, plans to introduce his own ESA amendments. It is unclear how the ESA will be amended, if at all. However, reform is needed in several areas.[56] First, private landowners need positive incentives to promote species preservation. Second, species should be identified as protected before they reach a critical state. Finally, Congress should provide the necessary resources for implementing agencies to be able to achieve their legislative mandates. The political climate in the current Congress and the leadership positions of legislators opposed to the goals of the ESA make the law's fate uncertain. However, moderate Republicans in both houses have been willing to defend environmental programs against legislative assaults. The 2006 midterm elections may prove critical to the existence of the Endangered Species Act.

Marine Mammal Protection Act

Clearly the federal government cannot mandate directly an international system of marine mammal protection, but in 1972, the government did institute such a program for the territorial waters of the United States. The reasons for such legislation are many. The primary reason was to provide protection and regulation of a commercial resource that was in danger of depletion. Another reason, stressed by ecologists and other scientists, was the ecological importance of marine mammals and the necessity to protect their ecological niche. Finally, an intensive lobbying effort arose from citizens concerned about the harvesting of mammals with apparently extraordinary intelligence and complex social arrangements.[57]

In 1972, Congress enacted the Marine Mammal Protection Act (MMPA), which "articulated only broad, general policy goals and implemented them with specific directions that were neither purely protectionist nor purely exploitive, but were almost always complex."[58] With some extremely specific exceptions, the keystone of the act was an absolute moratorium on the taking of marine mammals by United States citizens or by foreigners within the Fishery Conservation Zone of the United States. State control over marine mammals was preempted.[59]

Implementation of the act is split between the Secretary of Commerce and the Secretary of the Interior.[60] The Commerce secretary, who has delegated this authority to the National Marine Fisheries Service (NMFS), bears responsibility for all cetaceans (whales and porpoises) and for all pinnepedians (seals) except walruses. The Interior secretary has authority over all other marine mammals (manatees, dugongs, polar bears, sea otters, and walruses) and has delegated responsibility to FWS.

An independent advisory body, the Marine Mammal Commission, was established in the act. It became the focus of controversy during the first Reagan administration. The members of the commission had previously been highly respected marine scientists appointed by the president on the recommendation of the Council on Environmental Quality (CEQ), the Smithsonian, the National Science Foundation, and the National Academy of Sciences. Reagan appointed members chosen only by the CEQ, a debilitated organization controlled by the White House. In 1982, Congress made the appointments subject to Senate confirmation, and in 1984, Congress required that the three members be chosen from a list of marine specialists approved by the heads of the original recommending organizations.[61]

MMPA is unique in the rulemaking requirement it attaches to any consideration of a waiver by either secretary. Waivers are extremely specific, applying only to a particular species or population stock and then only to a limited amount. The rulemaking process the secretary must follow is the formal rulemaking process described in chapter 5: a full adversarial hearing conducted by an administrative law judge, allowing the presentation of evidence, cross examination of witnesses, and a full record. The hearing must cover the proposed waiver that will issue *after* the regulations are promulgated, as well as the regulations related to it, and the secretary must publish all scientific statements and all relevant studies and recommendations made by the Marine Mammal Commission. However, the waiver is rarely used, and Congress has provided a wide range of exceptions.[62]

Private interest groups have been highly visible in the protection of marine mammals. The plight of the whales has been publicized by Greenpeace, whose members cast themselves adrift between whaling ships and their prey. Harp seal hunts in Canada were halted by Greenpeace activists in often bloody confrontations with seal hunters, by protectionists spray painting the young seals to ruin their pelts during the harvest period, by a international boycott of Canadian fish products, and by the distribution of one of the most poignant animal posters ever made: a mother seal nuzzling the skinned carcass of her pup.[63] "Setting on" porpoises by tuna fishermen was halted in 1990 (or at least the tuna companies claimed that the practice had been stopped) due to a consumer boycott of tuna products: 1990 saw "Dolphin Safe" labels in the supermarket.[64] These interest groups are skilled at manipulating the policy process, providing trigger events, and using the media to increase public concern over marine mammal issues.

Federal Acquisition and Management of Wildlife Habitat

The federal government owns approximately one-third of the nation's land, but this ownership is heavily concentrated in the western states and Alaska. For wildlife to thrive, habitat must be available and protected. Federal wildlife habitat comes from three general areas of land management: lands expressly acquired for habitat, multiple-use lands, and special purpose federal lands, such as the national park system and military bases.

National Wildlife Refuge System

The Migratory Bird Treaty Act originally did not provide for land for bird refuges, but in 1929 new legislation rectified the oversight. Lands acquired under the Migratory Bird Conservation Act of 1929 were originally intended to be "inviolate sanctuaries" for the birds, but amendments have allowed the Secretary of the Interior to permit public hunting if compatible with other purposes. The Duck Stamp Act (Migratory Bird Hunting Stamp Act of 1934) provided funds for refuge acquisition; although other acts also authorize refuge acquisition, the Migratory Bird Conservation Act remains the primary source of authority for wildlife refuge acquisition.

Although wildlife refuges have existed since the creation of Pelican Island Wildlife Refuge in 1903, they were not drawn under one law until 1962, when Congress passed the Refuge Recreation Act. In 1966, Congress expanded the law by creating the National Wildlife Refuge System, which provides "a national network of lands and waters for the conservation, management and, where appropriate, restoration of . . . fish, wildlife, and plant resources and their habitats."[65] A wide variety of "compatible" uses are allowed. In 1997, the National Wildlife Refuge System Act established a hierarchy of management purposes with priority given to compatible wildlife-dependent activities such as hunting or wildlife education. Clearly the mandate behind the national wildlife refuges was to manage them as "dominant use" lands rather than as "single use" lands.[66] The system currently encompasses 90 million acres of lands and waters and is administered by the Fish and Wildlife Service.

Wetlands preservation is another important factor of wildlife habitat. Public perceptions about wetlands have changed dramatically since the 1860s when the Swamp Lands Acts gave federal wetlands to the states for development. Today, wetlands are usually purchased under the Migratory Bird Conservation Act with Duck Stamp Act funding. The 1961 Wetlands Loan Act allows advance appropriations to the Migratory Bird Conservation Fund for upland habitat surrounding wetlands and for some wetlands purchase as well. Other funds are available from the Land and Water Conservation Fund, supplied primarily by receipts for offshore oil and gas leases. A third source of wetlands protection is the Water Bank Act, which allows the Secretary of Agriculture to reimburse land owners who protect their wetlands and adjacent uplands. In 1990, Congress created a Wetlands Reserve Program which provides for federal purchases of conservation easements.[67]

Federal programs alone do not adequately address the problem of wetland loss to development; state programs funded under Pittman-Robertson and private organizations such as Ducks Unlimited are a significant factor in wetlands protection. Ducks Unlimited manages private lands throughout the Canadian-American migratory pathways and has conserved over 11 million acres of wetlands in North America.[68] The Nature Conservancy acquires wetlands to protect them from development, and the National Audubon Society manages bird refuges. The impact of groups such as these is not limited to their land acquisitions. Their intensive and skillful lobbying and political involvement also provides protection to the wetland habitats.

Multiple-Use Lands

The Forest Service manages 191 million acres, including half the big game and cold-water fish habitat. Wildlife conservation is a relatively recent addition to the Forest Service's responsibilities; the Multiple-Use Sustained-Yield Act (1960), the Forest and Rangeland Renewable Resources Planning Act (1974), and the National Forest Management Act (1976) include wildlife habitat for both game and nongame species as part of the Forest Service mission. The multiple-use mandate requires federal land management agencies to manage for recreation and wildlife habitat as well as for specific consumptive use such as timber harvesting.

Funding, always a problem, received some relief from the 1974 act that amended the Knutson-Vandenberg Act (1930). The original Knutson-Vandenberg Act required private purchasers of Forest Service timber to help pay for reforestation of the logged area. The amendment allowed the funds also to be used for protecting and improving fish and wildlife habitat. Although helpful, the funds have been restricted in use. Secondary impacts of logging activities are not mitigated, an issue that is particularly important in fish habitat management because of the heavy siltation that often accompanies timbering and road building. An additional criticism of the program is that funds are only generated by profitable timber sales; many sales are, on paper, financial losses to the federal government.[69]

The Bureau of Land Management (BLM) is the second agency required to protect wildlife under the multiple-use concept; like the Forest Service, its mandate comes from the Federal Land Policy and Management Act of 1976 (FLMPA). BLM manages about 60 percent of all lands under federal jurisdiction but is largely unknown in the eastern United States. Its lands are leftovers from the land disposals of the nineteenth century (discussed later in the section on federal land history). Most of the productive or economically valuable land was transferred into private hands, so the BLM holdings usually have low productivity and are not found in contiguous blocks of land. This makes BLM land decisions often controversial as they affect adjacent, privately held lands as well as blocks of federal land. Technically, BLM manages habitat rather than species (although it does have responsibility for wild horses and burros), with most management of resident species under state responsibility.

BLM policy implementation is also hampered by the condition of the land it manages. Grazing permits for BLM lands are issued to western ranchers at well below market value. The ranchers then have little incentive to improve or to maintain the public lands. As a result, typically the public grazing lands are not as well kept as the private lands, and political domination by the powerful livestock industry lobby has affected the BLM policy process. Formed in 1946 from the old Grazing Service and the General Land Office, the organizational history of the agency has earned it the nickname of "Bureau of Livestock and Mining." Efforts to reform the grazing laws and permit fees have been attempted without much success by many Secretaries of the Interior but have foundered on entrenched conservative ranching interests. However, the "New West" is less dependent on ranchers, and change—perhaps even progress—now seems possible.[70]

Special Purpose Lands

The National Park Service also has a stake in wildlife. The first national park, Yellowstone, was established in 1872. Even then hunting was an issue, and in 1883 the U.S. Army was used to protect the scenery and wildlife in Yellowstone. For the next thirty-three years, the Army tried, with varied success, to protect the newly established parks from hunting activities. In 1916, Congress enacted the National Park Service Organic Act, which listed wildlife protection as one of the purposes of the national parks.

Until the 1950s, wildlife management in the parks lacked an ecological perspective. "Good" animals were protected, but "bad" ones such as wolves and coyotes were killed. In the 1950s, an advisory board was appointed after the conservation community complained about Park Service management practices. In 1963, this group released the Leopold Report, which emphasized an ecological perspective for wildlife management.[71]

The Wilderness Act of 1964 applies to all of the federal land-management agencies. Wilderness protection is critical for habitat protection for wildlife, and this act was passed partly to overcome the reluctance of the Forest Service to designate wilderness areas in national forests. This is still a difficult issue, especially in the aftermath of several years of devastating fire seasons in the West, and given the probusiness administration of George W. Bush. Under the Wilderness Act, almost 40 million acres of National Park land alone have been designated as wilderness. The Land and Water Conservation Act, also passed in 1964, provides much needed money to purchase additional park land.

Military lands were incorporated into wildlife concerns through the Sikes Act Extension in 1974. Primarily aimed at the development of cooperative comprehensive plans with the departments of the Interior and Agriculture and state fish and game departments, the act provides an optional mechanism for cooperative wildlife management on military reservations. The Secretary of Defense may be brought in to work with the Secretary of the Interior and the state agencies to manage conservation on military reservations. Military bases supply surprisingly valuable habitat for wildlife; for example, more than 30 percent of endangered red-cockaded woodpeckers live on military bases.[72]

The final category of special lands is the vast holdings of the federal government on the outer continental shelf (OCS). The total area of the OCS is approximately 819.2 million acres, or 36 percent of the total dry land area of the United States.[73] The Outer Continental Shelf Lands Act of 1953 asserted national control of the OCS up to two hundred miles from the shore, excluding the three-mile territorial limit for the states established in the Submerged Lands Act of 1953.[74] Management is shared between BLM and the United States Geological Survey (USGS), with USGS having primary responsibility for tract-specific geologic, engineering, and economic evaluations.

The enabling legislation was amended in 1978 due to congressional dissatisfaction with Interior's administration of the 1953 Submerged Lands Act. The amendments required more flexible bidding procedures for oil and gas leases, expanded economic planning provisions, increased the role of state and local governments in planning lease sales, exploration, and development, and established a policy to favor small refiners. The 1978 amendments also created an Offshore Oil Pollution Compensation Fund, supported by a barrel tax at the point of production, to mitigate the costs of oil spills.

The OCS Lands Act establishes federal authority only over the mineral resources of the shelf and not over the fishing and navigation rights in the waters above. Although the OCS Lands Act does not convey authority to conserve wildlife, two related acts, the Fishery Conservation and Management Act of 1976 and the Marine Protection, Research, and Sanctuaries Act of 1972, do provide wildlife conservation authority.

PUBLIC LANDS

The federal lands comprise over 700 million acres, or about one-third of the United States.[75] This statistic is misleading as most of the federal land is in the western states and Alaska. In some western states, the federal government owns over half of the state's land. Thus federal land policies have a great impact on the states, especially the western states, as well as the national government. Federal jurisdiction over these lands is spread among several agencies (see Table 6.1: Public Lands of the U.S.).

Federal ownership of land arises from two sources. The first is Article I of the Constitution:

Table 6.1: Public Lands of the U.S.

land	Major enabling legislation	Management agencies (departments)
parks	National Park Service Organic Act (1916)	National Park Service (Interior)
grasslands, grazing, other public lands	[Taylor Grazing Act]; Federal Land Policy and Management Act (1976)	Bureau of Land Management (Interior)
forests	Forest and Rangeland Renewable Resources Planning Act (1974); Multiple-Use Sustained-Yield Act (1960); National Forest Management Act (1976)	National Forest Service (Agriculture)
preservation lands	Wilderness Act (1964); Wild and Scenic Rivers Act; Alaska National Interest Lands Conservation Act (1980)	National Forest Service, Bureau of Land Management, National Park Service
outer continental shelf	Outer Continental Shelf Act (1953)	Bureau of Land Management
wildlife refuges	National Wildlife Refuge System Administration Act (1966)	Fish and Wildlife Service (Interior)

[Congress shall have Power] . . . to exercise exclusive Legislation . . . over all Places purchased by the Consent of the Legislature of the State in which the Same shall be, for the Erection of Forts, Magazines, Arsenals, Dock-Yards, and other needful Buildings. . . . (Article I, § 8, cl. 17)

The power of the federal government over land that it acquired under Article I varies, depending upon reservations placed on the land at the time the land was ceded to the national government or on subsequent changes by Congress.

The second source of authority over lands is Article IV:

The Congress shall have Power to dispose of and make all needful Rules and Regulations respecting the Territory or other Property belonging to the United States; and nothing in this Constitution shall be so construed as to Prejudice any Claims of the United States, or of any particular State. (Article IV, § 3, cl. 2)

Federal power over these lands is virtually absolute. At one time the states were thought to exercise police power over federal land within their jurisdictions, just as they do over any other property owners, but the law is currently interpreted to mean that the federal government has sovereign power over these lands.

Since 1900, demands on the federal lands have increased dramatically. Increased leisure time, greater mobility, and the popularity of camping and hiking have increased public interest in all forms of outdoor activities, especially in wilderness experiences and wildlife observation. Shifts in population to the Sun Belt have created an enormous pressure on water supply and water quality. Competition among uses and user groups for federal land access is fierce. The outer continental shelf (see earlier discussion) has become increasingly important for mineral production. Demands on the national forests for timber have increased and continue to rise.

The statutes governing federal lands are as checkered as the federal land holdings. There is no uniform or controlling statute, which leaves the agencies with a fair amount of discretion but also subject to the vagaries of congressional whims. Although the public perception is that these lands are both managed and used by the federal government, in actuality most of the benefits from the federal lands go to private concerns through mining, grazing, recreation, and timbering. Mining and oil claims on federal land are developed by private individuals and corporations. Grazing permits are given to ranchers to expand their herds; the federal government does not run livestock on the federal grazing lands. Timber is purchased and cut by private timber companies, not the United States Forest Service. It is from "this interface between public ownership and private use of the same lands that the conflicts with federal policy arise and persist."[76]

The winning hand in these conflicts between public ownership and private use has changed many times since the colonial days. Marion Clawson, director of BLM from 1948 to 1953, divided the history of federal lands into five relatively distinct areas: acquisition, disposal, reservation, custodial and intensive management, and consultation and confrontation.

Acquisition

The early phase of acquisition was from the beginning of the republic through the 1860s: the Louisiana Purchase; the acquisition of Florida, the Southwest (including the Gadsden Purchase), the Pacific Northwest, and finally the acquisition of Alaska. While of course these acquisitions had the effect of increasing the lands held by the federal government, their primary purpose was imperialistic; the United States simply chose to purchase rather than to acquire by conquest.

Other forms of land acquisition by the federal government continued through the twentieth century. Under the Weeks Act of 1911, the national forests have been increased by purchases of private lands, and since 1961 the federal government has been purchasing land for national parks. There has been less opposition to these purchases than one might expect, because the private sector usually continues to have access to the benefits of the resources.

Disposal

Following the acquisition of large chunks of land, the federal government was eager to begin development on those lands. This necessitated subsidizing railroads to build railways to encourage homesteaders and ranchers to settle on the land. The government also removed Native Americans from the most profitable land, despite legal and moral arguments against such activities. Some land was given to war veterans, and some was auctioned.

Some was simply given away to homesteaders who would promise to live on the land and to improve it; eventually, more than a quarter of the public domain was distributed under the Homestead Act of 1862 and later laws (now repealed) such as the Timber Culture Act of 1873, the Desert Land Sales Act of 1877, the Timber and Stone Act of 1878, and the Stock-Raising Homestead Act of 1916. The period of American history from the early nineteenth century until the New Deal, in which land disposal took place, was tumultuous, and the "process of land disposal was a lusty affair—a headlong, even precipitous process, full of frauds and deceits, but one which transformed a great deal of land into valuable private property—and one which built a nation."[77]

Reservation

The Progressive Movement, and increasing demand by the public for conservation measures at the turn of the century, led to an interest in permanent reservation of part of the federal lands. The first large, systematic reservation was the national forest reserves created in 1891 by the Forest Reserve Act.[78] By 1897, nearly 40 million acres had been withdrawn for inclusion in the Forest Reserves.[79] The authority of the president to make these reservations was finally established by the Supreme Court when it ruled in *United States v. Midwest Oil Company* (1915) that "Congress, by failing to challenge a host of 19th century executive withdrawals, had in effect acquiesced to earlier presidents' claims that they held broad implied powers to withdraw public lands from disposal."[80] This presidential power was limited in the Federal Land Policy and Management Act (FLPMA) of 1976, which requires congressional review of proposed withdrawals and imposes other restrictions on the implied executive powers of withdrawal. Other reservations were established by the 1934 Taylor Grazing Act, which placed regulation of grazing on federal lands under the control of the Department of the Interior; in 1946, the department's Division of Grazing joined with the General Land Office to become the Bureau of Land Management.

Custodial and Intensive Management

Custodial management has been a characteristic of federal land management from the very beginning of the reservation period. During this period, federal land management focused on maintaining resources and allowing access for development, but active management was not a priority. It continues to reflect the earliest conservationist ideals of Gifford Pinchot, the first head of the Forestry Service, and his contemporaries. Pinchot wrote in 1910:

> The first great fact about conservation is that it stands for development . . . and for the prevention of waste. . . . The natural resources must be developed and preserved for the benefit of the many, and not merely for the profit of a few.[81]

Dissatisfied with the management competencies in the Department of the Interior, Pinchot took his Division of Forestry to the Department of Agriculture where it has continued to protect timber resources for private industry. The Forest Service emphasized its relationships with lumber concerns but it also encouraged recreational opportunities on forest lands.

When the National Park Service was established in 1916, it found itself in competition with the Forest Service, which was convinced that it was the logical guardian of the nation's parks. The Park Service responded by stressing its preservationist attitude (in contrast to the Forest Service's conservationist-utilitarian perspective) and by expanding the parks by adding Forest Service land as much as possible. During the New Deal, the Park Service benefited from the support of Roosevelt's close friend and advisor, Harold Ickes, who served as Secretary of the Interior. Ickes convinced Roosevelt to give a large portion of the Civilian Conservation Corps to Park Service management. Finally, in 1936, the Park Service won recognition of its recreational role with the passage of the Park, Parkway and Recreation Act. This act gave primary responsibility to the Park Service for federal recreation activities on all federal lands not controlled by the Department of Agriculture. It also identified the Park Service as the agency responsible for delivering federal aid for recreation projects to state governments.[82]

From about 1950 to 1960, the Park Service, Forest Service, and other land management agencies actively encouraged development and use of federal lands. Intensive management came to the Park Service in 1951 with the appointment of Conrad Wirth as director. He implemented Mission 66, a plan to upgrade the park facilities and to encourage increased use of the parks. More than 2,000 miles of road were built or upgraded during this period.[83] New and ambitious visitor centers were established in many parks, and Mission 66 was declared a success.

The Forest Service was also experiencing good times. Forest sale revenues increased, and in most years, the service showed a profit. During the 1950s, the Forest Service surplus was over $20 million.[84] Oil and gas leasing, mining, recreation, and grazing all also increased during this period, and in general the national forests experienced an economic boom. The land and its federal managers experienced increased pressures that in turn led inexorably to clashes with interest groups in the 1960s.

Consultation and Confrontation

To some extent, all of the previous phases of public land management continued from 1960 on. However, for reasons outlined in chapter 2, the public was no longer willing to allow federal agencies to manage resources without direct public input. Concerns with environmental quality were bound up in land management issues. Energy mining issues and air quality are interrelated, and preservation of the ocean ecosystems is imperiled by drilling on the outer continental shelf. Water supplies and watershed management became connected with safe disposal of hazardous and toxic wastes. All of these issues increased awareness of the impact of federal land-management policies for both environmentalists and commodity producers.

In 1960, Congress passed the Multiple-Use Sustained Yield Act that provided a legislative foundation for the institutional policies already in place in the Forest Service. Multiple use is an ambiguous concept that is not clarified in the legislative definitions. This is both a problem and an asset to the agencies required to manage under its instructions. It is a problem when uses conflict, as when critical habitat is also prime recreational or mining or timbering terrain. It is also an asset because, by leaving the term ambiguous, managers have discretion and, hence, flexibility.

The 1964 Wilderness Act, like the Multiple-Use Sustained Yield Act, was the result of controversy and compromise. It gave protection to wilderness areas within the national forests, protecting these areas from Forest Service redesignation. Lands managed by BLM were also considered for wilderness designation. Some extractive uses, such as coal mining, were allowed through the 1980s, and charges that under James Watt the Department of the Interior was deliberately building roads to exclude undeveloped land from wilderness consideration led to dramatic confrontations between environmental groups and Reagan's administration.[85]

Several acts, such as the Forest and Rangeland Renewable Resource

Planning Act of 1974 (RPA) and its successor, the National Forest Management Act of 1976, mandated long-range planning by the management agencies. The Forest and Rangeland Renewable Resource Planning Act requires that all renewable resources be assessed every ten years and that a national forest plan be submitted every five years. The Federal Land Policy and Management Act of 1976 (FLPMA) is also a planning act that increased the discretionary powers of BLM. It contains a multiple-use provision, includes BLM lands in wilderness consideration, and increases the requirements for public participation that were so characteristic of the legislation of the seventies.

The trend in federal land legislation was to turn away from agency initiatives and toward congressional initiatives, largely in response to the demands of special interest groups. Even the venerable Park Service was not immune from congressional assertions of power. Congress began to increase its power over the agency during the Nixon years, when the formerly cordial relations between the Park Service and the Congress deteriorated. As other forms of environmental benefits (such as new dams) for constituents decreased, congressional representatives increasingly found the national parks to be a vehicle for distributing goodies back home: one critic said:

> The Park Service has become a servant of Congress in the worst sense. It has become Congress' [sic] flunky in carrying out its pork barrel chores while it is supposed to be the guardian of the national interest. Unfortunately the Service doesn't have the power to uphold that interest.[86]

During the 1980s, public attention shifted to concerns about environmental quality, but the public lands, with their well-established "iron triangles," held their own in the policy process in Washington. Between 1970 and 1980, the number of acres included in the national parks increased by 169 percent. Over one hundred rivers were designated as wild and scenic, and another 10,000 miles were proposed for consideration. The National Wilderness Preservation System added significant amounts of land, primarily in Alaska. Wetlands were not such a success story; by 1995, about one half of the wetlands in the contiguous states had been eliminated,[87] and about 58,000 acres of wetlands continue to be lost annually.[88]

Although no major domestic legislation has been passed in the past ten years, looming fights over ESA and perhaps NEPA are indicators of possible seismic shifts in environmental policy. Environmental conflicts over public lands continue to make headlines. The use of snowmobiles in national parks has been a hot topic during the Clinton and Bush presidencies.[89] In 1996, President Clinton created the 1.7 million-acre Grand Staircase-Escalante National Monument—with no consultation with Utah's congressional delegation.[90] More recently, the Bush administration issued a rule giving state governors responsibility to retain continued "roadless area" designations for potential wilderness in their states by filing petitions with the federal government. Initially conservative western governors applauded the action. However, the cost of producing petitions is high; New Mexico has asked Congress for $500,000 for its roadless review process. In the end, the federal government will have the last word on approval, which it had before the rule was in place.[91] Governors critical of the process see this as a way to keep federal control while appearing to support state decisionmaking.

One of the most contentious issues over the past decade has been the prospect of drilling in the Arctic National Wildlife Refuge (ANWR). As part of the Alaska National Interest Lands Conservation Act (1980), gas and oil leasing and development in ANWR is prohibited unless authorized by Congress.[92] However, efforts to allow gas and oil exploration in ANWR began at least as early as 1981, when Secretary of the Interior James Watt tried unsuccessfully to transfer management responsibilities from the Fish and Wildlife Service to the United States Geological Survey so they could develop guidelines for resource exploitation.[93] By the late 1980s, a series of bills had been introduced to allow oil and gas leasing, but in 1992, the Clinton administration and the Democrat-controlled Congress blocked those efforts.

The story of ANWR is a classic tale of values in conflict. Proponents of drilling see less dependence on foreign oil and possible economic advantages to local populations. Opponents argue for habitat and species protection, conservation, and treaty obligations. When George W. Bush became president, he announced his intention to drill in ANWR, and his failure to bring Congress to heel has apparently turned ANWR development into a personal crusade. The latest rebuff was in December 2005 when the Defense Appropriations bill was blocked until the last-minute rider authorizing drilling in ANWR was removed. Coming from a Republican Senate, this was clear message that Congress is still interested in protecting ANWR.[94]

SUGGESTED READING

Bean, Michael, and Melanie Rowland. *The Evolution of National Wildlife Law*. 3rd ed. New York: Praeger, 1997. A tour de force essential for understanding wildlife law. The approach is legal, but it is clear and easily understood by the lay reader with a good background. This book and the Goble and Freyfogle book are about all you will need to understand wildlife law.

Clawson, Marion. *The Federal Lands Revisited*. Baltimore: Johns Hopkins University Press for Resources for the Future, 1983. Focused on the Forest Service and BLM lands, this book provides an historical look at federal lands.

Foresta, Ronald. *America's National Parks and Their Keepers*. Baltimore: Johns Hopkins University Press for Resources for the Future, 1984. A good companion for Clawson's book on the Forest Service and BLM.

Frederick, Kenneth, and Roger Sedjo, eds. *America's Renewable Resources: Historical Trends and Current Challenges*. Washington, DC: Resources for the Future, 1991. An excellent resource for historical background for water, forest, rangeland, cropland, and wildlife resources.

Goble, Dale, and Eric Freyfogle. *Wildlife Law: Cases and Materials*. New York: Foundation Press, 2002. A superb case book and, as far as I know, the only one. It is comprehensive and clear; we are fortunate that the only casebook in the field is of such high quality.

Jenkins, Matt, ed. *A People's History of Wilderness*. Paonia, CO: High Country News Books, 2004. A substantial collection of articles and essays on the politics of wilderness originally published in *High Country News*. (If you have any interest at all in western environmental issues, you should subscribe to *High Country News*. It comes out every two weeks, has online subscriptions, and covers the West better than anything else.)

Leopold, Aldo. *Game Management*. Madison: University of Wisconsin Press, 1986. This is a reprint of Leopold's classic 1933 work. A great deal of the book is technical information for game managers, but the chapters on the history of ideas in game management, economics, and policy and administration are masterpieces well worth reading today.

Smith, Jordan Fisher. *Nature Noir: A Park Ranger's Patrol in the Sierra*. Boston: Houghton Mifflin, 2005. Beautifully written and trenchant look at the life of a state park ranger.

NOTES

1. Unless otherwise noted, this discussion is drawn from Michael Bean and Melanie Rowland, *The Evolution of National Wildlife Law*, 3rd. ed. (New York: Praeger, 1997).

2. *Smith v. Maryland*, 59 U.S. 71 at 75.

3. *Manchester v. Massachusetts*, 139 U.S. 240 (1891).

4. The law specifically prohibited the dumping of nonliquid refuse; this law was never seriously enforced. Stephen Fox, *The American Conservation Movement: John Muir and His Legacy* (Madison: University of Wisconsin Press, 1981), 300.

5. At issue was whether Florida law or federal law governed commercial harvesting of sponges in Florida waters.

6. *United States v. Shauver*, 214 F.154 (E.D. Ark. 1914), *appeal dismissed*, 248 U.S. 594 (1919); *United States v. McCullagh*, 221 F. 288 (D. Kansas, 1915).

7. Under the Tenth Amendment to the Constitution, "the powers not delegated to the United States by the Constitution nor prohibited by it to the States, are reserved to the States respectively, or to the people," but the Constitution also provides that treaties "shall be the supreme law of the land . . . and anything in the Constitution or laws of any state to the contrary notwithstanding (Article VI)."

8. *Douglas v. Seacoast Products*, 431 U.S. 265 at 284.

9. Arthur McEvoy, *The Fisherman's Problem: Ecology and Law in California Fisheries, 1850–1980* (Cambridge, UK: Cambridge University Press, 1986), 117–118.

10. Thomas A. Lund, *American Wildlife Law* (Berkeley: University of California Press, 1980), 6.

11. However, the courts have continued to support federal authority over wildlife: for example, federally owned lands within state borders are not subject to state regulation (*Hunt v. United States*, 1928); the federal government may kill animals on national land without state permits (*New Mexico State Game Commission v. Udall*, 1969); and the interstate commerce clause gives Congress the power to protect wildlife in navigable waters when affected by dredge and fill operations conducted on *privately owned* riparian land (*Zabel v. Tabb*, 1970).

12. For the full story of the movement toward Pittman-Robertson, see U.S. Fish and Wildlife Service, *Restoring America's Wildlife 1937–1987: The First 50 Years of the Federal Aid in Wildlife Restoration (Pittman-Robertson) Act* (Washington, DC: USGPO, 1987).

13. Until 2002, a maximum of 8 percent of the funds collected could be used for administrative costs; between 1977 and 2001, administration costs for Pittman-Robertson averaged 6.4 percent. (U.S. Fish and Wildlife Service, "Deductions for Administration," http://federalasst.fws.gov/financialinfo/deductionsforadmin.htm [accessed 16 September 2005].) Following passage of the Wildlife and Sport Fish Restoration Programs Improvement Act of 2000, administrative expenses were no

longer based on a percentage of revenue. In FY2001, 2002, and 2003, specific administrative expenses caps were set. In FY2003 the cap was $16,424,000 for both the Wildlife and the Sport Fish programs, and the following years were assessed at this base plus an increase based on the Consumer Price Index. This is below the funding and staffing levels for administrations in previous years and caused some implementation headaches. An astute administrator can read between the lines of the FWS report to Congress on implementation of the changes: http://federalasst.fws.gov/financialinfo/2001reporttocongress.pdf.

14. ". . . no money apportioned under this chapter to any State shall be expended therein until its legislature . . . shall have . . . passed laws for the conservation of wildlife which shall include a prohibition against the diversion of license fees paid by hunters for any other purpose than the administration of said State fish and game department" (16 U.S.C. §669e).

15. Lonnie Williamson, "Evolution of a Landmark Law," in *Restoring America's Wildlife 1937–1987: The First 50 Years of the Federal Aid in Wildlife Restoration (Pittman-Robertson) Act* (Washington, DC: USGPO [U.S. Department of Interior Fish and Wildlife Service] 1987), 11.

16. Dian Olson Belanger, *Managing American Wildlife: A History of the International Association of Fish and Wildlife Agencies* (Amherst: University of Massachusetts Press, 1988), 50–51.

17. Williamson, "Evolution of a Landmark Law," 14.

18. Winston Harrington, "Wildlife: Severe Decline and Partial Recovery," in *American's Renewable Resources: Historical Trends and Current Challenges*, edited by Kenneth Frederick and Roger Sedjo, 205–246 (Washington, DC: Resources for the Future, 1991), 222–223.

19. Williamson, "Evolution of a Landmark Law," 14.

20. While this material is drawn from a number of sources, it relies primarily on William Chandler, "Federal Grants for State Wildlife Conservation," in *Audubon Wildlife Report 1986*, edited by Roger Di Silvestro (New York: National Audubon Society, 1986), 177–212; and Belanger, *Managing American Wildlife.* Pittman-Robertson funds are allocated to the states and to the Commonwealth of Puerto Rico, Guam, American Samoa, Northern Mariana Islands, and the Virgin Islands. Dingell-Johnson funds are also available to the states, Puerto Rico, the Virgin Islands, Guam, American Samoa, Northern Mariana Islands, and the District of Columbia. The focus of this section is the state-federal relationship, but when discussing administration of Pittman-Robertson, the term "states" is used to refer to all recipients of funds, although there are some administrative differences between the states and territories.

21. Some questions arose in the late 1950s over the second allocation formula: how was the term "paid license holder" to be interpreted? Initially the federal government interpreted this as the total number of licenses sold, but some states disaggregated their licenses (separate licenses for bow hunting and muzzle loaders, or for

deer and quail) to increase their share. Eventually the position of the Department of Interior prevailed: an individual license holder was only counted once regardless of how many licenses he held. *Udall v. Wisconsin*, 306 F. 2d 790 (D.C. Circuit 1962) *cert. denied*, 371 U.S. 969 (1963).

22. Ecologists may challenge this statement because so much of the emphasis of programs funded under this act is on game animals. However, the purpose of the act was to enhance hunting opportunities. It is funded by hunters and usually administered by game agencies. Success is traditionally measured by how well the implementation of a law fulfills the legislators' intent; under that criterion, this law is a success.

23. For example, in 1920, the wood duck was nearing extinction; today it is the most common breeding waterfowl on the American east coast. Pronghorn antelope increased from 25,000 or fewer in 1920 to over 750,000 today. U.S. Fish and Wildlife Service, *Restoring America's Wildlife* (brochure) (Washington, DC: USGPO), 8–9.

24. U.S. Fish and Wildlife Service, "Wildlife Restoration Apportionment History," http://federalasst.fws.gov/apport/WRAhistory.pdf (accessed 23 September 2005).

25. U.S. Fish and Wildlife Service, "Final apportionment of Pittman-Robertson Wildlife Restoration Funds for Fiscal Year 2005," http://federalasst.fws.gov/apport/WRFINALApportionment2005.pdf (accessed 23 September 2005).

26. Unless otherwise noted, this material is from Chandler, "Federal Grants for State Wildlife Conservation,"182–183; and Belanger, *Managing American Wildlife*.

27. Three other significant amendments have been made to the act: Transportation Equity Act of the 21st Century (EA-21), 1998; Coastal Wetland Planning, Protection, and Restoration Act, 1990; and Clean Vessel Act, 1992. See U.S. Fish and Wildlife Service, "Federal Aid in Sport Fish Restoration," athttp://federalasst.fws.gov/sfr/fasfr.html for more information on these amendments.

28. U.S. Fish and Wildlife Service, "Sport Fish Restoration Apportionment History," http://federalasst.fws.gov/apport/SFRAhistory.pdf (accessed 23 September 2005).

29. U.S. Fish and Wildlife Service, "Final apportionment of Dingell-Johnson Sport Fish Restoration Funds for Fiscal Year 2005," http://federalasst.fws.gov/apport/SFRFINALApportionment2005.pdf (accessed 23 September 2005).

30. Whit Fosburg, "Wildlife and the U.S. Forest Service," in *Audubon Wildlife Report 1985*, edited by Roger Di Silvestro, 307–341 (New York: National Audubon Society, 1987), 308. See also http://www.partnershipresourcecenter.org/resources/partnership-guide/chap3-3.html.

31. See http://www.doi.gov/pilt/ for information on Payments in Lieu of Taxes (PILT).

32. The preceding discussion is drawn from National Audubon Society, Audubon Wildlife Report 1985 (New York: National Society, 1985) and the 1986 and 1987 reports.

33. "Developer Fined for Destroying Bald Eagle Nest," TBO.com NEWS (*Tampa Tribune* [Florida]), 8 September 2005. http://news.tbo.com/news/ MGB5YJ5DCDE.html (accessed 22 September 2004).

34. The Forest Service program usually gets much less national publicity than the BLM program. However, in September 2005 the supervisor on the Apache-Sitgreaves National Forest proposed to capture and sell horses roaming in the forest. At issue is whether these are wild horses or horses that have moved on to the forest from adjacent tribal lands after the 2002 Rodeo-Chediski fire burned down the fences between the forest and the reservation. As this is written, a restraining order has halted Forest Service action. Jim Keyworth, "Fate of 'Wild' Horses Stalls in Legal Wrangling," *Payson Roundup*, 16 September 2005. http://paysonroundup.com/ sectioin/frontpage_lead/storypr/20467 (accessed 23 September 2005).

35. Betsy Cody, *Wild Horse and Burro Management*, CRS Report 97-370ENR, 19 March 1997.

36. Cody, *Wild Horse and Burro Management*, 1997.

37. Betsy Cody, *Wild Horse and Burro Management*, 1997.

38. Karen Sussman (Society for the Protection of Mustangs and Burros), quoted in Brett French, "Wild Horses' fans fear roundup will weaken herds," billingsgazette.com (*Billings Gazette* [Montana]), 20 August 2005. http://www. billingsgazette.com/index. Qhp?id=1+display=rednews/2005/08/20/build/state/ 35-horses.inc. Accessed 25 September 2005.

39. Karen Sussman, "Wild Horses' fans fear roundup will weaken herds," 2005.

40. S. Res. 452: Whereas the horse is a living link to the history of the United States; Whereas without horses, the economy, history, and character of the United States would be profoundly different; Whereas horses continue to permeate the society of the United States, as witnessed on movie screens, on open land, and in our own backyards; Whereas horses are a vital part of the collective experience of the United States and deserve protection and compassion; Whereas because of increasing pressure from modern society, wild and domestic horses rely on humans for adequate food, water, and shelter; and Whereas the Congressional Horse Caucus estimates that the horse industry contributes much more than $100,000,000,000 each year to the economy of the United States: Now, therefore, be it Resolved, That the Senate—(1) designates December 13, 2004, as 'National Day of the Horse,' in recognition of the importance of horses to the security, economy, recreation, and heritage of the United States; (2) encourages all people of the United States to be mindful of the contribution of horses to the economy, history, and character of the United States; and (3) requests that the President issue a proclamation calling on the people of the United States and interested organizations to observe the day with appropriate programs and activities.

41. Sale of Wild Free-roaming Horses and Burros, PL 108-447.

42. Only three American facilities slaughter horses for human consumption, but

the export of live horses for slaughter is more extensive. This bill stops both activities. One of the more egregious stories is that of the 1986 Kentucky Derby winner, Ferdinand, who was sold to a Japanese company. He did not perform well at stud and was slaughtered for human consumption.

43. Bean, *Evolution of National Wildlife Law*, 1983, 105.

44. Bean, *Evolution of National Wildlife Law*, 1983, 108.

45. In 1995, seventeen people in North Carolina pleaded guilty to violating the Lacey Act by bringing foxes into the state from Montana, Wyoming, North Dakota, Texas, and Indiana. One trader said, "I didn't know nothing until they raided my home. . . . I was just shocked. They kept talking about the Lacey Act, and I thought, 'What is the Lacey Act?'" The foxes were destined for enclosed "fox pens" where they are hunted by hounds. The letters to local newspapers were unanimous in defense of this sport; an attorney defending one of the pen operators said "It's just good old boys sitting around some fire and carrying on a harmless activity." Jeri Rowe, "Traders Don't Outfox Wildlife Officials," *Greensboro* [North Carolina] *News and Record*, 22 May 1995, B1.

46. Bean and Rowland, *Evolution of National Wildlife Law*, 196.

47. 50 C. F. R. § 402.2.

48. See Dale Goble and Eric Freyfogle, *Wildlife Law: Cases and Materials* (New York: Foundation Press, 2002), 1275–1287.

49. 16 U.S.C. § 1536(e).

50. Led by Tennessee Senator Howard Baker, in September 1979 Congress exempted the Tellico project from the Endangered Species Act (93 Stat. 437, 449–450 [1979]). George Cameron Coggins, Charles Wilkinson, and John Leshy, *Federal Public Land and Resources Law*, 3rd ed. (Westbury, NY: Foundation Press, 1993), 805–806.

51. See Bean and Rowland, *Evolution of National Wildlife Law*, 264, n. 337. An excellent movie about the Oregon timber sales exemptions request is *The God Squad and the Case of the Northern Spotted Owl* (Bullfrog Films, 2001).

52. U.S. Fish and Wildlife Service, "Threatened and Endangered Species System (TESS)," http://ecos.fws.gov/tess_public/TESSBoxscore (accessed 25 September 2005). This file is updated daily.

53. International Union for Conservation of Nature and Natural Resources (IUCN), "Red List of Threatened Species, Summary Statistics, Table 1: Numbers of threatened species by major groups of organisms (1996–2004)," http://www.redlist.org/info/tables/table1.html (accessed 25 September 2005).

54. Jeff Curtis and Bob Davison, "The Endangered Species Act: Thirty Years on the Ark," *Open Spaces Quarterly* 5(3)(2005). www.open-spaces.com/article-v5-n3-davison.php (accessed 13 March 2005).

55. Erica Werner, "House to Act on Endangered Species Law," Washingtonpost.com, 29 September 2005, http://www.washingtonpost.com/

wp-dyn/content/article/2005/09/29/AR2005092900295.html (accessed 2 October 2005). NEPA is also vulnerable. In the fall of 2005, the House Resources Committee (chaired by Rep. Richard Pombo, who is heading the fight to amend the ESA) held a series of public hearings on NEPA. Laura Paskus, "Bedrock Environmental Law Takes a Beating," *High Country News*, 22 August 2005, 3–4.

56. The points that follow are from Bean and Rowland, *Evolution of National Environmental Law*, 275–276.

57. Bean and Rowland, *Evolution of National Environmental Law*, 109–110.

58. Bean and Rowland, *Evolution of National Environmental Law*, 110–111.

59. MMPA is not the only legislation that protects marine mammals. The Endangered Species Act of 1973 provides protections for endangered and threatened marine mammals; the Marine Protection, Research, and Sanctuaries Act of 1972 provides habitat protection; and various international treaties, discussed in chapter 7, affect marine mammals.

60. "This split is a result of Executive Reorganization Plan No. 4 of 1970, which established the National Oceanic and Atmospheric Administration (NOAA) within the Commerce Department and transferred to it most of the functions vested in Interior's Bureau of Commercial Fisheries including management responsibility for oceanic marine mammals. Marine mammals considered land-oriented remained with Interior's Bureau of Sport Fisheries and Wildlife, which later was renamed the U.S. Fish and Wildlife Service (FWS)." Michael Weber, "Marine Mammal Protection," in *Audubon Wildlife Report 1985*, edited by Roger Di Silvestro (New York: National Audubon Society, 1985), 189–190.

61. 16 U.S.C. 1401 §201. Bean and Rowland, *Evolution of National Wildlife Law*, 112–113.

62. Bean and Rowland, *Evolution of National Wildlife Law*, 119–121.

63. Humane Society of the United States, http://www.protect seals.org.

64. However, international policies under the General Agreement on Tarriffs and Trade (GATT) have substantially weakened American attempts to regulate international trade in products harvested by environmentally unacceptable methods. See James Salzman and Barton Thompson Jr., *Environmental Law and Policy* (New York: Foundation Press, 2003), 217–224.

65. 16 U.S.C.§ 668dd(a)(2).

66. Bean and Rowland, *Evolution of National Environmental Law*, 288.

67. Bean and Rowland, *Evolution of National Environmental Law*, 436.

68. Ducks Unlimited, "State Facts Sheet," http:// www.ducks.org/StateFactSheets/Nation.pdf (accessed 23 September 2005).

69. National Audubon Society, *Audubon Wildlife Report 1985*, 311.

70. See, for example, Tony Davis, "Rangeland Revival," *High Country News*, 5 September 2005, 6–12; and April Reese, "The Big Buyout," *High Country News*, 4 April 2005, 8–13, 19.

71. A. S. Leopold, S. A. Cain, C. M. Cotton, I. N. Gabrielson, and T. L. Kimball, *Wildlife Management in the National Parks: The Leopold Report* (Washington, DC: U.S. Department of the Interior, Advisory Board on Wildlife Management, 1963.)

72. Laura Tangley, "Bases Loaded," *National Wildlife* (Oct/Nov. 2005), 38-45.

73. Walter J. Mead, Asbjorn Moseidjord, Dennis Muraoka, and Philip Sorensen, *Offshore Lands: Oil and Gas Leasing and Conservation on the Outer Continental Shelf* (San Francisco: Pacific Institute for Public Policy Research, 1985), 7.

74. Texas and the west coast of Florida have state control for three marine leagues or 10.4 miles. These states are entitled to the wider boundary because they held those lands at the time of their admission as states.

75. Unless otherwise noted, this material is from Marion Clawson, *The Federal Lands Revisited* (Baltimore: Johns Hopkins University Press for Resources for the Future, 1983), esp. chapters 1 and 2.

76. Clawson, *Federal Lands Revisited*, 4.

77. Clawson, *Federal Lands Revisited*, 25.

78. Although Yellowstone National Park was established in 1872, Clawson (p. 28) notes that this was an isolated instance of reserving land not otherwise in demand. He quotes John Ise, *Our National Park Policy* (Baltimore: Johns Hopkins University Press for Resources for the Future, 1961), 17–18:

> The establishment of Yellowstone was, of course, due partly to the efforts of few of these idealists, several of them men of influence. Reservation was possible because most private interests were not looking so far west at this early date, for there were no railroads within hundreds of miles of Yellowstone. Lumbermen had moved into the Lake States and were too busy slashing the pine forests there to reach out for timber lands in this inaccessible region; the hunters and trappers were here, but were not an important political force; the cattlemen, who have been in recent years so powerful an influence against some conservation legislation, were not yet invading the Far West in large numbers; the water-power interests that have been among the most serious threats to a few later national parks were not interested here. With Indians still a lurking danger, the 'poor settlers' had not ventured into this region in great numbers and were not calling for Congressional consideration.

79. One of my favorite Teddy Roosevelt stories is the "Midnight Forests." Congress had passed a law limiting presidential power to add forest reserves in western states. Roosevelt had to sign it, but before he did, he and Gifford Pinchot stayed up far into the night, drawing new maps and adding over 16 million acres to the existing reserves. President Clinton accomplished the same thing; he "created more public lands for recreational and conservation purposes than any other presidency in U.S. history"—50 million new acres protected and 65 million acres designated as roadless areas (and therefore reserved for possible wilderness designation). Walter

A. Rosenbaum, *Environmental Politics and Policy*, 6th ed. (Washington DC: CQ Press, 2005), 312.

80. Tom Arrandale, *The Battle for Natural Resources* (Washington, DC: Congressional Quarterly, 1983), 41, citing *United States v. Midwest Oil Company*, 236 U.S. 459 (1915).

81. Gifford Pinchot, *The Fight for Conservation* (Garden City, NY: Harcourt, Brace, 1919), quoted in Roderick Nash, *American Environmentalism: Readings in Conservation History* 3rd ed. (New York: McGraw-Hill, 1990), 76–78.

82. Ronald A. Foresta, *America's National Parks and Their Keepers* (Baltimore: Johns Hopkins University Press, 1984), 45–46 (notes omitted).

83. Foresta, *America's National Parks*, 54.

84. Clawson, *Federal Lands Revisited*, 37–38.

85. See, for example, Perri Knize, "Chainsaw Environmentalism," *Backpacker*, November 1987, 55–59. The title tells it all.

86. Quoted in Foresta, *America's National Parks*, 79.

87. Walter A. Rosenbaum, *Environmental Politics and Policy*, 3rd ed. (Washington, DC: CQ Press, 1995), 74.

88. Michael Kraft and Norman Vig, "Environmental Policy from the 1970s to the Twenty-First Century," in *Environmental Policy: New Directions for the Twenty-First Century*, 6th ed. (Washington, DC: CQ Press, 2006), 23. This is a slower rate of loss than in previous years: mid-1950s to mid-1970s: 458 acres per year; 1970s to 1980s: 290,000 acres per year. Nancy Kubasek and Gary Silverman, *Environmental Law*, 5th ed. (Upper Saddle River, NJ: Pearson, 2005), 379–380.

89. See James Rasband, James Salzman, and Mark Squillance, *Natural Resources Law and Policy* (New York: Foundation Press, 2004), 584–586.

90. Rasband et al., *National Resources Law and Policy*, 599–602.

91. April Reese, "Western Governors Wary of Roadless Forest Mess," *High Country News*, 25 July 2005, 4.

92. 16 U.S.C § 3142–3143. The amount of energy resources available from ANWR is uncertain. Drilling there might violate several environmental treaties: for example, the 1987 Caribou Agreement (United States, Canada) which protects the Porcupine Caribou herd that migrates through the refuge; the 1973 Agreement on the Conservation of Polar Bears (United States, Canada, Denmark, Norway, USSR); and several migratory bird treaties that require habitat protection in ANWR. See Benjamin Sovacool, "The Coming Costs of Drilling in Arctic Refuge," *Roanoke Times* [Virginia], 18 March 2003, 9.

93. See *Trustees for Alaska v. Watt*, 524 F. Supp. 1303 (D. Alaska 1981), aff'd 690 F. 2d 1279 (9th Cir. 1982) (Refuge Administration Act requires the Fish and Wildlife Service to administer all refuges).

94. For further discussion of ANWR, see Rosenbaum, *Environmental Politics and Policy*, 6th ed., 285–289.

CHAPTER SEVEN

International Environmental Policy and Law

Government policymakers are moving toward a more global view of the world environment, triggered by the recognition of problems such as climate change, depletion of atmospheric ozone, acid precipitation, and destruction of the tropical rainforests. Governments are often working more cooperatively: large construction projects with impacts that cross national boundaries are now usually assessed for their international effect. Nations notify each other when transporting toxic materials across national boundaries. Environmental treaties, conventions, and "soft-law" options—customary procedures that are not formalized through treaties or other binding documents—have proliferated.[1]

Governmental approaches to international environmental problems have also been affected by the dominance of economic considerations and economic analysis. Multinational corporations overshadow national governments in many international spheres. National sovereignty often yields to corporate interests in the world economy: never before in world history have corporate interests unconnected with the interests of some nation-states regularly determined international policies.[2] The technological revolution in communication affects government decisionmaking as well, because instant telecommunications, independent of cables and other physical connections, make global assessment of the environment possible. Such electronic information exchange is rapid and difficult to control; this provides equal access to information and a common vocabulary of events and interpretation that may overwhelm regional and national differences.

Although few issues are truly global, many issues have physical impacts that cross national boundaries. Even a problem that is limited geographically may have international or global ramifications, such as the changes in weather caused by volcanic eruptions. Some issues are beyond the practical jurisdiction of any one national government (for example, mining on the deep seabed and issues of outer space). Other issues are extremely localized but occur in many jurisdictions, and therefore international cooperation is to the advantage of all concerned (for example, containing outbreaks of contagious disease). Finally, some local or regional issues have global repercussions. Developed nations dominate international policy in all policy areas, and their constituencies will not usually become involved with third world concerns until they perceive some direct impact on themselves. For example, destruction of tropical rainforests is believed to affect global climate; this belief has led international financing for third world governments to encourage rainforest protection.

For environmental concerns to become international issues, they first must become national issues. Sovereign nations have many issues of international importance and, until there is consensus within the country that environmentalism is important, a nation will not expend its limited international resources to address the problems. In addition, national governments need some assurance or expectation that international policies for environmental problems could be successful. The scientific community recognizes the interdependence of Earth's subordinate ecosystems and the impact of human activity, but translating scientific knowledge into effective policy is a perpetual stumbling block.

This chapter provides an introduction to the international institutions and legal processes that affect environmental law and policy. Entire graduate degree programs and law school curricula are devoted to this topic; it would be impractical to attempt a comprehensive survey of international treaties and other agreements that govern international environmental concerns.[3] My task here is twofold. First, I want to acquaint readers with the roles of key players: the United Nations and nongovernmental organizations. The second task is to illustrate how these players have affected environmental policy by discussing two specific policy areas: the global commons of the oceans and the atmosphere.[4] For example, the United States is one of the chief contributors of emissions that cause climate change. By withdrawing from the Kyoto Protocol in

2001, the government has protected American manufacturers and American energy producers as well as signaled a willingness to be isolated—at least in this one policy area—from its traditional European partners.[5] Similarly, the American failure to ratify the Biodiversity Convention has paved the way for draconian amendments to the Endangered Species Act. It is important for environmental managers to recognize these consequences and to see how domestic policies may be affected.

International and global commons are particular kinds of resource domains[6] that contain common pool resources. International commons such as Antarctica are domains shared by several nations; global commons are resource domains such as the oceans, atmosphere, or outer space to which all states have access. The use of international treaties and other forms of international accommodation is the only way to address the problems raised by the commons. They present especially thorny policy and law problems because there is intense competition for the right to exploit their resources, but there is no established, enforceable law to regulate access and use.

I have chosen global commons as illustrations (resource domains that do not lie within the jurisdiction of any one nation) for several reasons. First, these areas have traditionally been *open access*, which means that the right to exploit them (high-seas fisheries) or to despoil them (air pollution) is open to all. When anyone can exploit a resource but no one cares for it, the usual result is that the resource supply diminishes, often to dangerously low levels. Second, the oceans and the atmosphere are areas that are critical to the long-term health of the planet. For example, spewing pollutants into the atmosphere has reduced clean air to such a degree that the planet's climate is affected. Third, these are relatively modern legal regimes. Finally, the human response to vast areas of valuable resources unfettered by legal rights recognized by the dominant culture historically has been appropriation by governments and individuals, followed by exploitation as soon and as rapidly as physical force and technology would permit. Global commons have remained exceptions only because access to them has been difficult and resources have been either plentiful or not valuable enough to justify the effort to claim them. Today, however, technology has caught up with desire. Fortunately, the vulnerability of the global commons can be addressed in an era of relative peace among the superpowers, and decisions are made at the negotiation table rather than on the battlefield.

INTERNATIONAL ORGANIZATIONS

Environmental institutions and advocacy groups have known for over half a century that unilateral national actions were not enough to protect endangered species and to halt pollution. For example, Africa cannot protect its endangered species without help from the countries that provide a market for luxury furs. The industrial states cannot prevent acid deposition from blowing over their borders, and—as Chernobyl taught the world—no one is safe from radiation once it gets into the atmosphere. With this realization came more vigorous efforts to expand issues from national to international agendas.

The United Nations

The United Nations began to respond to these concerns in the mid-1960s. Environmentalism had become a salient issue not just in the United States but also across the globe, especially in other industrialized democracies such as Canada, France, Japan, Sweden, West Germany, and the United Kingdom. These countries had writers like Rachel Carson to expose the dangers of pollution: Jean Dorst in France wrote *Before Nature Dies* (1965), and in Sweden, Rolf Edberg wrote *On the Shred of a Cloud* (1966).[7] The *Torrey Canyon* disaster in 1967 brought home to western Europe the dangers that could result from ignoring the environment.

In 1966, the General Conference of the United Nations Education, Scientific, and Cultural Organization (UNESCO) adopted a resolution that the *biosphere* was a social concern as well as a geophysical one. At the 1968 Biosphere Conference in Paris, members declared that environmental concerns, especially issues regarding air, soil, and water pollution in industrialized countries, were becoming critical and that short-term solutions were no longer satisfactory. They also asserted the importance of using social sciences as well as science and technology to fashion remedies.

In 1969, the Secretary-General of the United Nations gave his state of the environment report. He announced that Stockholm would be the site for an international conference on the environment in 1972. For two years the Preparatory Committee and subcommittees met, and in 1971 they set the final agenda for the conference. The preliminary meetings had produced some consensus on the issues, and when the delegates assembled in

Stockholm, they had an agenda designed to promote achievements rather than simple discussion.

Biosphere protection and social and economic development were the two foci of the conference, and the achievements of the Stockholm Conference in these two areas were substantial. First, the United Nations Environment Programme (UNEP) was established in the Secretariat to provide an integrated mechanism to coordinate worldwide environmental concerns. Second, the delegates achieved general consensus on four major documents: the Declaration on the Human Environment, the Declaration of Principles, 109 Recommendations for Action, and—perhaps most critical of all—a Resolution of Institutional and Financial Arrangements. Of course, all the participants did not accede to all the proposals. France vowed to continue to test nuclear weapons, Japan decided to continue whaling, and the United States refused to commit funds for environmental protection in developing countries. By most accounts, however, Stockholm was a success:

> It avoided foundering on antagonisms born of Third World resentment over First World "injustice." The price of this avoidance was incorporation of environmental protection into the Third World's development priorities. Yet this First World concession introduced a new environmental element into the conventional interpretation of development. The development concept was thus enlarged, and delegates were exposed to evidence that many social and economic problems had environmental connections.[8]

That same year, the United Nations General Assembly adopted the report of the Stockholm Conference. The site of UNEP was moved from Geneva to Nairobi as a concession to the developing nations. By 1974, UNEP was attempting to implement the Stockholm resolutions. UNEP has become the accepted international forum for examining environmental problems, and the existence of a third world majority in its membership has continued to allay the suspicions of developing nations. The primary accomplishment has been the promotion of treaties; for example, UNEP helped forge the Convention on International Trade in Endangered Species (CITES) in 1973.

Twenty years passed before another major international environmental conference was convened. In the interim, international perspectives on the environment changed significantly. The ecological crisis worsened; scientific knowledge about the environment and its interrelationships increased; the role of poverty as a cause of environmental degradation, especially in developing countries, became clearer; and new formal institutions such as UNEP and the European Community (now the European Union [EU]) became prominent actors in the international arena.[9]

In June 1992, the United Nations Conference on Environment and Development (UNCED, or the Earth Summit, or the Rio Conference) convened in Rio de Janeiro. It was the largest international conference ever held, with representatives from 179 nations at the conference. The NGOs held a parallel conference; representatives of more than 2,500 interest groups attended the Global Forum. President George H. W. Bush was conspicuous by his absence; he refused to attend until he was sure the Climate Change Convention would not impose binding targets on carbon dioxide emissions.[10]

Even without Bush, the American presence was disruptive:

> U.S. opposition to targets and deadlines for limiting emissions of greenhouse gases continued to exasperate leaders from other industrialized countries. . . . But in the end they yielded to the U.S. position in order to secure its signing of the Climate Change Convention. To those who argued that the United States should reduce its consumption of fossil fuels and other natural resources, the Bush administration refused to compromise.[11]

The conference conveners were overly ambitious. A major obstacle was the fight between the developed nations of the North and the less-developed Southern countries. The divisions between North and South revolved around financing for environmental initiatives. The developing nations made their position clear: they were unwilling to support environmental controls unless the developed countries provided funding and technology transfers.[12] The Global Environment Facility (GEF), set up by the World Bank, was a first step toward financing the policies set at Rio; by the mid-1990s, GEF funding was targeted on biodiversity, climate, degradation of international waters, and ozone depletion.[13]

Five major documents resulted from the Rio Conference: Agenda 21, a lengthy document that spelled out comprehensive goals and objectives for the world environment at an estimated annual cost of $125 billion;[14] a nonbinding statement of twenty-seven principles in the Rio Declaration on Environment and Development; the Climate Change Convention; the Biodiversity Convention; and a statement on forest principles. The most significant institutional outcome was the creation of the United Nations Commission on Sustainable Development, whose main purpose is to provide a venue for further discussions on biodiversity.

The Rio Conference has had little impact on American national policy. The nonbinding agreement on climate change was not honored; the only significant American legislation to address the problems of greenhouse gas emissions was the Clean Air Act Amendments of 1990. Bush refused to sign the Biodiversity Convention, and although Clinton signed the treaty, the Senate failed to ratify it.

While the contributions of the United Nations are substantial, the organization itself labors under severe handicaps. First, global governance is essentially a matter of administration, and treaties may be stumbling blocks rather than useful guidelines for several reasons. Second, the need for consensus and compromise often leads to the acceptance of the lowest common denominator for policy objectives, and third, even after a treaty has been negotiated, nations may delay ratification or even fail to ratify the treaty at all.[15]

Problems with ratification may occur for a number of reasons: other national priorities may move ratification down on the formal agenda, internal bureaucracies may object, or special-interest groups may interfere. On occasion, treaty negotiators forge agreements that exceed their mandates. In other cases, the government that sent the negotiators may fall or the administration may change. This was clearly the case when George W. Bush withdrew from the Kyoto Protocol in 2001. Finally, governments involved in negotiations may not have been negotiating in good faith; their agreements may be deliberate deceptions or mere expressions of solidarity with allies.

To encourage cooperation and participation in international regimes, several inventive strategies have been used. Treaties and conventions may contain incentives to promote a higher level of cooperation or attainment than is strictly required by the treaty, a sort of international extra-credit assignment. Treaties may impose unequal demands on nations in recognition that the nations involved have unequal resources or levels of technology. Treaty standards may also be put in place before ratification is complete, either through provisional treaty application or by "soft law," which sets agreed-on rules without the formal treaty apparatus. Governments may also assign responsibility for regime governance to an intergovernmental organization such as the International Whaling Commission (IWC).

Enforcing treaties is problematic because there is no central sovereign at the international level; nations comply with treaties to ensure they will be able to enter into other international agreements or to avoid sanctions. (The ultimate sanction is war.) The United Nations is primarily a deliberative body; its members are instructed by their national governments and must return to their national governments for approval of decisions. It is perhaps more helpful to think of international law as a process through which authoritative decisions are made in the transnational arena rather than the authoritative, enforceable set of rules that characterize national law. Numerous policy actors (including nation-states, nongovernmental organizations, and international governmental organizations) signal their acceptance of a particular international regime through custom, by incorporation of the principles of international law in treaties and conventions, by judicial decisions in both national and international courts, by the articulation of general principles of law, and by unilateral declarations.[16]

Nongovernmental Organizations

Nongovernmental organizations (NGOs) at both the national and international levels have substantial influence on design and implementation of international resource regimes. Often environmental policy networks have large popular bases that cut across national boundaries, and NGOs now have a significant role in the initiation of international environmental programs. For example, the 1992 Global Forum held in conjunction with UNCED generated thirty-three alternate treaties covering a wide array of topics such as forestry, biodiversity, and climate change.[17] NGOs frequently play a significant role in the initiation of international environmental programs. They may have observer status at international meetings, and official government delegations sometimes contain NGO members, as when a Greenpeace representative served on the New Zealand delegation to the 1972 Convention on the Prevention of Marine Pollution by Dumping of Wastes and other Matter (London Convention).[18] NGOs provide scientific or technical assistance: for example, the Recognized Private Operating Agencies (RPOAs) provide technical information to the formal Study Groups of the Standardization Bureau of the International Telecommunication Union, and they pay for the privilege. The benefit they receive is access to the policy-making process in the telecommunications regime. The impact of NGOs is substantial. Policies adopted in large part because of NGO influence include the designation of Antarctica as a world park, establishment of the Southern Ocean Whale Sanctuary, and a moratorium on high-seas drift-net fishing.[19] They may also affect implementation; for example, the World Conservation Union (IUCN) drafted the proposed Covenant on Environment and Development (1995) which codified the existing status of international environmental law.[20]

The scientific community has also had an important role in the formation and legitimation of international regimes. Certainly the Antarctic regime was a child of the scientists; their insistence on the research focus of the regime and the exclusion of military concerns has helped maintain the stability of the regime. Of course, the scientific community has its own agenda in maintaining an avowedly neutral, scientific presence in environmental regimes. Protection of research funds, government jobs, and access to policy decisions rest on refusing to take sides in political disputes. There is also a culture of political neutrality within the sciences, just as practitioners of public administration frequently claim to hold policy-neutral positions, often in the face of overwhelming evidence to the contrary.

INTERNATIONAL AND GLOBAL COMMONS

Much of human history can be described as an effort by individuals to establish absolute control over items of value, whether land or cattle or jewels or people. The notion of commonly held property has an equally long but less flamboyant pedigree. Communal wells in arid regions, ancient irrigation systems, common pastures in medieval English villages, Shaker settlements in the New World, and neighborhood automobile-parking ordinances are all examples of common pool resource regimes. These are, however, small scale; the usual response to common pool resources has been appropriation and exploitation. The global commons of the twentieth century are, in large part, an exception because their resources were so vast that they seemed inexhaustible and they were not within national boundaries.

In the past, physical access to international and global commons has been difficult; for example, Antarctica is unbearably cold, the high seas were impossible to monitor, deep outer space was beyond the reach of even our dreams. In addition, the value of the resources within each domain has not always been clear; while the Antarctic seal and whale harvests were profitable, the existence of deep sea mineral nodules are a comparatively recent discovery, and to date there is little known economic value in deep space exploration. The political climate has also changed, and developing countries now assert their rights to share in the resources within these global commons.

The first part of this section provides an introduction to property rights in international law as they affect international and global commons. The remaining sections describe the current management regimes for oceans and the atmosphere.

Property Rights and Regimes

In the American national system of environmental administration and law, property rights are defined by the Constitution and legislation, but in the international arena, rights are less clearly defined, in part because there is no clear enforcement mechanism. International law cannot be defined as "the command of the sovereign backed by a sanction" because there is no sovereign, and international sanctions are applied with great reluctance. To understand the acquisition, exploitation, and conservation of resource systems in international environmental law, it is customary—and helpful—to think of property rights in economic terms.[21] The property right to a resource is not a single right but rather a bundle of rights, such as rights of access, exclusion, extraction, or sale of the captured resources, or the right to transfer one's rights to a second person. The specific composition of each bundle of rights varies. For example, all nations that are members of the Antarctic Treaty System have the right to establish Antarctic research stations in their bundle of rights, but they cannot transfer their access rights to non-member states. In contrast, nations that have been assigned geostationary orbit slots may lease those slots to other countries. Both groups have rights to the resource, but one may transfer access rights and the other may not.

Property rights may also be exclusive or nonexclusive. Exclusive rights imply that access to the resource is limited; others can be excluded from the resource. For example, the United States asserts control of fishing within its coastal jurisdiction. A nonexclusive right gives access to the resource to all the members of a specific pool of users rather than to individuals. For example, all members of the Antarctic Treaty have a nonexclusive right to explore the southern continent. Access to high-seas fisheries has historically been virtually unrestricted; therefore, the right to exploit these fisheries has been nonexclusive. Similarly, access to outer space is open to anyone with the technology to launch a rocket.

In international environmental law, it is important to base political or legal analysis on property rights and the legal regimes that administer them rather than on simply the physical resources. Thus the consideration of ocean fisheries must specify the resource regime: the bundle of rights in the high-seas regime includes the nonexclusive right of virtually unlimited access, while the bundle of rights in coastal fisheries allows only limited access.

Nations choose to share, or to continue to share, a resource domain for several reasons. First, the costs of defining and enforcing property rights (for example, the time and diplomatic costs of negotiating specific rights for each state) may be more than the individual nations are willing or able to bear. Second, individual nations may simply be unwilling to accept the consequences of unilateral assumption of property rights; they might be risking economic sanctions or even war. Finally, the resource itself may be difficult to divide (the atmosphere) or it may be in such large supply (the high-seas fisheries in the nineteenth century, or outer space) that clearly defined property rights seem unnecessary. If there are no access rights or extraction rules, then the resource domain is an *open-access resource* and liable to overexploitation. If all nations have legal access to the resource domain and have agreed to management rules, then it is a global commons (high seas or outer space), but if access is shared by a limited number of nations, the resource domain is an international commons (Mediterranean Sea or Antarctica).[22] Outer space is the last true global commons; no national property rights have been established in this domain. As technology improves and profitable exploitation becomes feasible, outer space will probably become an international commons subject to a legal regime with exclusionary rights.

Regimes for international and global commons do not develop in a policy vacuum. Nations have many diplomatic concerns and must reconcile domestic interests as well as international ones. For example, the United States refused to sign the Law of the Sea Treaty partly to protect domestic business interests in deep-sea mining. There is also a great deal of uncertainty about the scientific data on many international and global commons. Relatively straightforward information on populations and breeding habits of many ocean fish, for example, often is either lacking or conflicting. It is difficult to set catch limits without knowing how much harvest pressure a fishery can tolerate.

Another problem arises with risk assessment. Risk assessment involves estimating the probability that a given policy will produce harmful results; decisionmakers have different levels of risk they are willing to accept.[23] Early disagreement over the interaction of chlorofluorocarbons and ozone depletion points up this problem; the data were clear, but the scientific community could not agree on its interpretation.[24]

To provide an introduction to the processes by which international environmental law is made, the following sections describe the management regimes of two global commons: the oceans and the atmosphere.

Oceans

The ocean regime is the most complex of all the global commons regimes. Every nation with a coastline is concerned with the regime; nations have gone to war to gain access to critical seas. The oceans contain an elaborate array of resources, and even in this day of air and space travel, they are the premier international highways. For millennia, the oceans have been a dump for waste, and they are critical in maintaining weather patterns and atmospheric quality. Given this complexity—and the complete story of the oceans is vastly more complex than can be portrayed here—it is impossible to outline the development of the entire ocean regime. Unlike the evolution of the Antarctic regime, which is coherent, modern and relatively stable, the ocean regime has evolved over centuries and is based on a patchwork of customs and multilateral treaties. Two of the concerns addressed by those treaties are discussed in this section: living resources of the oceans and marine pollution.

The present law of the sea is the result of a series of international conferences. In 1958, the first United Nations Conference on the Law of the Sea (UNCLOS I) passed a set of conventions that, while technically binding only on the nations that ratified them, were in effect codifications of existing customary law. Two years later, in 1960, UNCLOS II was convened to resolve issues that had not been decided at UNCLOS I; a major issue was the size of the territorial seas—the distance from shore that a nation claims as sovereign territory.[25] Little was accomplished at UNCLOS II, although a compromise on the question of fishing zones and the limits of the territorial seas was almost reached.

After several years of preparatory meetings and negotiations, UNCLOS III began in 1973, continuing in a series of twelve sessions until 1982. The task was to design a new legal regime for the oceans. The design of the conference was flawed because it tried to reach agreement on two completely different resource domains: the sea and the deep seabed.[26] Deep seabed mining was especially problematic. Various actors in the international arena, especially the United States and the other major industrialized nations, were watching the arrangements carefully, concerned that whatever was decided for deep seabed mining would set precedent for other global or international commons such as the Antarctic, outer space, the moon, and the electromagnetic and satellite orbits. Resolution of the seabed issue was almost impossible, and by linking the two, issues of the ocean regime were dragged under as well.[27]

A coherent ocean regime is necessary because much of the world's population depends on ocean resources for both income and protein, and overfishing has depleted many fisheries stocks to unsustainable levels. International efforts to regulate the living resources of the seas is a constant source of controversy among nations.

Living Resources

While preparations for the 1982 UNCLOS were under way, several treaties relating to conservation were negotiated.[28] These and the 1980 World Conservation Strategy and the 1982 World Charter for Nature set the stage for the fisheries concerns reflected in the 1982 UNCLOS negotiations.

The issues of conservation and territorial seas are closely linked. They were finally addressed in the 1982 UNCLOS. One of the most useful accomplishments of the 1982 UNCLOS was the clarification of territorial limits: the twelve-mile limit for the territorial sea; the contiguous zone extended to twenty-four nautical miles; the continental shelf to its natural margin or to two hundred nautical miles, whichever is farther; and an Exclusive Economic Zone (EEZ) not to exceed two hundred nautical miles. The EEZ is subject to the control of the coastal state and the waters are therefore no longer an open-access regime, but this has clearly not been sufficient to promote effective conservation. For example, in 2003, the Georges Bank cod fishery off the coast of Newfoundland was closed completely because of fisheries depletion. Observers apportioned blame generously: inshore fishers blamed offshore trawlers for indiscriminate overfishing, while offshore fishermen accused the inshore fishers of cheating on quotas. Canadians blamed the Europeans for taking migratory fish in international waters in violation of the Northwest Atlantic Fisheries Organization regulations, but Canada had also contributed to the problem by subsidizing its fleet and processing plants since 1977.[29]

CASE DISCUSSION 7.1

Fishy Tales

Tuna boats set their nets on dolphins because tuna are often found in the ocean below dolphins. Because dolphins are mammals, they drown when entangled in the tuna seine nets. Prior to the passage of the Marine Mammal Protection Act of 1972 (MMPA), over 300,000 dolphins were killed annually. The act helped curtail American slaughter, but foreign tuna fleets were unaffected. Amendments to MMPA in 1988 imposed a mandatory embargo on importation of yellowfin tuna from countries whose fleets failed to meet congressional standards for dolphin protection (16 U.S.C. § 1371 [a][2]).

The standards required that the incidental kill rate of the foreign fleet could not be more than twice the American rate for 1989 and no more than one and a quarter times the American rate for subsequent years. In addition, for the eastern spinner dolphin subspecies, the total eastern spinners killed could not be more than 15 percent of the total number of mammals killed by that fleet.

In March 1990, the National Marine Fisheries Service (NMFS) issued a new regulation that announced, first, that 31 July was the deadline for providing dolphin kill data for the previous year, and second, if a foreign nation were embargoed, the Secretary of Treasury may reconsider the embargo based only on the data from the next six months. In other words, a country that killed too many dolphins in 1989 would be embargoed in July 1990, but the embargo could be lifted immediately if the data for January to July 1990 showed acceptable incidental kill rates.

On 25 July 1990, Earth Island Institute filed for an injunction to force a National Marine Fisheries Service embargo on Mexican tuna. The

(continued)

CASE DISCUSSION 7.1 (*continued*)

agency said it needed more time to process the data. On 28 August 1990, the court granted the injunction. On 6 September, NMFS imposed the embargo. On 7 September, NMFS lifted the embargo based on the January 1 to June 30 data for 1990.

Ten days later, on 17 September 1990, Earth Institute applied for a temporary restraining order, and on 4 October, the district court granted the injunction, saying the March regulation modifying the embargo rules violated the MMPA.

Does the *Chevron* doctrine support the agency's action in issuing the regulation? The government argued that the six-month reconsideration was an incentive to foreign countries to comply with American standards. Do you agree?

(Source: *Earth Island Institute v. Mosbacher, Secretary of Commerce*, 929 F. 2d 1449 [1991])

In July 1993, a United Nations conference on global fisheries management reached agreement on the problem but not on the solutions. As the fisheries conference emphasized, global fisheries were (and still are) in a perilous state. Current policies for managing marine living resources have "developed on an ad hoc basis with little, if any, of the coordination and integration required for effective conservation or the insistence that it be based on scientific advice."[30] This is caused in part by the imperfect match between the resource domain and political jurisdiction, as well as by the inevitable problem of economically rational fishers maximizing return on investment with no regard for sustainability. By 1994, no fish stocks were underfished.[31] In 1995, an attempt was made to address some of the high-seas issues with negotiations on the Agreement on Straddling and Highly Migratory Fish Stocks ("U.N. Fish Stocks Agreement").[32] This agreement emphasizes sustainable use and the precautionary principle in deciding conservation goals and increases cooperation.[33] However, overfishing continues to deplete fish stocks. A particularly contentious area is the North Sea, where the European Union's Common Fisheries Policy has dropped some fish stocks to dangerous levels. Resentment and even violence has flared between fishermen on their traditional, national fishing grounds and foreign fishermen from other EU states who are allowed to fish the same waters. In 1998, the EU joined UNCLOS and seems to be making progress on improved fisheries management.[34]

Management of sustainable fisheries may prove to be an elusive dream. Scientific data on fisheries stocks are often incomplete or inconclusive. To make matters worse, fishermen frequently choose to ignore management recommendations, either because they disbelieve the data, or they cannot afford to alter their activities, or because short-term economic gains are more important than long-range stock preservation. Some fishery policies are designed to protect nontarget species (e.g., turtle excluder devices), and fishermen see compliance with these policies as having little economic benefit and high economic cost. Developing nations are often dependent on catches for both internal consumption and for export. Overlapping political jurisdictions and the highly migratory habits of some species only exacerbate the problems.

Marine Pollution

Control of marine pollution is a significant part of the ocean regime. The immediate impact of these pollutants ranges from unsafe and unsightly waste-strewn beaches to fishing stocks that are depleted or unfit for consumption. Marine pollution stems from several sources: discharges from the land and from ships, waste disposal, and oil drilling. Land discharges include sewage, radioactive waste, industrial wastes, and agricultural pollutants (e.g., herbicides, pesticides, and fertilizers). Ship discharges include contaminants from ballast, invasive species, garbage, sewage, and spills of fuel, oil, and other cargoes. Some marine pollution is the result of official policies that allow ocean dumping or ocean-based incineration to dispose of various wastes. Because the ocean currents are found throughout the water column, these pollutants are distributed not only across the surface of the oceans but also from the surface to unmeasured depths. It is clear that the ocean cannot be used as an inexhaustible sink for waste disposal or pollution.

Because these pollutants arise from so many sources, international control has been troublesome to establish. Some pollutants such as agricultural runoff are nonpoint source pollutants that cannot be easily reduced even on a national level, while others, such as spills from offshore oil drilling or industrial waste disposal, originate from activities with such high economic value that strong regulatory statutes are difficult to enact and, given the location of the problems, almost impossible to enforce. As with most pollution, the costs are often borne by ecosystems far from the point of origin, and penalties for generating negative externalities are hard to impose, especially across international boundaries. Early efforts to contain marine pollution failed; draft conventions negotiated in 1926 and 1935 never entered into force. The 1954 International Convention for the Prevention of Pollution of the Sea by Oil (London) focused on pollution from oil tankers.[35] Even with amendments in 1962 and 1969, the convention was not very successful because there were no incentives for ratification or sanctions for noncompliance. However, the many treaties and conventions agreed upon in the past forty years have made significant progress in controlling marine pollution. Most scholars accept the argument that the 1982 UNCLOS incorporated the London Dumping Convention of 1972[36] and the International Convention for the Prevention of Marine Pollution from Ships (both are discussed later) into the Law of the Sea, and that nations are under an international obligation to protect the ocean environment.[37]

In October 1983, the 1954 London Convention was superseded when the International Convention for the Prevention of Marine Pollution by Ships (MARPOL) entered into force. MARPOL was first adopted in 1973 and amended in 1978, partly to expedite adoption.[38] It follows the London Convention focus of technological solutions to the discharge of oil into the marine environment, but it also covers non-oil discharges, such as garbage from cruise ships; its enforcement provisions are more effective. Unfortunately, many ships are now registering with developing countries, which allows them to sidestep some international controls.[39]

Dumping hazardous waste at sea is also controlled by treaty. The Convention on the Prevention of Marine Pollution by Dumping of Wastes and Other Matter (London Convention of 1972) and the Convention for the Prevention of Marine Pollution by Dumping from Ships and Aircraft (Oslo Convention of 1972)[40] apply to the high seas and the northeast Atlantic, respectively. The London Convention distinguishes some harmful wastes (the "black list," e.g., organohalogenic compounds, mercury) that are absolutely prohibited, from other, less harmful products (the "grey list," e.g., lead, arsenic, copper, pesticides) that may be dumped if the appropriate permit is obtained.[41] A third category of waste requires only a general permit.

The Oslo Convention has a similar structure. The London Convention is widely ratified and applies to all marine areas not considered territorial waters, so the regime it establishes is a global regime.[42]

Neither convention prohibits dumping absolutely, but the continued acceptance of ocean dumping is doubtful. For centuries water has been an economical medium for waste disposal, and free-flowing rivers will indeed self-cleanse of some natural waste products. However, production of large volumes of wastes that are not biodegradable has eliminated the utility of water dumping. Scientific uncertainty regarding cumulative and latent effects of wastes, the increasing awareness of how social, economic, and environmental costs shift from polluters to second parties, and the strengthening voices of developing countries unwilling to accept these costs have all changed the international focus on ocean dumping. In 1993, a ban on all ocean dumping of industrial waste by 1995 went into effect.[43]

Other agreements that control ocean dumping apply to particular geographic regions, for example, the Protocol for the Protection of the Mediterranean Sea against Pollution from Land-Based Sources (Athens).[44] These conventions are focused on land-based sources of pollution such as agricultural runoff and urban sewage.

Atmosphere

Atmospheric issues are truly global. As we might expect, international controls for atmospheric problems have been extremely difficult to negotiate for a variety of reasons. Issues of sovereignty have plagued the policy arena from the start, and scientific data have been both conflicting and confusing. Developed and developing countries have disagreed over acceptable levels of pollution, with some developing countries viewing air pollution as proof their country was on the road to industrialization and an improved economy. Pollution control technology is expensive, and the costs of monitoring and enforcing regulation have been high. Businesses with strong political influence have successfully blocked regulatory efforts.[45] The transboundary nature of air pollution and other atmospheric problems has aggravated the difficulties, with transboundary air pollution only one of many policies subject to international horse-trading. Finally, lack of established international organizations charged with the coordination of transboundary air policy has delayed progress toward resolution of the problem.

Although transboundary air pollution is, strictly speaking, a negative externality or spillover and not an issue of resource use, the impact of such issues on international law regarding the global commons is significant. This discussion of the atmosphere addresses three areas. The first section looks at acid deposition, and the second examines the problems of ozone depletion in the upper atmosphere. The final section looks at the problem of climate change and the Kyoto Protocol.

Acid Deposition

Acid deposition ("acid rain")[46] became an international issue when the impact of fossil fuels and air-borne radiation became apparent in countries that had not caused them. The first modern warning signs appeared in Sweden and Norway in the late 1960s, when some lakes no longer could support plant and animal life or normal biological processes.[47] Scientists determined that the acid deposition affecting these lakes had originated in Europe and in other parts of Scandinavia. In the next twenty years, evidence showed similar and increasing problems with acid deposition throughout the European continent and North America. Acid deposition also destroys forests, increases the vulnerability of plants to pests and disease, and damages the built environment.

In 1980, the United States and Canada signed a memorandum of intent indicating that each would reduce the sulfur and nitrogen emissions from coal-fired furnaces. However, the newly elected Reagan administration immediately backed away from the agreement and advocated more study to confirm the connection between coal-fired furnaces and acid deposition. This was a difficult position for the White House to maintain, given a number of reports from the American scientific community that confirmed the connection.[48]

Sweden, Finland, and Norway were practically alone in their drive to establish international controls on the major causes of acid deposition, sulfur dioxide, and nitrous oxides. Industrialized nations that were heavily dependent on coal-fired utilities, such as the United States and the United Kingdom, vetoed any agreements that might force their energy costs up. A small step was made in 1979 when the Geneva Convention on Long-Range Transboundary Air Pollution was signed. The convention was widely viewed as a "toothless agreement" that did not regulate acid deposition adequately.[49] It is so general that, for example, the United States' continued pollution in Canada is not a violation of the convention.[50]

Discouraged by the slow pace of international programs, some nations have taken the unusual step of committing to additional restrictions outside the larger treaty systems. In Ottawa in 1984, ten nations formed the "Thirty-Percent Club" and pledged that they would reduce 1980 sulfur dioxide emission levels by 30 percent by 1993. The group then provided a forum for negotiations that led to the Helsinki Protocol on the Reduction of Sulphur Emissions or Their Transboundary Fluxes by at Least 30 Percent (1985).[51] Unfortunately, neither the United States, Poland, nor the United Kingdom, all major sources of transboundary sulfur dioxide pollution, were parties to this convention.

The United States was unwilling to accede to substantial reductions in nitrogen oxide emissions, claiming that unilateral reductions had already fulfilled any American obligations. In 1988, a second protocol was added to the Geneva Convention: the Sofia Protocol Concerning the Control of Emissions of Nitrogen Oxides or Their Transboundary Fluxes.[52] The Sofia Protocol mandated an emissions freeze at 1987 levels but allowed many countries, such as the United States, to delay compliance until 1994 to compensate for earlier reductions. However, not all nations that signed the Geneva Convention are party to these protocols, and even those that are party often do not fully implement protocol provisions.

Since then the international evidence of the impact of transboundary pollution has mounted. Forests in the eastern United States are endangered, and in Germany over half of the trees are damaged from acid deposition. Eastern Europe is also plagued with damaged areas, the extent of which is becoming apparent as the political regimes change.[53]

One stumbling block for international cooperation to stem acid deposition is the great difficulty nations have had in reaching internal agreement on their own remedies. For example, in the United States, conflicts between industry and environmentalists, among coal-producing regions, and between coal-burning and acid deposition–receiving regions complicate any legislative attempts to deal with the problem. It was not until the Clean Air Act Amendments of 1990 that the United States finally passed a legislative scheme to reduce acid deposition. Stricter standards were imposed on 110 coal-burning electric utility plants, and nitrous oxide emissions were also scheduled for reduction.[54]

Ozone Depletion

Another transboundary air pollution issue with global implications is the diminishing level of ozone in the stratosphere. Stratospheric ozone shields the planet's surface from ultraviolet radiation, affecting temperature gradients and weather patterns across the Earth, and is reduced by the interaction of chlorine and ozone. Lower levels of stratospheric ozone are dangerous because ultraviolet radiation can penetrate to the planet surface more easily. This increases the incidence of skin cancers, reduces some crop yields, and has numerous other negative effects on living organisms. For example, reduction of ozone protection over the southern pole allowed ultraviolet radiation to penetrate more deeply into the ocean, not only reducing the productivity of the phytoplankton but also increasing genetic damage in the organisms.[55] This issue may be one of the few success stories in international environmental policy, although it is too soon to be sure. Identified in the 1970s as a potential problem, by 2005 production of ozone-depleting chemical had fallen by 95 percent,[56] and the amount of stratospheric chlorine (a major cause of ozone depletion) is leveling off.[57]

National action to curtail ozone loss predated the international efforts by several years. In 1974, two scientific studies hypothesized a dangerous connection between release of chlorine from chlorofluorocarbons (CFCs) and the reduction of stratospheric ozone.[58] In 1977, the United States imposed some limits on CFC use under the Clean Air Act Amendments. Federal regulations limited the use of CFCs in aerosols in 1978, and Canada, Norway, and Sweden followed suit.[59] The European Community proposed a slower reduction extended over a longer time; several observers attribute this reluctance to industry pressures and a lack of public interest.[60]

In 1985, compromise was reached through the Vienna Convention for the Protection of the Ozone Layer, which called for an economic workshop, information exchange, and further research.[61] As in the Transboundary Air Pollution Convention, serious questions of economic equity between developing and developed nations were at issue. In 1985, no practical substitute for CFCs was available, and their use in industrial processes and refrigeration were critical in technology transfers to developing countries. This led to a weak convention that was an "empty framework" of vague measures.[62] Nonetheless, the convention is important for its ecosystem approach and its emphasis on prevention rather than on simple remedies.[63]

Scientific data continued to accumulate that indicated a dramatic decrease in stratospheric ozone. The world environmental community was shocked at the 1985 reports of an enormous ozone hole over the Antarctic.[64] The hole was so extensive that the scientists had delayed publishing their report while they rechecked the data: American satellite measurements had not observed the dissipation because their computers were programmed to ignore losses of such magnitude as anomalies.[65] The hole eventually exposed an area equal to the size of the continental United States,[66] and a similar but smaller hole exists over the Arctic.

In September 1987, twenty-four nations (including the major CFC-producing countries) plus the European Community Commission signed the Montreal Protocol on Substances that Deplete the Ozone Layer.[67] The Protocol was especially notable because "for the first time the international community reached agreement on control of a valuable economic commodity to prevent future environmental damage."[68] The Protocol imposed substantial reductions in the use of CFCs when no replacement chemical was available, bypassing the customary "best available technology" approach in favor of a standard that recognized the urgency of the ozone problem.[69] The Protocol was widely accepted by the international community, in part because of the selective, built-in incentives; for example, the Soviet Union was "grandfathered" for factories under construction, and developing countries were allowed to delay compliance for ten years.[70] Also expectations for funding contributions from each country were adjusted according to the United Nations' global assessment scale that is based on each country's economic, geographic, and demographic characteristics.[71]

The Montreal Protocol was revised in 1990. The amendments accelerated the timetable for phasing out CFCs; the United States implemented this change in Title VI of the 1990 Clean Air Act Amendments. The amendments also adopted an incentive program to encourage developing countries to change to CFC substitutes and new technologies as rapidly as possible. A second set of negotiations in 1992 advanced the schedule even further, calling for a total ban by 2030 and adding controls for methyl bromide.[72]

The Montreal Protocol represents a major shift in the relationship between scientific certainty and public policy decisionmaking. The political and economic pressures to resist establishing policies to reduce CFCs and related compounds were intense. Richard Benedick, chief United States negotiator for the ozone protection treaties, attributes the success of the negotiations to several factors, among which were the close relationships between atmospheric scientists and the government officials, the education and use of public opinion to sway politicians, leadership from the United Nations Environmental Programme and from financially influential countries such as the United States, and consideration of the needs of developing countries.[73]

Climate Change

Climate change is probably the most complex and intractable environmental issue on the planet. Scientists are fairly confident that ozone depletion can eventually be reversed, but they are not sure that increasing global temperatures can be effectively moderated or, even if they are, that physical changes such as new patterns for ocean currents will ever return to their familiar configurations.

Climate change (global warming) is an anticipated increase in the average planetary temperature caused by three major sources: increased atmospheric carbon dioxide and nitrous oxides (by-products of fossil fuel combustion); methane, primarily originating in agricultural processes, especially animal wastes and paddy farming; and chlorofluorocarbons (CFCs), which are also implicated in the loss of stratospheric ozone.[74] Increased carbon dioxide levels are also affected by destruction of the rainforest (where trees absorb carbon dioxide) and the reduced capacity of the world's oceans to absorb carbon dioxide. Although the scientific community has still not reached consensus over the relative weights of various causes of climate change, scientists generally agree that human activities are exacerbating the global warming trend.[75] Recent research points toward a complex relationship between climate and massive oscillations in ocean currents in the North Atlantic and Pacific. Some scientists assert that the planet moves through warming and cooling cycles independent of human activity and that the current warming trend is simply part of the planet's natural cycle, but as the global warming trend continues despite cooler ocean currents, the likelihood that human activities are the main culprit has increased.[76] While the cumulative impact is uncertain, changes in patterns of agriculture and in sea levels seem likely, and the problem comes not from climate change alone but from the *rate* of change.

In 1908, Svante Arrhenius was the first scholar to connect human industrial processes, carbon dioxide emissions, and world temperatures.[77] Climate change remained a minor item on the world environmental agenda until well after World War II. Weather data collection had become more sophisticated to provide information for military and commercial aviation, and cold war fears of a possible "nuclear winter" led scientists to examine climate data carefully. Concurrent research on oceans suggested that they were not an inexhaustible carbon dioxide sink,[78] and in 1957 the first permanent monitoring station for carbon dioxide was established at Mauna Loa, Hawaii.

By 1979, a scientific consensus was emerging that carbon dioxide and other greenhouse gases were inclining to dangerous levels. In 1985, an international conference at Villach, Austria, concluded that climate warming appeared inevitable, and participants began to talk of a climate convention. After the Villach Conference, the pace of policy formation picked up considerably. The same year, British scientists discovered a large "hole" in stratospheric ozone over the Antarctic; this provided a dramatic underscoring to the idea that human activities could damage Earth's atmosphere. In 1987, the United Nations Environment Programme (UNEP) and the WMO created the Intergovernmental Panel on Climate Change (IPCC) to study global warming.

Politicians jumped on the bandwagon: American President Reagan signed the short-lived Global Climate Protection Act (January 1988), British Prime Minister Thatcher discussed global warming in a public speech (September 1988), and presidential candidate George H. W. Bush made global warming a campaign issue. However, once elected, Bush proved less enthusiastic, and in an example of spectacular political misjudgment, his administration ordered National Aeronautics and Space Administration (NASA) scientist James Hansen to alter his testimony to Congress to suggest scientific uncertainty about the effect of greenhouse gases on global climate. Hansen went public, and the ensuing publicity brought global warming to the political forefront. Despite increasing international pressures, the United States continued to oppose a climate change convention.

In December 1988, the United Nations General Assembly passed the Resolution on Protection of the Global Climate.[79] Three months later, an international panel of Legal and Policy Experts on the Protection of the Atmosphere met in Toronto, Canada, and supported an international convention on climate change. In 1990, the final report from the IPCC's first Working Group presented a relatively united front from the world's atmospheric scientists that increasing levels of carbon dioxide were having a deleterious effect on the world climate. Many nations took this conclusion very seriously: between May and December, a majority of the Organization for Economic Cooperation and Development (OECD) member states had begun to curb greenhouse emissions.[80]

In the same year, the Second World Climate Conference met in Geneva to address global climate change issues.[81] Representatives from over 130 nations called for an international convention on global warming; this call eventually resulted in the 1992 Earth Summit (UNCED) in Rio de Janeiro, where the Framework Convention on Climate Change opened for signature. Parties to this convention agreed to limit and mitigate carbon dioxide emissions and to provide technology transfer and financial assistance to developing nations. As a concession to American policy, the convention contains no quantified emissions targets.

Movement toward a climate change convention was extraordinarily susceptible to domestic politics.[82] The climate change conversations, essentially an extension of the acid deposition and ozone debates, were shrouded in scientific uncertainty. The same coalitions that had opposed acid deposition policies were also opposed to climate change programs because the same domestic economic interests were threatened. For example, the OPEC nations did not support the convention because they feared the development of alternative energy sources (especially nuclear power) that would cut into their exports. The United States relies heavily on cheap fossil fuels, and for America, the potential economic costs of the convention were high. The developed nations did not present a united front either. The newly industrialized countries were willing to accept emissions limits only in exchange for the most current technology, while some smaller states, especially the Alliance of Small Island States (AOSIS), wanted strict international controls at any price because they are so vulnerable to even the smallest elevation in sea level.

The doomsday scenarios for climate change include alterations in areas of agricultural productivity, increased global precipitation, more severe storm events, rising sea levels, and wider distribution of tropical diseases. Although the precautionary principle was a strong motivator for the Montreal Protocol, it has not had the same effect on climate change policies, primarily because the economic interests are more diverse and have strong incentives to delay any agreement. In 1997, the Kyoto Protocol called for a reduction in greenhouse gas emissions to pre-1990 levels. Although President Clinton was in favor of a climate treaty and had worked toward the Kyoto Protocol, the Senate would not ratify it. As soon as George W. Bush took office, he began to back away from American commitments to climate change programs. In mid–March 2001, he withdrew the United States from the Kyoto Protocol. It took the signature of Russia in 2004 to finally bring Kyoto into effect: it entered into force on 16 February 2005.

SUGGESTED READING

Axelrod, Regina, David Downie, and Norman Vig, eds. *The Global Environment: Institutions, Law, and Policy.* Washington, DC: CQ Press, 2005. An excellent selection of essays on global issues. The focus is on institutions rather than on policy areas.

Birnie, Patricia, and Alan Boyle. *International Law & the Environment.* 2nd ed. Oxford, UK: Clarendon Press, 2002. You really can't pick this one up to read it, but it is the most thorough, accurate, and clear book available on this subject. An essential addition to your library.

Buck, Susan. *The Global Commons.* Washington, DC: Island Press, 1998. It is perhaps immodest to recommend my own book. However, it expands the discussions here on global commons and includes Antarctica as well as outer space, an area that is interesting and increasingly important.

Jordan, Andrew, ed. *Environmental Policy in the European Union: Actors, Institutions and Processes.* 2nd ed. London: Earthscan, 2005. This book provides in-depth case studies as well as an assessment of the European Union's capacity to deal with environmental challenges.

Ostrom, Elinor. *Governing the Commons; The Evolution of Institutions for Collective Action.* Cambridge, UK: Cambridge University Press, 1990. If I could only have one book on the commons, this would be it. The focus is on small-scale common pool resources. The analytic framework, based on empirical data, has wide application. Very readable.

Peterson, D. J. *Troubled Lands: The Legacy of Soviet Environmental Destruction.* Boulder, CO: Westview, 1993. A superb, detailed look at the environmental degradation in the former Soviet Union. It is remarkably readable and essential for understanding the institutions, political processes, and policies that let to such devastation. Highly recommended.

Wallace, Helen, and William Wallace, eds. *Policy Making in the European Union.* 4th ed. Oxford, UK: Oxford University Press, 2000. A very comprehensive textbook with extensive case studies.

NOTES

1. See Peter Sand, *Lessons Learned in Global Environmental Governance* (Washington, DC: World Resources Institute, June 1990). In this chapter, citations for international treaties are from Patricia Birnie and Patrick Boyle, *International Law & the Environment*, 2nd ed. (Oxford, UK: Oxford University Press, 2002).

2. The modern corporation itself is a recent legal invention. To give a profit-oriented enterprise the legal rights of human beings is a development that does not astonish us only because we have grown accustomed to its face.

3. While there are many comprehensive law school texts on international law and international environmental law, my recommendation for a starting point for serious study is Birnie and Boyle, *International Law & the Environment*.

4. Outer space is also a global commons. Antarctica shares many of the characteristics of a global commons, although it is in fact an international commons since many nations have conflicting sovereignty claims on the continent. I chose the oceans and the atmosphere because they are, for now, the most important, and because they will be most familiar to American readers.

5. As a child of the cold war, I found it painfully ironic that the final signature that brought Kyoto into effect was Russia.

6. Resources are located in fixed spatial dimensions known as *resource domains*. For example, fish are a natural resource found in the ocean resource domain. Geostationary orbits are resources found in the space resource domain. In some situations, the domain and the resource are coterminous. For example, when sailors use the oceans as roads to transport people and goods, the oceans themselves are a resource. When the sailors are fishing, the oceans are also a resource domain and the fish stocks are the resource.

7. Jean Dorst, *Before Nature Dies*, translated by Constance D. Sherman (Boston: Houghton Mifflin, 1970); Rolf Edberg, *On the Shred of a Cloud*, translated by Sven Åhman (Alabama: University of Alabama Press, 1969).

8. Lynton Caldwell, *International Environmental Policy* (Durham, NC: Duke University Press, 1984), 53.

9. Marvin Soroos, "From Stockholm to Rio: The Evolution of Global Environmental Governance," in *Environmental Policy in the 1990s*, 2nd ed., edited by Norman Vig and Michael Kraft (Washington, DC: CQ Press, 1994), 299–321, 300–301.

10. Norman Vig, "Presidential Leadership and the Environment: From Reagan and Bush to Clinton," in *Environmental Policy in the 1990s*, 2nd ed., edited by Norman Vig and Michael Kraft (Washington, DC: CQ Press, 1994), 71–95, 87.

11. Marvin Soroos, "From Stockholm to Rio," 316, notes omitted.

12. As Kim says to Mahbub Ali: "I will change my faith and my bedding, but thou must pay for it." Mahbub Ali was so amused that he almost fell off his horse laughing; the developed nations at Rio did not have a similar reaction. Rudyard Kipling, *Kim* (New York: Dell, 1959), 132.

13. Nancy Kubasek and Gary Silverman, *Environmental Law*, 5th ed. (Upper Saddle River, NJ: Pearson/Prentice Hall, 2005), 416.

14. Richard Tobin, "Environment, Population, and Economic Development," in *Environmental Policy in the 1990s*, 2nd ed., edited by Norman Vig and Michael Kraft (Washington, DC: CQ Press, 1994, 275–297), 293.

15. See Sand, *Lessons Learned in Global Environmental Governance*.

16. See Anthony D'Amato, "What 'Counts' as Law?" in *Law-Making in the Global Community*, edited by Nicholas Onuf (Durham, NC: Carolina Academic Press, 1982), 99–103.

17. "Chronological Summary: Events of 1992," *Colorado Journal of International Environmental Law and Policy* 4 (1993): 232.

18. Grant Hewison, "Environmental Non-Governmental Organizations," in *Ocean Governance: Strategies and Approaches for the 21st Century*, edited by Thomas Mensah (Honolulu: Law of the Sea Institute, 1996, 115–137, 129.

19. Hewison, "Environmental Non-Governmental Organizations," 137.

20. Birnie and Boyle, *International Law & the Environment*, 68.

21. There are hidden dangers in the use of economic analysis: apparently the mere study of economics diminishes cooperative behavior. Reporting on a study by Robert Frank, Thomas Gilovich, and Dennis Regan ("Does Studying Economics Inhibit Co-operation?" *Journal of Economic Perspectives* [Spring 1993]), *The Economist* notes that economists and economics students are less concerned about fairness, give less to charity, and are more likely to cheat than their colleagues in other disciplines. "How do you mean, 'fair'?" *The Economist*, 29 May 1993, 71.

22. Modern international commons were once global commons, but as technology and developing markets made them profitable to exploit, the legal right of access was assumed by states with the technology or the power to enforce it, and then access was denied to other nations.

23. See Mary Douglas and Aaron Wildavsky, *Risk and Culture* (Berkeley: University of California Press, 1982).

24. An interesting case study on this topic is Forest Reinhardt, "Du Pont Freon® Products Division," in *Managing Environmental Issues: A Casebook*, edited by Rogene Buchholz, Alfred Marcus, and James Post (Englewood Cliffs, NJ: Prentice-Hall, 1992), 261–286.

25. The "cod war" between Iceland and Great Britain was the trigger event for UNCLOS II. Iceland asserted a 12-mile limit that excluded the British fishing fleet from its traditional fishing grounds. At one point in the dispute, British fishermen were accompanied in disputed waters by armed escort vessels.

26. Robert A. Goldwin, "Common Sense vs. 'The Common Heritage.'" In *Law of the Sea: U.S. Policy Dilemma*, edited by Bernard Oxman, David Caron, and Charles Buderi (San Francisco: ICS Press, 1983), 60.

27. The seabed mining regime that was finally adopted in 1994 is designed to be a combination of private property regime and cooperative property regime. Private

mining operations can establish leases (a substantial bundle of property rights) but at the price of technology transfer and financing the cooperative regime, contributing costly information on explorations and paying fees to the international organization in charge of mining (the Enterprise). The regime will be extremely difficult to implement. While forecasting is an uncertain business, it seems unlikely that the seabed minerals regime will survive without substantial modification.

28. Especially important are the following: 1973 Convention on International Trade in Endangered Species of Wild Fauna and Flora (CITES), (Washington, DC), 993 UNTS 243; 12 ILM 1085 (1973), in force 1 July 1975; 1979 Convention on the Conservation of Migratory Species of Wild Animals (Bonn), 19 ILM (1980) 15, in force 1 November 1983; 1979 Convention on the Conservation of European Wildlife and Natural Habitats (Berne), UKTS 56 (1982), Cmnd. 8738, ETS 104, in force 1 June 1984; and 1980 Convention on the Conservation of Antarctic Marine Living Resources (Canberra) (CCAMLR), TIAS. 10240; 19 ILM (1980) 837, in force 7 April 1981.

29. Scott Brennan and Jay Withgott, *Environment: The Science behind the Stories* (San Francisco: Pearson/Benjamin Cummings, 2005), 407.

30. Birnie and Boyle, *International Law & the Environment*, 646.

31. S.M. Garcia and R. Grainger, FAO Fisheries Technical Paper 359 (1996), cited in Brennan and Withgott, *Environment: The Science behind the Stories*, 407.

32. 34 ILM 1542 (1995), not in force.

33. Birnie and Boyle, *International Law & the Environment*, 673.

34. Birnie and Boyle, *International Law & the Environment*, 662–663.

35. 327 UNTS 3; UKTS 54 (1958), Cmnd. 595, 12 UST 2989, TIAS 4900, in force 26 July 1958.

36. 26 UST 2403; TIAS. 8165. Amended 12 October 1978, TIAS. No. 8165; 18 ILM 510 (1979), in force 30 August 1975. Birnie and Boyle, *International Law & the Environment*, 420.

37. Birnie and Boyle, *International Law & the Environment*, 419–422.

38. Birnie and Boyle, *International Law & the Environment*, 362.

39. Birnie and Boyle, *International Law & the Environment*, 363.

40. 932 UNTS 3, UKTS 119 (1975), Cmnd. 6228, 11 ILM 262 (1972), in force 7 April 1974.

41. Alexandre Kiss and Dinah Shelton, *International Environmental Law* (Ardsley-on-Hudson, NY: Transnational Publishers, 1991), 182.

42. Birnie and Boyle, *International Law & the Environment*, 420. This convention will be replaced by the 1996 Protocol, which is not yet in force.

43. Birnie and Boyle, *International Law & the Environment*, 421.

44. 19 ILM (1980) 869, in force 17 June 1983.

45. Ozone depletion was relatively simple to address because individuals perceived personal harm (higher rates of skin cancer) and the primary manufacturer of chloro-

fluorocarbons (CFCs) was an American company eager to corner the market on CFC substitutes. See Reinhardt, "Du Pont Freon® Products Division," 261–286.

46. The correct term is *acid deposition* because acid is found in fog and clouds as well as in rain.

47. Walter Rosenbaum, *Energy, Politics, and Public Policy*, 2nd ed. (Washington, DC: CQ Press, 1987), 117.

48. *New York Times*, 28 June 1983, quoted by Walter Rosenbaum, *Environmental Politics and Policy* (Washington, DC: CQ Press, 1985), 135. The most comprehensive report on acid deposition is the National Acid Precipitation Assessment Program (NAPAP), a ten-year study sponsored jointly by the Environmental Protection Agency; NOAA; the departments of Agriculture, Energy, the Interior; and the CEQ. Patricia Irving, ed., *Acid Deposition: State of Science and Technology, Summary Report of the United States National Acid Precipitation Assessment Program* (Washington, DC: USGPO, September 1991), cited in Jacqueline Vaughn Switzer, *Environmental Politics: Domestic and Global Dimensions* (New York: St. Martin's Press, 1994), 259.

49. Gareth Porter and Janet Welsh Brown, *Global Environmental Politics*, 2nd ed. (Boulder, CO: Westview Press, 1996), 69.

50. Birnie and Boyle, *International Law and the Environment*, 509.

51. 27 ILM (1998) 707, in force 2 September 1987.

52. 27 ILM (1988) 698, in force 14 February 1991.

53. See Peterson, *Troubled Lands: The Legacy of Soviet Environmental Destruction* for a superb, detailed look at the environmental degradation in the former Soviet Union.

54. In the United States, the Clean Air Act Amendments (1990) not only strengthened existing legislation but also added several new areas to federal regulatory control. They also established the innovative emissions trading program, which applied market-based strategies to the problems of air pollution. Each major coal-fired plant was allocated a set amount of permissible sulfur dioxide emissions, which might be traded, bought, or sold.

55. Keith Schneider, "Ozone Depletion Harming Sea Life," *New York Times*, 16 November 1991, 6, col. 6.

56. Brennan and Withgott, *Environment: The Science behind the Stories*, 341.

57. Brennan and Withgott, *Environment: The Science behind the Stories*, 343.

58. Chlorine is released from chlorofluorocarbons (CFCs), which are nonpoisonous and relatively inert chemicals used in refrigerants and as aerosol propellants. CFCs are especially stable and can remain in the atmosphere for decades or longer. As solar radiation breaks the CFCs down, chlorine is released, which reacts with ozone (O_3) to create oxygen (O_2). The chlorine molecule is then free to react with another ozone molecule, setting off a chain reaction in the stratosphere. Richard Stolarski and Ralph Cicerone, "Stratospheric Chlorine: A Possible Sink for

Ozone," *Canadian Journal of Chemistry* 52 (1974): 1610–1615; Mario Molina and F. Sherwood Rowland, "Stratospheric Sink for Chlorofluoromethanes: Chlorine Atom Catalysed Destruction of Ozone," *Nature* 249 (1974): 810–812. Both cited in Richard Elliot Benedick, *Ozone Diplomacy: New Directions for Safeguarding the Planet* (Cambridge, MA: Harvard University Press, 1991), 10.

59. Benedick, *Ozone Diplomacy*, 24.

60. Markus Jachtenfuchs, "The European Community and the Protection of the Ozone Layer," *Journal of Common Market Studies* 28, no. 3 (March 1980): 263; David Pearce, "The European Community Approach to the Control of Chlorofluorocarbons," Paper submitted to UNEP Workshop on the Control of Chlorofluorocarbons, Leesburg, Virginia, 8–12 September 1986, 12. Both cited by Benedick, *Ozone Diplomacy*, 24–25.

See also Thomas B. Stoel Jr., Alan S. Miller, and Breck Milroy, *Fluorocarbon Regulation* (Lexington, MA: D.C. Heath, 1980), 205; and J. T. B. Tripp, D. J. Dudek, and Michael Oppenheimer, "Equality and Ozone Protection," *Environment* 29, no. 6 (1987): 45; Benedick, *Ozone Diplomacy*, 28.

61. Vienna Convention for the Protection of the Ozone Layer, UNEP Doc. 1G.53/5; 26 ILM 1529 (1987), in force 22 September 1988.

62. Birnie and Boyle, *International Law & the Environment*, 519.

63. Birnie and Boyle, *International Law & the Environment*, 519.

64. J. C. Farnau, B. G. Gardiner, and J. D. Shanklin, "Large Losses of Total Ozone in Antarctica Reveal Seasonal ClO_x/NO_x Interaction," *Nature* 315 (1985): 207–210.

65. Benedick, *Ozone Diplomacy*, 18–19. The ozone hole was more severe over the Antarctic because the air there is the coldest on Earth, and the chemical reaction that removes ozone from the atmosphere is accelerated in cold temperatures. The hole now exposes an area equal to the size of the continental United States. Joel S. Levine, "A Planet at Risk," Public Lecture, 20 February 1993, Greensboro, North Carolina. According to Dr. Levine, global warming will do nothing to alleviate this problem as the impact of global warming is felt at the Earth's surface and, in fact, global warming leads to increasingly cold temperatures in the upper atmosphere.

66. Kiss and Shelton, *International Environmental Law*, 339.

67. Protocol (to the 1985 Vienna Convention) on Substances that Deplete the Ozone Layer (Montreal), 26 ILM 1540 (1987), in force 1 January 1989.

68. Orval Nangle, "Stratospheric Ozone: United States Regulation of Chlorofluorocarbons," *Environmental Affairs* 16 (1989): 546.

69. Benedick, *Ozone Diplomacy*, 1.

70. Peter Sand, "International Cooperation: The Environmental Experience," in *Preserving the Global Environment: The Challenge of Shared Leadership*, edited by

Jessica Tuchman Mathews (New York: Norton, 1991), 242.

71. Sand, "International Cooperation," 245.

72. Jacqueline Vaughn Switzer, *Environmental Politics: Domestic and Global Dimensions*, 4th ed. (Belmont CA: Thomson/Wadsworth, 2004), 296.

73. Richard Elliot Benedick, "Protecting the Ozone Layer: New Directions in Diplomacy," in *Preserving the Global Environment: The Challenge of Shared Leadership*, edited by Jessica Tuchman Mathews (New York: Norton, 1991), 113–153, esp. 143–149.

74. Clive Ponting, *A Green History of the World* (New York: Penguin, 1991), 387–388.

75. See "International Panel on Climate Change, Summary for Policy Makers" at http://www.ipcc.ch/pub/un/syreng/spm.pdf (accessed 15 October 2005). See also Michele Betsill, "Global Climate Change Policy: Making Progress in Spinning Wheels?" in *The Global Environment: Institutions, Law, and Policy*, edited by Regina Axelrod, David Downie, and Norman Vig (Washington, DC: CQ Press, 2005), 103.

76. William Stevens, "Study of Ocean Currents Offers Clues to Global Climate Shifts," *New York Times*, 18 March 1997 (http://www.nytimes.com).

77. Svante Arrhenius, *Worlds in the Making* (New York: Harper, 1908), cited in Matthew Paterson, *Global Warming and Global Politics* (New York: Routledge, 1996), 19–20.

78. Roger Revelle and Hans Suess, "Carbon Dioxide exchange between atmosphere and ocean, and the question of an increase in atmospheric CO_2 during the past decade," *Tellus* 9 (1957): 18–27, cited in Matthew Paterson, *Global Warming and Global Politics* (New York: Routledge, 1996), 22.

79. *General Assembly Resolution on Protection of the Global Climate for Present and Future Generations of Mankind*, A/Res/44/207.

80. Ian Rowlands, *The Politics of Global Atmospheric Change* (Manchester, UK: Manchester University Press, 1995), 79.

81. The first conference was held in Geneva in 1979.

82. Unless otherwise noted, this discussion is from Paterson, *Global Warming and Global Politics*, 78–110.

AFTERWORD

This book was written to explain the history of environmental law, the process by which our laws are made and amended, the role of the agencies in implementing the laws, and the role of the courts in interpreting them. Environmental managers who read this book already have a thorough knowledge of their own policy areas, but it is educational and perhaps comforting to realize that environmental managers in all agencies and in all levels of government face similar issues. Whether those managers are administering a Forest Service timber sale or supervising the cleanup of a Superfund site, their jobs are embedded in a legal and political context that they must understand if they are to perform their jobs well. The purpose of this book has been to help managers understand that context.

Members of the environmental movement of the 1960s took Bob Dylan's anthem to heart: "For the times they are a-changin'!" However, they would have been better served by reading French novelist Alphonse Karr, who wrote in 1849 that "the more things change, the more they are the same" (*plus ça change, plus c'est la même chose*). What environmentalists failed to realize is that issues may change fairly rapidly, but institutions such as governments and markets evolve at a glacial pace. They confused short-term resolution of issues with long-term institutional reform. The institutional structure within which the environmental movement works has not changed much over the last fifty years—a few new agencies, a few new laws—and the forces that control that institutional structure remain. They have simply shifted emphases.

In 1901, with the help of President Theodore Roosevelt (a Republican, but one with a proconservation bent nurtured by his own love of outdoors adventure), the fledgling environmental movement briefly embraced both conservation and preservation. By 1920, the two had split as John Muir clashed with Gifford Pinchot over the Hetch Hetchy Valley, a part of Yosemite National Park that was ultimately flooded to provide water for San Francisco. Pinchot was the scion of a northeastern timber family, trained in German forestry methods and tempered in France's highly bureaucratic forestry system. He was wealthy and ambitious, and his utilitarian view of America's natural resources was irreconcilable with Muir's almost religious fervor for unspoilt wilderness. The two factions—conservation versus preservation—have never achieved more than an uneasy truce, and the underlying philosophical dispute—moral values versus economic rationality—is still the basis of much of the political discord in the field today.

By the late 1950s, environmentalists were adding pollution and regulation of toxic and hazardous materials to their concerns (see chapter 5). Even these issues had overtones of the conservation-preservation split. In 1964, Rachel Carson began *Silent Spring* with the story of nature dying; the chemical industry countered with the economic utility of simple and cheap pest control. The naive slogan "think globally, act locally" failed to notice the proliferation of new technology, industrialization and urbanization, the growing influence of global markets, the new European Community (who guessed that as the European Union they would be contemplating a constitution by the end of the century?), gentle integration of China into the world community, and the maturing economies of India and Brazil. Despite the oil shortage of the mid-1970s, the larger environmental community did not realize the importance of Middle East politics; they knew it was a factor, but their hands were full with domestic disputes. "Maybe later," they thought, but of course the time to begin planning was not *later*, but *now*.

While the environmentalists were protecting wildlife, creating wilderness reserves, and regulating chemicals, public attitudes about the environment were changing. The environmental movement successfully infiltrated national political and educational institutions, but by becoming mainstream, they lost the shock value and media access of the early days. As new issues were brought up, the public somehow assumed the old ones had been solved, perhaps because most Americans confuse passage of a law with its successful implementation, or else the public had become complacent because of visible improvements, such as reduced lead or safer drinking water. By 2000, public support was tempered even further by economic considerations. Conservation is relatively cheap; federal costs are substantial, but they are primarily used for maintenance. However, environmental regulation is expensive, both in government outlay and in costs to business and industry, and the costs are increasing sharply. Solutions, if there are any, are complicated by uncertain and perhaps tainted scientific information, the lack of international cooperation, and global market forces.

The work of environmental managers is more complex than ever before. In the first two editions of this book, I stressed the importance of knowing institutional history, current law, and cultural norms as well as balancing the demands of political superiors with the demands of agency constituents and learning general principles of public administration. These are still important, but they are not enough. In the coming century, environmental managers will confront some of the most pressing and vital problems that have ever faced society. Two of the most important questions for environmental managers to ask regularly are *why*? and *what if*?[1]

While this book was being written, in late August of 2005 Hurricane Katrina hit the Gulf states, imposing a staggering toll on the natural world. It was a shocking illustration of the price paid for destroyed wetlands and unwise siting of dangerous industrial complexes. If no one asks *why* New Orleans was so devastated, then no one will be looking for useful policy changes as the city is rebuilt. If some had asked *what if*? the destruction and misery caused by Katrina might have been less.

It is difficult to be generally optimistic about the current state of the world. Small successes abound, but the specter of climate change looms over everything. As the Arctic ice floes break up earlier and faster, polar bears caught too far out drown as they attempt to swim to safety. The Gulf Stream is altering its course. Newly industrialized nations are adding damaging emissions; even if they were using the best available technology (and they are not), the extent of the new industrial processes means more air and water pollution. In the United States, government scientists are resigning because of inappropriate political interference with their work. If Shellenberger and Nordhaus are correct (see the end of chapter 2), a new intellectual framework is necessary to confront the serious global challenges. Our roles as citizens give us opportunities to influence decisions on the grand scale. However, our roles as environmental managers are usually more mundane. We are making site visits to wetlands or writing comprehensive land use plans for cities. We are monitoring commercial salmon pens in the Pacific Northwest or helping the Cree Nation in Quebec with mine contamination.

To do well, we need to understand what underlies the current situation and how our actions will affect it. It is especially critical that managers learn to exercise their administrative discretion appropriately.[2] At the federal level, environmental managers may be caught between their obligations to meet statutory mandates and the goals of their political superiors. The solution may lie with influential advocacy groups or a strategically placed lawsuit. At the state or local level, the courts are not used as readily, and external pressures can be more subtle.[3]

To be successful, environmental managers must take the long view, looking back at the processes and events that have shaped Earth's environment to its present condition and predicting how these processes will shape and be shaped by events still unknown. Taking the long view helps managers see the cyclical nature of politics and public opinion. If times are hard for environmental managers now, the odds are they have been better in the past and will be better again in the future. The managers' responsibility is to be so well informed that they can encourage and support progress as it occurs.

Despite the sometimes grim tone of this afterword, I am hopeful for the future. Colleges and universities are full of bright people interested in environmental issues; they are found not only in the environment-related disciplines, such as agriculture, biology, geography, and environmental science/studies, but also in economics (!), business, architecture, and political science. Advancements in technology have made "green" buildings profitable; recycling is becoming a corporate norm;[4] organic foods are now competitive; most of the world is committed to mitigating the causes of climate change. Environmental management is both a challenge and an opportunity: environmental managers are placed so that, if they are clever and conscientious, they can change the world—or their part of it—for the better. Few of us are so fortunate.

NOTES

1. One of the most useful books I have ever read is Richard Neustadt and Earnest May, *Thinking in Time* (New York: Free Press, 1986). The subject matter is American foreign policy, but the analytic techniques in the book are as applicable to environmental policy. If you decide to read it, go all the way to the end, where you will find a summary of the techniques in an appendix.

2. If you are interested in learning how public managers can think through ethical performance of their administrative responsibilities, read John Rohr, *Ethics for Bureaucrats*, 2nd ed. (New York: Marcel Dekker, 1989). Rohr's thesis is that public

employees take an oath to uphold the Constitution and that the fundamental ethical norms embedded in the Constitution can be used to guide ethical bureaucratic decisions.

3. I know of one case in which a city's parks and recreation department received an unexpected budget cut. The department promptly reduced one citywide program that was especially popular in minority neighborhoods. Within two weeks, their budget was fully restored.

4. For example, Hewlett-Packard encloses a postage-paid recycling envelope with every ink cartridge.

FINDING CASE LAW*

After reading this book, you surely have a more comprehensive view of how environmental law is developed and administered. There are hundreds of court cases that deal with environmental issues. While those mentioned in this book are certainly important, they may not have a direct impact on your own area of environmental policy. So how do you find the cases that will allow you to understand what must be done to meet the guidelines of federal and state government regulations? What is a case citation? What does it mean? Are there different sources for state and federal court cases? This essay provides a beginner's guide to finding case law.

To find a case, you must first know how to read a case citation. For example, a typical *U.S. Reports* citation would look like this: 504 U.S. 555 (1992); this case is *Lujan v. Defenders of Wildlife.* Case citations consist of volume numbers (504), a court reporter reference (U.S., which is *United States Reports*), page number (555), and year of the opinion (1992). To find the case you would locate *U.S. Reports* in the library, find volume 504 (printed on the spine of the book), and turn to page 555. This will be the first page of the case you are researching. All citations are read like this; a list of the more common reporters and their abbreviations is found in Table A.1. Cases may be reported in several reporters; for example, United States Supreme Court cases are found in *U.S. Reports* (official), *Supreme Court Reporter*, and the annotated *United States Supreme Court Reports, Lawyers' Edition.*

There are several ways to find case law. The easiest, at least to those who are fond of computers, is to use the two online legal research services, Westlaw

---

*This material was substantially revised and updated by Marian Kshetrapal, JD, MLIS; the original material used in the second edition was prepared by John Ehmig.

Table A.1: Citation examples

U. S. Reports	452 U.S. 490 (1981)
U. S. Supreme Court Reports, Lawyers' Edition	87 L. Ed. 626 (1943)
U. S. Supreme Court Reports, Lawyers' Edition 2d	82 L. Ed. 2d 221 (1984)*
Supreme Court Reporter	115 S. Ct. 714 (1995)
Federal Cases	19 F. Cas. 1348 (1819)
Federal Reporter	221 Fed. 288 (1915) or 226 F. 137 (1920)
Federal Reporter, Second Series	449 F. 2d 1109 (1960)
Federal Supplement	100 F. Supp. 140 (1965)

*The "second series" or "2d." designation has no legal significance. It just indicates a new series of volume numbers.

and LexisNexis. Both of these services offer full-text coverage of all Supreme Court cases dating back to 1790 and other federal cases found in the earliest volumes of *Federal Cases* (___ F. Cas. ___). Both Westlaw and LexisNexis make the opinions available as soon as they are released by the courts and make any necessary typographical changes, headnotes, or references when the case is ready to be published in print. A case can be searched by any of its citations, by title, or even by subject matter. The major drawbacks to using Westlaw and LexisNexis are, of course, cost and availability. Online access is restricted to institutions and individuals who have paid a significant annual fee, and cost for each session depends on the number of searches.

Another computer-based source of cases, especially useful for U.S. Supreme Court cases, is the Internet. Cases may be located through one of several free websites that have the seal of approval throughout the legal community and academia. These websites are updated frequently, and they provide convenient access to the full text of federal and state case law. It is important to include a word of caution, however. While case opinions obtained from websites are generally created verbatim from print versions of cases, the print versions always control when there are differences between the print and electronic copies.

The first site, Findlaw, is maintained by Thomson—the same company that produces the fee-based site Westlaw mentioned above. Through the "Federal and State Cases" section of the site, users can search all of the federal court case law, including Supreme Court, United States Court of Appeals, and district court decisions. Unfortunately, as of 2005, the site only contains apellate court case law from the last six to eleven years, depending on which court heard the case. The 8th Circuit opinions, for

Table A.2: Internet addresses

Findlaw	http://www.findlaw.com
WashLaw	http://www.washlaw.edu
Legal Information Institute	http://www.law.cornell.edu/lii.html

example, are only available from 1995 through the current year. All U.S. Supreme Court Cases are available. Opinions are searchable by date, party names, docket number, case citation, and/or keyword. Searching capabilities vary by court system.

The second site, WashLaw, is a product of the staff at Washburn School of Law Library. This site differs from Findlaw in that it does not provide access to the full text of court opinions but instead contains links to outside sites where the full text may be found. Most links are to official court-sponsored websites, but there are links to nonofficial sites such as the Legal Information Institute (LII) of Cornell University School of Law's site. LII provides access to U.S. Supreme Court decisions from 1990 through the present and to over 600 historic cases decided prior to 1990 that are searchable by keyword.

For those who are neither computer oriented nor have access to online services, there are still several ways to find case law using a case citation. The first place to look to find a United States Supreme Court case is in the official reporter of the Supreme Court, the *United States Reports* (___ U.S. ___). *United States Reports* is updated with several new volumes every year; unfortunately advance sheets and volumes appear in print very slowly. Bound versions of Court opinions appear nearly three years after the opinion is issued. Because of the lag between the decision and its publication, several commercial publishers produce unofficial reports that come out much more quickly. *U.S. Law Week*, as its name implies, is the most current. West Publishing Company, which also produces the Westlaw computerized service, publishes several unofficial reporters. It publishes the *Supreme Court Reporter* (___ S. Ct. ___), which includes a synopsis of the case and also contains a table of words and phrases to allow you to find a case without knowing a specific case citation or name. A similar reporter that also contains detailed annotations especially useful to lawyers is the *United States Supreme Court Reports, Lawyers' Edition* (___ L. Ed. ___ or ___ L. Ed. 2d ___), published by the Lawyers Co-operative Publishing Company. These reporters allow lawyers and other interested researchers to have access to decisions in a matter of weeks instead of years.

For federal cases that have not reached the Supreme Court, there are the *Federal Reports* (___ Fed. ___ and, after 1924, ___ F. 2d ___) and the *Federal Supplement* (___ F. Supp.___). The *Federal Reports* cover selected cases from the U.S. Courts of Appeals, and the *Supplement* covers selected cases from the U.S. District Courts.

State court decisions also have official and unofficial reporters. Like the federal system, most of the official reports are published extremely slowly. Therefore, most researchers rely on the unofficial reports. Westlaw and LexisNexis both contain state court decisions and are excellent sources, if you have access to them. Published reporters include West's National Report System for state court systems, which now has seven reports published according to geographic regions. Some states are large enough to have their own supplements to the regions court reports.

These are some of the best sources for case law in the United States, on both the state and the federal level. More information is available electronically each day as Internet access becomes more prevalent in homes, businesses, and libraries. The printed copies of case reports are still accessible in most public or university libraries and can also be found in many courthouse law libraries. To make sure that a case is a current statement of the law and that it has not been overturned by another case, ask a law librarian for assistance in finding the case's more recent history. Enjoy the search and good luck!

ADDITIONAL READING

Berring, Robert, and Elizabeth Edinger. *Finding the Law.* 12th ed. St. Paul, MN: West Publishing Company, 2005.

Sloan, Amy. *Basic Legal Research: Tools and Strategies.* 2nd ed. Gaithersburg, MD: Aspen Publishers, 2003.

GLOSSARY

acid deposition. Droplets of sulfuric acid and nitric acid dissolved in rain, snow, or other forms of precipitation. Formed when sulfur dioxide and nitrogen oxide combine with water vapor.

acid rain. See *acid deposition.*

action forcing. Characteristic of environmental legislation that requires agencies and businesses to take positive action rather than simply to avoid harmful actions.

administrative law judge (ALJ). Hearing examiners established in the federal system under the Administrative Procedure Act who are specialists in their substantive fields and who conduct administrative hearings. They are protected under the civil service system but lack the extensive constitutional protections of Article III judges. Many state agencies also employ ALJs.

agenda. Issues that have been identified as meriting public attention. The *systemic agenda* consists of all items perceived by the general public as meriting attention and within governmental authority. The *institutional agenda* consists of items up for the active consideration of political decisionmakers.

alienation. The transfer of property from one owner to another.

ancient lights. The doctrine that, if a building's windows have existed for at least twenty years, the light going into those windows may not be blocked.

Article I Court. An administrative court established by the executive branch of the federal government, which is itself established by Article I of the Constitution. Examples are Tax courts and Admiralty courts.

Article III Court. A judicial court established under the Judiciary Article (Article III) of the Constitution. The Supreme Court of the United States is an Article III court.

attention group. Citizens who are concerned about specific issues but are not concerned about public issues in general. This is the first level of public to which an issue is expanded.

attentive public. Citizens who are generally informed and interested in public issues of all sorts; this is the second group to which an issue is expanded after it reaches an attention group.

beneficent degradation. The economically desirable level of pollution in a body of water.

Best Practicable Environmental Option. In British environmental policy, the notion that regulatory authorities should select the option for disposal of pollution that provides the least harm, given present scientific, technical, practical, economic, and geographic factors.

Best Practicable Means. In British environmental policy, the concept that pollution control must employ the most efficient and reasonable technology currently available, subject to scientific, technical, and economic considerations.

biosphere. The notion that the entire planet is ecologically interrelated.

black letter law. Written law, found in constitutions, statutes, administrative regulations, executive orders, treaties, and appellate court decisions. Also, a term referring to a legal principle that is firmly established and is unlikely to face successful challenge.

brief. (1) A law school brief is a short (usually one page) summary of the key facts and legal holdings of a case; (2) a lawyer's brief is a lengthy (often 50 pages) legal memorandum filed with a court to support a motion made by the attorney to the judge.

bubble policy. Concept under the Clean Air Act that sets air quality standards for an imaginary enclosed area or "bubble" within which area industrial plants may adjust emission levels as long as the overall air quality within the bubble does not deteriorate. See *emissions offset policy.*

captured agency. An agency that identifies so closely with the interests of the industries it regulates that it forgets its responsibilities to society.

cetacean. Animal belonging to the order Cetacea, which includes fishlike aquatic mammals such as the whale and porpoise.

Chevron doctrine. Based on *Chevron v. Natural Resources Defense Council* (1984), this doctrine affirms the use of agency discretion when the intent of Congress is not clear and the agency action is reasonable.

circumstantial reactors. Initiators who take advantage of unanticipated events or "trigger events" to create or to magnify issues.

civil law. A legal system in which decisions are based on statutes rather than on previous cases (common law system). Also called *continental law.*

coming to the nuisance. Building or developing property near a previously existing nuisance.

common law. A legal system relying on custom and on the development of precedent derived from court decisions. Contrast with *civil law.*

commons. Resource domains in which *common pool resources* are found, such as oceans.

common pool resources. Subtractable resources managed under a property regime in which a legally defined user pool cannot be efficiently excluded from the *resource domain*.

competitive regulatory policy. Public policy that limits the right to provide specific goods and services to a few companies chosen from a group of competitors; the selected companies are then regulated; for example, the allocation of routes to the airline industry, prior to deregulation.

concurring opinion. A written judicial opinion that agrees with the decision of the majority but presents different reasoning.

Congressional Record. The daily publication of the U.S. Congress that carries the official account of congressional proceedings.

continental law. See *civil law*.

covenant. A restriction that appears in the deed or title document on the uses of real property to which owners agree as a condition of ownership; for example, banning children from a retirement community.

convention. A binding written agreement between two or more nations. Conventions may also be called *treaties* or *protocols*, although protocols are usually additions to existing treaties.

discretion. The power of administrators acting in a ministerial capacity to make substantive or procedural decisions they deem advisable as long as they do not act in an arbitrary or capricious manner.

dissenting opinion. A written judicial opinion that disagrees in whole or in part with the decision of the majority.

distributive policy. Public policy that supports private activities beneficial to society as a whole, but that would not usually be undertaken by the private sector; for example, grazing subsidies.

do-gooders. In the context of the public policy process, initiators who use events to publicize issues but who gain no personal benefit.

due process. The constitutional obligation of government to follow existing rules, principles, and procedures established in the law when taking action to deprive any persons of "life, liberty, or property."

due process explosion. A marked increase in the judicial demands for the extension of due process protections for entitlements as well as property, signaled by the U.S. Supreme Court's decision in *Goldberg v. Kelly* (1970).

easement. The right to make limited use of another's property, such as a right-of-way.

eminent domain. The right of the sovereign or state to take private property for public purposes. The Fifth and Fourteenth amendments to the U.S.

Constitution provide that citizens are entitled to just compensation when eminent domain is exercised by the national or state governments.

emissions offset policy. A policy under the Clean Air Act that allows a new firm to enter an area and to pollute to a predetermined degree if an established firm will agree to reduce its emissions by the same amount. See *bubble policy*.

endangered species. Any species in danger of extinction throughout all or a significant portion of its range, other than a pest that poses an overwhelming and overriding risk to humans. See *threatened species*.

environmental impact statement (EIS). Under the National Environmental Policy Act, a formal evaluation of any proposed, major, federal project and its alternatives, including a "no action" alternative, in terms of its potential impact on the natural and human environment.

evaluation. Comparing the desired outcomes of a policy with the actual outcomes. *Formative evaluation* occurs while the policy is being formulated and implemented and allows for midcourse corrections. *Summative evaluation* is used when a program is completed and measures how closely the goals of a program were achieved.

executive order. Formal presidential directive with the force of law.

exploiters. In the context of the public policy process, initiators who manufacture issues for their own gain.

Federal Register. Government publication that prints presidential proclamations, reorganization plans, executive orders, notices of proposed and final rules and regulations, and administrative orders.

federalism. A form of government in which power is shared between the central government and relatively autonomous constituent governments. The United States and Canada are examples of federal systems.

global commons. Resource domains to which all nations have legal access, such as the atmosphere or outer space. See *international commons*.

groundwater. Water that percolates through the soil and is often stored in aquifers. It is the source for wells and springs.

hearing examiner. See *administrative law judge*.

identification group. The narrowest kind of public, consisting of people with a detailed awareness of specific issues.

initiators. People who use situations to place issues on the agenda.

international commons. Resource domains shared by several nations, such as the Mediterranean Sea and Antarctica. See *global commons*.

iron triangle. See *subgovernment*.

judicial review. The power of a court to determine the legality and constitutionality of an action of a government official, agency, or legislative body.

legislative history. The formal record of all legislative hearings, testimonies, debates, committee reports, and votes preceding the enactment of a statute.

mass public. The general public; the portion of the population that is less active, less interested, and less informed than the other, smaller group publics. The last group to which an issue is expanded.

natural oil seepage. Oil that rises to the surface of the ocean floor without any human disturbance such as drilling.

non-attainment region. Under the Clean Air Act, regions that have not achieved primary ambient air-quality standards by a deadline set forth in the statute. Such regions face potential restrictions on new pollution discharges.

nonpoint source pollution. Pollution without readily identified egress points, such as agricultural runoff.

nuisance. An action that unreasonably impairs the legal property rights of another. *Private nuisance* is the unreasonable interference with the use or enjoyment of another's land. A *public nuisance* is an activity that adversely affects the health, morals, safety, welfare, comfort, or convenience of the public in general.

outer continental shelf (OCS). The submerged and relatively accessible land adjacent to the coastline. The federal government claims jurisdiction from the three-mile state territorial limit to an outer ten-mile limit.

ozone layer. Layer of gaseous ozone in the upper atmosphere that protects living organisms by filtering ultraviolet radiation.

pelagic. Occurring in open oceans or seas rather than inland waters or adjacent to coastal lands.

pinnipedia. Animal belonging to the order Pinnipedia; aquatic mammals including seals, walruses, and similar animals having finlike flippers as organs of locomotion.

point source pollution. Pollution with a readily isolated egress point such as a sewer treatment plant or an oil tanker.

police power. The power of the government to protect public health, safety, and welfare. In the American federal system, this power is reserved to the states.

polluter pays. The concept that whoever generated the pollution must bear the costs of removing the pollution and remedying its bad effects.

pollution rights. Legal permission to discharge a given amount of pollution. These rights may be transferred.

precautionary principle. A policy-decision rule stating that actions should not be taken without a full understanding of the possible consequences. "Better safe than sorry."

precedent. A legal judgment stated in the resolution of a case that is used as a standard in subsequent, similar cases.

primary air pollutants. Air pollutants, such as carbon monoxide, that are harmful as soon as they enter the atmosphere.

procedural due process. The forms and procedures followed by government when exercising its legitimate functions.

property. Any *tangible* item to which the owner has an enforceable right of use, or *intangible* right to which the owner has legal title; the removal of either kind of property by government requires due process.

protective regulatory policy. Public policy that regulates the conditions under which private activities may occur, such as setting emission standards for coal-fired plants.

protocol. A binding written agreement between two or more nations, usually an addition to an existing treaty and often specifying technical standards for the treaty. Protocols must be ratified separately. They may also be called *treaties* or *conventions*.

public trust doctrine. The common law concept that the tidelands, the navigable waters, and the wildlife found in them are held by the sovereign in trust for the people.

ratcheting. The practice of administrative regulatory agencies repeatedly increasing pollution control standards imposed on industries that have already spent resources to comply with earlier standards. This increases compliance costs and frustrates cooperative industries.

readjustors. Policy initiators who perceive a real imbalance or inequity and strive to correct it.

redistributive policy. Public policy that changes the allocation of valued goods and services, such as money, property, or rights, among different groups; an example is affirmative action.

resource domain. The fixed spatial dimension in which resources are found; for example, tuna (*resource*) are found in the oceans (*resource domain*).

rule. Agency statement of general or particular applicability and future effect designed to implement, interpret, or prescribe law or policy. *Substantive rules* implement or prescribe law or policy, for example, safety requirements for nuclear power plants. *Procedural rules* describe the organization, procedure, or practice requirements of an agency, for example, defining who may intervene in an agency adjudication. *Interpretive rules* are statements issued by agencies that present the agency's understanding of the meaning of the language in its regulations or the statutes it administers.

rulemaking. The process of promulgating rules. *Informal rulemaking* follows Section 553 of the Administrative Procedure Act and requires notice and comment. *Formal rulemaking* follows sections 556 and 557 of APA and requires a full administrative hearing. *Hybrid rulemaking* combines informal and formal rulemaking; its key requirement is the creation of a formal record. *Negotiated rulemaking* brings stakeholders into the rulemaking process before the proposed rule is formulated.

Sagebrush Rebellion. A movement in the early 1980s by some western states to regain control of the federal lands within their boundaries.

scope of review. The extent to which a court examines questions of law, interprets constitutional and statutory provisions, and determines the meaning or applicability of the terms of an agency action.

secondary air pollutants. Pollutants formed from the chemical reaction of several air components, such as *acid deposition*.

snail darter. A species of minnow declared endangered in 1975, halting the construction of the Tellico Dam in Tennessee.

spatial-extension resources. Resources that have value because of their location, such as geostationary orbits or Antarctic research stations.

standing. The legal right of a party to have a case heard; defined in common law as having suffered an actual injury in fact to a legally protected right.

state ownership doctrine. In American wildlife law, wildlife found within a state's borders are the property of the state rather than of the individual on whose property the wildlife is found. This doctrine was substantially modified in the twentieth century.

subgovernment. A coalition of interest groups, relevant agencies in the executive branch, and the appropriate congressional committee or subcommittee that is concerned with a given policy area. Also known as *iron triangles*.

substantial evidence. The amount of evidence—more than a mere token, but less than a preponderance, which would outweigh the evidence presented by opposition—that an agency must present to a reviewing judge or *ALJ* to justify its decisions.

substantive due process. The constitutional doctrine that all government action must be fair and reasonable and must fall within a sphere of activity that is a legitimate government concern.

sunk costs. Resources expended on a project prior to completion that could not be recovered if the project were abandoned.

surface water. Water that does not penetrate the ground or return to the atmosphere, for example, lakes, ponds, many rivers and streams, and wetlands.

technology forcing. Legislation that requires businesses to develop new technology in order to meet statutory and regulatory standards on pollution control.

threatened species. Any species likely to become endangered within the foreseeable future throughout all or a significant portion of its range. See *endangered species*.

tort. A private or civil wrong or injury for which the injured party is entitled to damages.

treaty. A binding written agreement between two or more nations. Treaties may also be called *conventions* or *protocols*, although protocols are usually additions to existing treaties.

trigger event. An unexpected occurrence that provides an opportunity for an issue to be expanded to larger publics.

waste. Acts committed upon the land that are harmful to the rights of the party not in possession, such as a tenant cutting down all of a landlord's trees without permission.

zoning. Dividing a community into districts, which are then subject to regulation concerning permissible uses and types or sizes of buildings.

ACRONYMS

ABA	American Bar Association
AOSIS	Alliance of Small Island States
ANWR	Arctic National Wildlife Refuge
APA	Administrative Procedure Act
ASPA	American Society for Public Administration
BAT	Best Available Technology
BLM	Bureau of Land Management
BMP	Best Management Practices
BNA	Bureau of National Affairs
BPEO	Best Practicable Environmental Option
BPM	Best Practicable Means
CAA	Clean Air Act
CAFO	Concentrated Animal Feeding Operation
CCAMLR	Convention on the Conservation of Antarctic Marine Living Resources (Southern Ocean Convention)
CEQ	Council on Environmental Quality
CERCLA	Comprehensive Environmental Recovery, Compensation, and Liability Act
CFC	chlorofluorocarbon
CITEJA	International Technical Committee for Aerial Legal Experts
CITES	Convention on International Trade in Endangered Species of Wild Fauna and Flora
CWA	Clean Water Act
DEQ	Department of Environmental Quality
EC	European Community (see EEC and EU)
EEC	European Economic Community (see EC and EU)
EEZ	Exclusive Economic Zone
EIS	Environmental Impact Statement
EPA	Environmental Protection Agency

EPCRA	Emergency Planning and Community Right to Know Act (see SARA)
ESA	Endangered Species Act
EU	European Union (see EC and EEC)
FAO	Food and Agricultural Organization (United Nations)
FCC	Federal Communications Commission
FDA	Food and Drug Administration
FIFRA	Federal Insecticide, Fungicide, and Rodenticide Act
FLPMA	Federal Land Policy and Management Act
FONSI	Finding of No Significant Impact (NEPA)
FTC	Federal Trade Commission
FWPCA	Federal Water Pollution Control Act
FWS	U.S. Fish and Wildlife Service
GATT	General Agreement on Tariffs and Trade
GAO	Government Accounting Office
GEF	Global Environment Facility (World Bank)
GOO	Get Oil Out
GPO	Government Printing Office
HCP	Habitat Conservation Plan
HUD	Housing and Urban Development, Department of
ICC	Interstate Commerce Commission
IPCC	Intergovernmental Panel on Climate Change
ISA	International Seabed Authority
IUCN	International Union for Conservation of Nature and Natural Resources
IWC	International Whaling Commission
LOS	Law of the Sea
LULU	Locally Undesirable Land Use
LUST	Leaking Underground Storage Tank
MARPOL	International Convention for the Prevention of Pollution by Ships
MMPA	Marine Mammal Protection Act
NAAQS	National Ambient Air Quality Standards
NASA	National Aeronautics and Space Administration
NCP	National Contingency Plan
NEPA	National Environmental Policy Act
NGO	Nongovernmental Organization
NLDC	New London Development Corporation
NMFS	National Marine Fisheries Service (now NOAA, Fisheries)
NOAA	National Oceanic and Atmospheric Administration

NOAA, Fisheries	National Oceanic and Atmospheric Administration, Fisheries (formerly NMFS)
NPL	National Priority List (Superfund)
NPS	National Park Service
OECD	Organization for Economic Cooperation and Development
OCS	Outer Continental Shelf
OMB	Office of Management and Budget
OPEC	Organization of Petroleum Exporting Countries
OSHA	Occupational Safety and Health Administration
OTA	Office of Technology Assessment
PCB	polychlorinated biphenyl
PSD	Prevention of Significant Deterioration
PRP	Potentially Responsible Parties
RARG	Regulatory Analysis and Review Group
RCRA	Resource Conservation and Recovery Act
RPA	Forest Rangeland Renewable Resource Act
RPOA	Recognized Private Operating Agency
SARA	Superfund Amendment and Reauthorization Act
SCRAP	Students Challenging Regulatory Agency Procedures
SDWA	Safe Drinking Water Act
SEA	Single European Act
SIP	State Implementation Plan
SPM	Suspended Particulate Matter
TMI	Three Mile Island
TSCA	Toxic Substances Control Act
TVA	Tennessee Valley Authority
UNCED	United Nations Conference on the Environment (1992)
UNEP	United Nations Environmental Programme
UNESCO	United Nations Educational, Scientific, and Cultural Organization
UNCLOS	United Nations Conference on the Law of the Sea (I, 1958; II, 1960; III, 1973–1982)
USDA	United States Department of Agriculture
USGS	United States Geological Survey
UST	Underground Storage Tank
WQBEL	Water Quality-Based Effluent Standards

LIST OF CASES

American Banana Co. v. United States Fruit Co., 213 U.S. 347 (1909).

American Cetacean Society v. Baldridge, 768 D.C. Cir. 426, 604 F. Supp. 1398 (1985).

American Textile Manufacturers Institute et al. v. Donovan, Secretary of Labor, et al., 452 U.S. 490 (1981).

Association of Data Processing Service Organizations v. Camp, 397 U.S. 150 (1970).

Babbitt v. Sweet Home Chapter of Communities for a Greater Oregon, 515 U.S. 687 (1995).

Baldwin v. Montana Fish and Game Commission, 436 U.S. 371 (1978).

Berman v. Parker, 348 U.S. 26 (1954).

Bi-Metallic Investment Co. v. State Board of Equalization, 239 U.S. 441 (1915).

Bivens v. Six Unknown, Named Agents of the Federal Bureau of Narcotics, 403 U.S. 388 (1971).

Board of Regents v. Roth, 408 U.S. 564 (1972).

Boomer v. Atlantic Cement Co., 26 N.Y. 219 (1970).

Boyce Motor Lines v. United States, 342 U.S. 337 (1952).

Calvert Cliffs Coordinating Committee, Inc. v. United States Atomic Energy Commission, 449 F. 2d 1109, 146 U.S. App. D.C. 33 (1971).

Chatham Steel Corp. v. Sapp, 858 F. Supp. 1130 (1994).

Chevron U.S.A., Inc. v. Natural Resources Defense Council, 467 U.S. 837 (1984).

Ciba-Geigy Corp. v. United States Environmental Protection Agency, 874 F. 2d 277 (1989).

City of Milwaukee v. State, 193 Wis. 423, 214 N.W. 820 (1927).

Concerned Area Residents for the Environment v. Southview Farm, 34 F. 3d 114 (1994).

Commonwealth [PA] v. Koczwara, 155 A. 2d 825 (1959).

Dalehite v. United States, 346 U.S. 15 (1953).

Dolan v. City of Tigard, 114 S. Ct. 2309 (1994).

Donovan v. Dewey, 452 U.S. 594 (1981).

Dooley v. Town Plan and Zoning Commission of Fairfield, 151 Conn. 304, 197 A. 2d 770 (1964).

Douglas v. Seacoast Products, 431 U.S. 265 (1977).

Dow Chemical Co. v. United States, 476 U.S. 227 (1986).

Dred Scott v. Sandford, 60 U.S. (19 How.) 393 (1857).

Duke Power Company v. Carolina Environmental Study Group, Inc., 438 U.S. 59 (1978).

Earth Island Institute v. Mosbacher, 929 F. 2d 1449 (1991).

Environmental Defense Fund v. Massey, 986 F. 2d 528 (1993).

Equal Employment Opportunity Commission v. Arabian American Oil Co., 229 U.S. 244 (1991).

Euclid v. Ambler Realty Co., 272 U.S. 365 (1926).

Federal Crop Insurance Corp. v. Merrill, 332 U.S. 380 (1947).

First English Evangelical Lutheran Church of Glendale v. City of Los Angeles, 487 U.S. 1211 (1987).

Flast v. Cohen, 392 U.S. 83 (1968).

Foley Bros. v. Filardo, 336 U.S. 281 (1949).

Fontainebleau Hotel Corp. v. Forty-Five Twenty-Five, Inc., 114 So. 2d 357 (1959).

Foster-Fountain Packing Co. v. Haydel, 278 U.S. 1 (1926).

Geer v. Connecticut, 161 U.S. 519 (1896).

Goldberg v. Kelly, 397 U.S. 24 (1970).

Gould v. Greylock Reservation Commission, 350 Mass. 410, 215 N.E. 2d 114 (1966).

Griswold v. Connecticut, 381 U.S. 479 (1965).

Hawaii Housing Authority v. Midkiff, 467 U.S. 229 (1984).

Hunt v. United States, 278 U.S. 96 (1928).

Illinois Central Railroad Co. v. Illinois, 146 U.S. 387 (1892).

Just v. Marinette County, 56 Wis. 2d 7, 201 N.W.2ed. 761 (1972).

Kelo et al. v. City of New London et al., 125 S. Ct. 2655 (2005).

Kleppe v. New Mexico, 426 U.S. 529 (1976).

Kyllo v. United States, 553 U.S. 27 (2001).

Lochner v. New York, 198 U.S. 45 (1905).

Londoner v. Denver, 210 U.S. 373 (1908).

Lucas v. South Carolina Coastal Council, 112 S. Ct. 2886 (1992).

Lujan v. Defenders of Wildlife, 504 U.S. 555 (1992).

Lujan v. National Wildlife Federation, 497 U.S. 871 (1990).

Lykes Bros., Inc. v. United States Army Corps of Engineers, 821 F. Supp. 1457 (M.D. Fla. 1993).

Manchester v. Massachusetts, 139 U.S. 240 (1891).

LEGISLATION

Administrative Procedure Act 1946
U.S.C. 2000 Title 5, §§ 551 et seq., 701 et seq.

Air Quality Act 1967
U.S.C. 2000 Title 42, § 7401 et seq.

Alaska National Interest Lands Conservation Act 1980
U.S.C. 2000 Title 16, § 3101 et seq. and throughout titles 16 and 43

Bald Eagle Protection Act 1940
U.S.C. 2000 Title 16, § 668 et seq.

Black Bass Act 1926 (Interstate Transportation)
U.S.C. 2000 Title 16, § 851 et seq.

Clean Air Act (amended 1970, 1990)
U.S.C. 2000 Title 42, § 7401 et seq.

Clean Water Act 1972 (amended 1977, 1987)
U.S.C. 2000 Title 33, § 1251 et seq.

Coastal Zone Management Act 1972
U.S.C. 2000 Title 16, § 1451 et seq.

Comprehensive Environmental Response, Compensation, and Liability Act 1980 [Superfund]
U.S.C. 2000 Title 26, § 4611 et seq.
U.S.C. 2000 Title 42, § 9601 et seq.

Deepwater Port Act 1974
U.S.C. 2000 Title 33, § 1501 et seq.

Duck Stamp Act 1934 [Migratory Bird Hunting Stamp Act]
U.S.C. 2000 Title 16, § 718 et seq.

Endangered Species Act 1973
U.S.C. 2000 Title 16, § 1531 et seq.

Endangered Species Conservation Act 1969
U.S.C. 2000 Title 16, § 668aa et seq.

Endangered Species Preservation Act 1966
U.S.C. 2000 Title 16, § 668aa et seq.

Federal Aid in Sport Fish Restoration (Dingell-Johnson) Act 1950
16 U.S.C. § 777 et seq.

Federal Aid in Wildlife Restoration (Pittman-Robertson) Act of 1937
16 U.S.C § 669 et seq.

Federal Environmental Pesticide Control Act 1972
U.S.C. 2000 Title 7, § 135 et seq.

Federal Insecticide, Fungicide, and Rodenticide Act 1947
U.S.C. 2000 Title 7, § 135 et seq.

Federal Land Policy and Management Act 1976
U.S.C. 1988 Title 43, § 1701 et seq.

Federal Water Pollution Control Act 1972
U.S.C. 2000 Title 33, § 1251 et seq.

Fish and Wildlife Conservation (Forsythe-Chafee or Nongame) Act of 1980
U.S.C. 2000 Title 16, § 2901 et seq.

Fish and Wildlife Coordination Act 1934
U.S.C. 2000 Title 16, §§ 661–667e

Fishery Conservation and Management Act 1976
U.S.C. 2000 Title 16, §§ 971, 1362, 1801, 1802, 1811–1813, 1821–1825, 1851–1861, 1881
U.S.C. 2000 Title 22, §§ 1972, 1973

Forest and Rangeland Renewable Resources Planning Act 1974
U.S.C. 2000 Title 16, § 1600 et seq.

Forest Reserve Act 1891
U.S.C. 2000 Title 16, § 471a et seq.

Freedom of Information Act 1966 [part of Administrative Procedure Act]
U.S.C. 2000 Title 5, § 552

Government in the Sunshine Act 1976 [part of Administrative Procedure Act]
U.S.C. 2000 Title 5, § 552b

Homestead Act 1862
U.S.C. 2000 Title 43, §§ 161 et seq., 890–892

Knutson-Vandenburg Act 1930
U.S.C. 1988 Title 16, §§ 576–576b

Lacey Act 1900 (Game)
U.S.C. 2000 Title 16, § 701

Land and Water Conservation Act 1964
U.S.C. 2000 Title 16, §§ 460d, 4601–4604 et seq.

Lea Act 1948 (Wildlife Areas)
U.S.C. 2000 Title 16, § 695 et seq.

Marine Mammal Protection Act 1972
U.S.C. 2000 Title 16, § 1361 et seq.

Marine Protection, Research, and Sanctuaries Act 1972
U.S.C. 2000 Title 33, § 1401 et seq.

Migratory Bird Act 1913
Mar. 4, 1913, c. 145, 37 Stat. 828, repealed 1918

Migratory Bird Conservation Act 1929
U.S.C. 2000 Title 16, § 715 et seq.

Migratory Bird Hunting Stamp Act 1934 [Duck Stamp Act]
U.S.C. 2000 Title 16, §§ 718–718h

Migratory Bird Treaty Act 1918
U.S.C. 2000 Title 16, §§ 703–711
U.S.C. 2000 Title 18, § 43

Multiple-Use Sustained-Yield Act 1960
U.S.C. 2000 Title 16, § 528 et seq.

National Environmental Policy Act 1969
U.S.C. 2000 Title 42, § 4321 et seq.

National Forest Management Act 1976
U.S.C. 2000 Title 16, § 1600 et seq.

National Park Service Organic Act 1916
U.S.C. 1988 Title 16, § 1 et seq.

National Wildlife Refuge System Administration Act 1966
U.S.C. 2000 Title 16, §§ 668dd–668ee

Negotiated Rulemaking Act of 1996
U.S.C. 2000 Title 5, § 581 et seq.

Outer Continental Shelf Lands Act 1953
U.S.C. 2000 Title 43, § 1331 et seq.

Park, Parkway and Recreation Area Study Act 1936
June 23, 1936, c. 735, 49 Stat. 1894

Privacy Act 1974 [part of Administrative Procedure Act]
U.S.C. 2000 Title 5, § 552a

Refuge Recreation Act 1962
U.S.C. 2000 Title 16, § 460k

Resource Conservation and Recovery Act 1976
U.S.C. 2000 Title 42, § 6901 et seq.

Resource Recovery Act 1970
U.S.C. 1970 Title 42, § 3251 et seq.

Rivers and Harbors Act 1899
U.S.C. 2000 Title 16, §§ 460d, 492
U.S.C. 2000 Title 22, § 275a
U.S.C. 1976 Title 31, § 680
U.S.C. 2000 Title 33
U.S.C. 2000 Title 48, § 1399

Safe Drinking Water Act 1974
U.S.C. 2000 Title 42, §§ 300f–300j–309

Sikes Act 1960 (conservation on military reservations)
U.S.C. 2000 Title 16, § 670a et seq.

Stock-Raising Homestead Act 1916
U.S.C. 2000 Title 43, § 291 et seq.

Submerged Lands Act 1953
U.S.C. 2000 Title 43, § 1301 et seq.

Superfund 1980 [Comprehensive Environmental Response, Compensation, and Liability Act]
U.S.C. 2000 Title 26, § 4611 et seq.
U.S.C. 2000 Title 42, § 9601 et seq.

Superfund Amendment and Reauthorization Act 1986
Oct. 17, 1986, P.L. 99–499, 100 Stat. 1613

Surplus Grain for Wildlife Act 1961
Aug. 17, 1961, P.L. 87–152, 75 Stat. 389

Swamp Land Acts 1849, 1850, 1860
U.S.C. 2000 Title 43, § 981 et seq.

Tariff Act 1930
U.S.C. 1958 Title 19, § 1001 et seq.

Taylor Act 1934 (grazing)
U.S.C. 2000 Title 43, § 315 et seq.

Toxic Substances Control Act 1976
U.S.C. 2000 Title 15, § 2601 et seq.

Waterfowl Depredations Act 1956
July 3, 1956, P.L. 654, c. 512, 70 Stat. 492

Weeks Act 1911 (protection of watersheds)
U.S.C. 2000 Title 16, §§ 480, 500, 515 to 519, 521, 552, 563

Wetlands Loan Act (waterfowl) **1961**
U.S.C. 2000 Title 16, § 715k–3 et seq.

Wild Free-Roaming Horses and Burros Act 1971
U.S.C. 2000 Title 16, § 1331

Wilderness Act 1964
U.S.C. 2000 Title 16, § 1131 et seq.

BIBLIOGRAPHY

Althaus, Helen. *Public Trust Rights*. Washington, DC: GPO, November 1978.

Arrandale, Thomas. *The Battle for Natural Resources*. Washington, DC: Congressional Quarterly, 1983.

Arrhenius, Svante. *Worlds in the Making*. New York: Harper, 1908.

Attorney General's Committee Report. *Administrative Procedure in Government Agencies*. Preface by Charles K. Woltz. Charlottesville: University Press of Virginia, 1968.

Ault, W. O. *Open-Field Farming in Medieval England*. London: Allen and Unwin, 1972.

Bayard, Louis, Ryan Cree, Barbara Elkins, Betsy Loyless, Mary Minette, and Chuck Porcari, eds. *2003 National Environmental Scorecard*. Washington, DC: League of Women Voters, February 2004.

Bean, Michael J. *The Evolution of National Wildlife Law*. New York: Praeger, 1983.

Bean, Michael J., and Melanie Rowland. *The Evolution of National Wildlife Law*. 3rd ed. New York: Praeger, 1997.

Belanger, Dian Olson. *Managing American Wildlife: A History of the International Association of Fish and Wildlife Agencies*. Amherst: University of Massachusetts Press, 1988.

Benedick, Richard Elliot. *Ozone Diplomacy: New Directions in Safeguarding the Planet*. Cambridge, MA: Harvard University Press, 1991.

Benedick, Richard Elliot. "Protecting the Ozone Layer: New Directions in Diplomacy." In *Preserving the Global Environment: The Challenge of Shared Leadership*, edited by Jessica Tuchman Mathews, 112–153. New York: Norton, 1991.

Betsill, Michele. "Global Climate Change Policy: Making Progress in Spinning Wheels?" In *The Global Environment: Institutions, Law, and Policy*, edited by Regina Axelrod, David Downie, and Norman Vig, 103–124. Washington, DC: CQ Press, 2005.

Birnie, Patricia, and Alan Boyle. *International Law & the Environment*. 2nd ed. Oxford, UK: Clarendon Press, 2002.

Brennan, Scott, and Jay Withgott. *Environment: The Science behind the Stories*. San Francisco: Pearson/Benjamin Cummings, 2004.

British Information Services. *The London Conference on Substances that Deplete the Ozone Layer*. New York: British Consulate General, 28 June 1990.

Buck, Susan J. "Cultural Theory and Management of Common Property Resources." *Human Ecology* 17 (1989): 101–116.

Buck, Susan. "Environmental Policy in the United Kingdom." In *International Public Policy Sourcebook*. Vol. 2, *Education and Environment*, edited by Fredric Bolotin, 310–333. New York: Greenwood Press, 1989.

Buck, Susan. "Interjurisdictional Management in Chesapeake Bay Fisheries." *Coastal Management* 16 (1988): 151–166.

Buck, Susan. "No Tragedy on the Commons." *Environmental Ethics* 7 (Spring 1985): 49–61.

Buck, Susan J., and Edward Hathaway. "Designating State Natural Resource Trustees under SARA." In *Regulatory Federalism, Natural Resources and Environmental Management*, edited by Michael Hamilton, 83–94. Washington, DC: ASPA, 1990.

Bureau of Land Management. "BLM Announces First Sale of Wild Horses Under New Law." 18 March 2005. http:/www.blm.gov/nlp/news/releases/pages/2005/pr050301_whb.htm (accessed 16 September 2005).

Bureau of Land Management. "Fact Sheet in the BLM's Management of Wild Horses and Burros." 19 August 2005. http://www.blm.gov/nhp/spotlight/whb_authority/fact_sheet.htm (accessed 16 September 2005).

Bureau of National Affairs. *U.S. Environmental Laws, 1988 Edition*. Washington, DC: Bureau of National Affairs, 1988.

Caldwell, Lynton. *International Environmental Policy*. 2nd ed. Durham, NC: Duke University Press, 1990.

Carson, Rachel. *Silent Spring*. New York: Houghton Mifflin, 1962.

Chandler, William. "Federal Grants for State Wildlife Conservation." In *Audubon Wildlife Report 1986*, edited by Roger Di Silvestro, 177–212. New York: National Audubon Society, 1986.

Clawson, Marion. *The Federal Lands Revisited*. Baltimore: Johns Hopkins University Press, 1983.

Cobb, Roger, and Charles Elder. *Participation in American Politics*. Boston: Allyn and Bacon, 1972.

Cody, Betsy. "Wild Horse and Burro Management." CRS Report 97-370ENR, 19 March 1997.

Coggins, George Cameron, Charles Wilkinson, and John Leshy. *Federal Public Land and Resources Law*. 3rd ed. Westbury, NY: Foundation Press, 1993.

Cohen, Steven. "Defusing the Toxic Time Bomb: Federal Hazardous Waste Programs." In *Environmental Policies in the 1980s: Reagan's New Agenda*, edited by Norman Vig and Michael Kraft, 273–291. Washington, DC: Congressional Quarterly, 1984.

Colbern, Theo, Dianne Dumanoski, and John Myers. *Our Stolen Future*. New York: Dutton, 1996.

Colorado Journal of International Environmental Law and Policy 4 (1993): 232. "Chronological Summary: Events of 1992."

Cooper, Phillip. *Public Law and Public Administration*. 2nd ed. Englewood Cliffs, NJ: Prentice Hall, 1988.

Cooper, Phillip. *Public Law and Public Administration*. 3rd ed. Itasca, IL: Peacock, 2000.

Corkery, Michael, and Ryan Chittum. "Eminent-Domain Uproar Imperils Projects." *Wall Street Journal*, 3 August 2005, B1.

Cox, Susan Jane Buck. "No Tragedy on the Commons." *Environmental Ethics* 7 (Spring 1985): 49–61.

Curtis, Jeff, and Bob Davison. "The Endangered Species Act: Thirty Years on the Ark." *Open Spaces Quarterly* 5(3) 2005. http://www.open-spaces.com/article-v5n3-davison.php (accessed 13 March 2005).

Dales, J. H. *Pollution, Property & Prices: An Essay in Policy-Making and Economics*. Toronto: University of Toronto Press, 1968.

Daley, Beth. "On Energy and Environment, a Vast Divide." *Boston Globe*, 19 October 2004, A 20.

D'Amato, Anthony. "What 'Counts' as Law?" In *Law-Making in the Global Community*, edited by Nicholas Onuf, 83–107. Durham, NC: Carolina Academic Press, 1982.

Davis, Tony. "New Grazing Rules Ride on Doctored Science: Veteran Scientists Leave the BLM in Frustration." *High Country News*, 25 July 2005, 3.

Davis, Tony. "Rangeland Revival." *High Country News*, 5 September 2005, 6–12.

Dorst, Jean. *Before Nature Dies*. Translated by Constance D. Sherman. Preface by Prince Bernard. Boston: Houghton Mifflin, 1970.

Douglas, Mary, and Aaron Wildavsky. *Risk and Culture*. Berkeley: University of California Press, 1982.

Ducks Unlimited. "State Facts Sheet." http://www.ducks.org/StateFactSheets/Nation.pdf (accessed 23 September 2005).

Dunning, Harrison, ed. *The Public Trust Doctrine in Natural Resources Law and Management*. Davis: University of California, 1981.

Earthworks. "Gold Mine to Dump Mine Waste in Pristine Alaskan Lake." *Yubanet*, 24 June 2005. http://yubanet.com/artman/publish/printer_22140.shtml (accessed 29 July 2005).

Economist, "How Do You Mean, 'Fair'?" 29 May 1993, 71.

Edberg, Rolf. *On the Shred of a Cloud*. Translated by Sven Åhman. Montgomery, AL: University of Alabama Press, 1969.

Farnau, J. C., B. G. Gardiner, and J. D. Shanklin. "Large Losses of Total Ozone in Antarctica Reveal Seasonal ClO_x/NO_x Interaction." *Nature* 315 (1985): 207–210.

Findley, Roger, and Daniel Farber, eds. *Cases and Materials on Environmental Law*. 4th ed. St. Paul, MN: West, 1995.

Foresta, Ronald A. *America's National Parks and Their Keepers*. Baltimore: Johns Hopkins University Press, 1984.

Fox, Stephen. *The American Conservation Movement: John Muir and his Legacy*. Madison: University of Wisconsin Press, 1981.

French, Brett. "Wild Horses' Fans Fear Roundup Will Weaken Herds." billingsgazette. com, (*Billings* [Montana] *Gazette*) 20 August 2005. http://www.billingsgazette.com/index.php?id=1&display=rednews/2005/08/20/build/state/35-horses.inc (accessed 22 September 2005).

Gaba, Jeffrey M. *Environmental Law*. Black Letter Series. St. Paul, MN: West, 1994.

Garcia, S. M., and R. Grainger. FAO Fisheries Technical Paper 359 (1996). Cited in Brennan and Withgott, *Environment: The Science behind the Stories*, 407.

Global Marine Oil Pollution Information Gateway. "Sources of Oil to the Sea." http://oils.gpa.unep.org/facts/sources.htm (accessed 1 August 2005).

Goble, Dale, and Eric Freyfogle. *Wildlife Law: Cases and Materials*. New York: Foundation Press, 2002.

Goldwin, Robert A. "Common Sense vs. 'The Common Heritage.'" In *Law of the Sea: U.S. Policy Dilemma*, edited by Bernard Oxman, David Caron, and Charles Buderi, 59–75. San Francisco: ICS Press, 1983.

Gonner, E. C. K. *Common Land and Inclosure*. 2nd. ed. London: Cass, 1966.

Hamilton, Michael, ed. *Regulatory Federalism, Natural Resources and Environmental Management*. Washington, DC: ASPA, 1990.

Hardin, Garrett. "The Tragedy of the Commons." *Science* 162:1243–1248.

Harney, Kenneth. "Eminent Domain Ruling Has Strong Repercussions." *Washington Post*, 23 July 2005, F1.

Harrington, Winston. "Wildlife: Severe Decline and Partial Recovery." In *American's Renewable Resources: Historical Trends and Current Challenges*, edited by Kenneth Frederick and Roger Sedjo, 205–246. Washington, DC: Resources for the Future, 1991.

Hartwick, John, and Nancy Olewiler, *The Economics of Natural Resource Use*. New York: Harper & Row, 1986.

Hattam, Jennifer. "Highway Robbers: Make-Believe Roads Threaten Real Wilderness." *Sierra*, July/August 2003, 11.

Heclo, Hugh. "Issue Networks and the Executive Establishments." In *The New

American Political System, edited by Anthony King, 87–124. Washington, DC: American Enterprise Institute, 1978.

Heffron, Florence, and Neil McFeeley. *The Administrative Regulatory Process*. New York: Longman, 1983.

Heinzerling, Lisa. "Action Inaction: Section 1983 Liability for Failure to Act." *University of Chicago Law Review* 53 (Summer 1986): 1047–1073.

Henry, Marguerite. *Brighty of the Grand Canyon*. New York: Rand McNally, 1953.

Hewison, Grant. "Environmental Non-Governmental Organizations." In *Ocean Governance: Strategies and Approaches for the 21st Century*, edited by Thomas Mensah, 115–137. Honolulu: Law of the Sea Institute, 1996.

Hunter, David B. "An Ecological Perspective on Property: A Call for Judicial Protection of the Public's Interest in Environmentally Critical Resources." *Harvard Environmental Law Review* 12 (1988): 311–383.

International Union for Conservation of Nature and Natural Resources (IUCN). "Red List of Threatened Species, Summary Statistics, Table 1: Numbers of Threatened Species by Major Groups of Organisms (1996–2004)." http://www.redlist.org/info/tables/table1.html (accessed 25 September 2005).

Irving, Patricia, ed. *Acid Deposition: State of Science and Technology, Summary Report of the United States National Acid Precipitation Assessment Program*. Washington, DC: USGPO, September 1991. Cited in Switzer, *Environmental Politics: Domestic and Global Dimensions*.

Ise, John. *Our National Park Policy*. Baltimore: Johns Hopkins University Press, 1961.

Jachtenfuchs, Markus. "The European Community and the Protection of the Ozone Layer." *Journal of Common Market Studies* 28, no. 3 (March 1980): 263. Cited in Benedick, *Ozone Diplomacy*, 24.

Janofsky, Michael. "Pentagon is Asking Congress to Loosen Environmental Laws." *New York Times*, 11 May 2005, A 16.

Jenkins, Matt, ed. *A People's History of Wilderness*. Paonia, CO: High Country News Books, 2004.

Jenkins, Matt. "The Public Pays to Keep Water in a River." *High Country News*, 4 April 2005, 6.

Keefe, William, Henry Abraham, William Flanigan, Charles O. Jones, Morris Ogul, and John Spanier. *American Democracy: Institutions, Politics, and Policies*. Homewood, IL: Dorsey Press, 1983.

Keyworth, Jim. "Fate of 'Wild' Horses Stalls in Legal Wrangling." *Payson Roundup*, 16 September 2005. http://paysonroundup.com/section/frontpage_lead/storypr/20467 (accessed 23 September 2005).

Kingdon, John W. *Agendas, Alternatives, and Public Policies*. 2nd ed. New York: Longman, 2002.

Kipling, Rudyard. *Kim*. New York: Dell, 1959.

Kiss, Alexandre, and Dinah Shelton. *International Environmental Law*. Ardsley-on-Hudson, NY: Transnational Publishers, 1991.

Knight, Alfred. *The Life of the Law*. Oxford, UK: Oxford University Press, 1996.

Knize, Perri. "Chainsaw Environmentalism." *Backpacker*, November 1987, 55–59.

Kraft, Michael, and Norman Vig. "Environmental Policy from the 1970s to the 1990s: Continuity and Change." In *Environmental Policy in the 1990s*, 2nd ed., edited by Norman Vig and Michael Kraft, 3–29. Washington, DC: CQ Press, 1994.

Kraft, Michael and Norman Vig. "Environmental Policy from the 1970s to the Twenty-First Century." In *Environmental Policy: New Directions for the Twenty-First Century*, 6th ed., edited by Norman Vig and Michael Kraft, 1–33. Washington, DC: CQ Press, 2006.

Kubasek, Nancy, and Gary Silverman. *Environmental Law*. 5th ed. Upper Saddle River, NJ: Pearson, 2005.

Lash, Jonathan,. Katherine Gillman, and David Sheridan. *A Season of Spoils: The Reagan Administration's Attack on the Environment*. New York: Pantheon, 1984.

"Legal Winds of Change: Business and the New Clean Air Act." Videoconference Resource Materials, presented by Environmental Protection Agency, PBS Adult Learning Satellite Service, Public Television Outreach Alliance, and the University of North Carolina at Greensboro. 28 November 1990.

Leopold, A. S., S. A. Cain, C. M. Cotton, I. N. Gabrielson, and T. L. Kimball. *Wildlife Management in the National Parks: The Leopold Report*. U.S. Department of the Interior, Advisory Board on Wildlife Management, 1963.

Levine, Joel S. "A Planet at Risk." Public Lecture, Greensboro, North Carolina, 20 February 1993.

Lockhart, William B., Yale Kamisar, and Jesse Choper. *The American Constitution: Cases–Comments–Questions*. St. Paul, MN: West, 1970.

Lund, Thomas A. *American Wildlife Law*. Berkeley: University of California Press, 1980.

Mazmanian, Daniel, and Paul Sabatier. *Implementation and Public Policy*. Glenview IL: Scott, Foresman & Company, 1983.

McCord, J. M. "'Sound Science' in Doubt at Yucca Mountain." *High Country News*, 18 April 2005, 3.

McEvoy, Arthur. *The Fisherman's Problem: Ecology and Law in California Fisheries, 1850–1980*. Cambridge, UK: Cambridge University Press, 1986.

Mead, Walter J., Asbjorn Moseidjord, Dennis Muraoka, and Philip Sorenson. *Offshore Lands: Oil and Gas Leasing and Conservation on the Outer Continental Shelf*. San Francisco: Pacific Institute for Public Policy Research, 1985.

Miller Jr., G. Tyler. *Living in the Environment*. 5th ed. Belmont, CA: Wadsworth, 1988.

Molina, Mario, and F. Sherwood Rowland. "Stratospheric Sink for Chlorofluoromethanes: Chlorine Atom Catalysed Destruction of Ozone." *Nature* 249 (1974): 810–812. Cited in Benedick, *Ozone Diplomacy*, 10.

Naff, John. *Journal of the American Bar Association* 58 (1972): 820. Reprinted in Christopher Stone, *Earth and Other Ethics*. New York: Harper & Row, 1987.

Nangle, Orval. "Stratospheric Ozone: United States Regulation of Chlorofluorocarbons." *Environmental Affairs* 16 (1989): 531–580.

Nash, Roderick. *American Environmentalism: Readings in Conservation History*. 3rd ed. New York: McGraw-Hill, 1990.

National Audubon Society. *Audubon Wildlife Report*. New York: National Audubon Society, 1985, 1986, 1987.

Neustadt, Richard, and Earnest May. *Thinking in Time*. New York: Free Press, 1986.

Nie, Martin. "Administrative Rulemaking and Public Lands Conflict: The Forest Service's Roadless Rule." *Natural Resources Journal* 44 (Summer 2004): 687–742.

New York Times. "Carolina Power Is Top Buyer," 31 March 1993, C2.

New York Times. "Law Students Buy and Hold Pollution Rights," 31 March 1995, B13.

O'Leary, Rosemary. *Environmental Change: Federal Courts and the EPA*. Philadelphia: Temple University Press, 1993.

Ostrom, Elinor. *Governing the Commons*. Cambridge, UK: Cambridge University Press, 1990.

Ostrom, Elinor. *Understanding Institutional Diversity*. Ewing, NJ: Princeton University Press, 2005.

Paskus, Laura. "Bedrock Environmental Law Takes a Beating." *High Country News*, 22 August 2005, 3–4.

Paskus, Laura. "Bush's Second-Term Shake-ups." *High Country News*, 7 February 2005, 3.

Paskus, Laura. "Congress Touts 'Green Energy,' but Bill Is Black and Blue." *High Country News*, 16 May 2005, 2.

Paskus, Laura. "'Sound Science' Goes Sour." *High Country News*, 23 June 2003, 7–12.

Paterson, Matthew. *Global Warming and Global Politics*. New York: Routledge, 1996.

Pearce, David. "The European Community Approach to the Control of Chlorofluorocarbons." Paper submitted to UNEP Workshop on the Control of Chlorofluorocarbons, Leesburg, Virginia, 8–12 September 1986. Cited by Benedick, *Ozone Diplomacy*, 25.

Peters, Guy. *American Public Policy: Promise and Performance*. 2nd ed. Chatham, NJ: Chatham House Publishers, 1986.

Peterson, D. J. *Troubled Lands: The Legacy of Soviet Environmental Destruction*. Boulder, CO: Westview Press, 1993.

Pinchot, Gifford. *The Fight for Conservation*. Garden City, NY: Harcourt, Brace, 1919.

Plater, Zygmunt, Robert Abrams, and William Goldfarb. *Environmental Law and Policy: Nature, Law, and Society*. St. Paul, MN: West, 1992.

Plater, Zygmunt, Robert Abrams, William Goldfarb, and Robert Graham. *Environmental Law and Policy: Nature, Law, and Society*. 2nd ed. St. Paul, MN: West Group, 1998.

Ponting, Clive. *A Green History of the World*. New York: Penguin, 1991.

Porter, Gareth, and Janet Welsh Brown. *Global Environmental Politics*. 2nd ed. Boulder, CO: Westview Press, 1996.

Rasband, James, James Salzman, and Mark Squillance. *Natural Resources Law and Policy*. New York: Foundation Press, 2004.

Reed, Tom. "Hunting: It's Not about the Gun." *High Country News*, 11 October 2004, 19.

Reese, April. "The Big Buyout." *High Country News*, 4 April 2005, 8–13, 19.

Reese, April. "Western Governors Wary of Roadless Forest Mess." *High Country News*, 25 July 2005, 4.

Reinhardt, Forest. "Du Pont Freon® Products Division." In *Managing Environmental Issues: A Casebook*, edited by Rogene Buchholz, Alfred Marcus, and James Post, 261–286. Englewood Cliffs, NJ: Prentice-Hall, 1992.

ReVelle, Penelope, and Charles ReVelle. *The Environment: Issues and Choices for Society*. Boston: Jones and Bartlett Publishers, 1988.

ReVelle, Penelope, and Charles ReVelle,. *The Global Environment: Securing a Sustainable Future*. Boston: Jones and Bartlett Publishers, 1992.

Revelle, Roger and Hans Suess. "Carbon Dioxide exchange between atmosphere and ocean, and the question of an increase in atmospheric CO_2 during the past decade." *Tellus* 9 (1957): 18–27. Cited in Paterson, *Global Warming and Global Politics*.

Ring, Ray. "As Washington Waffles, Western States Go Green." *High Country News*, 25 July 2005, 5–6.

Ripley, Randall, and Grace Franklin. *Congress, the Bureaucracy, and Public Policy*. Homewood, IL: Dorsey Press, 1984.

Rodgers Jr., William H. *Handbook on Environmental Law*. St. Paul, MN: West, 1977.

Rogers, Paul. "The Clean Air Act of 1970." *EPA Journal*, January–February 1990. http://www.epa.gov/history/topics/caa70/11htm (accessed 22 December 2005).

Rohr, John. *Ethics for Bureaucrats*. 2nd ed. New York: Marcel Dekker, 1989.

Rosenbaum, Walter A. *Energy, Politics, and Public Policy*. 2nd ed. Washington, DC: Congressional Quarterly, 1987.

Rosenbaum, Walter A. *Energy, Politics, and Public Policy*. 3rd ed. Washington, DC: Congressional Quarterly, 1995.

Rosenbaum, Walter A. *Environmental Politics and Policy.* 5th ed. Washington, DC: CQ Press, 2002.

Rosenbaum, Walter A. *Environmental Politics and Policy.* 6th ed. Washington, DC: CQ Press, 2005.

Rosenbaum, Walter A. "Improving Environmental Regulation at the EPA: The Challenge in Balancing Politics, Policy, and Science." In *Environmental Policy: New Directions for the Twenty-First Century.* 6th ed., edited by Norman Vig and Michael Kraft, 169–192. Washington, DC: CQ Press, 2006.

Rowlands, Ian. *The Politics of Global Atmospheric Change.* Manchester, UK: Manchester University Press, 1995.

Rowe, Jeri. "Traders Don't Outfox Wildlife Officials." *Greensboro* [North Carolina] *News & Record*, 22 May 1995, B1.

Sagoff, Mark. "At the Shrine of Our Lady of Fatima or Why Political Questions Are Not All Economic." In *Environmental Ethics: Readings in Theory and Applications*, edited by L. P. Pojman, 443-450. Boston, MA: James and Bartlett, MA, 1994.

Salzman, James, and Barton H. Thompson Jr. *Environmental Law and Policy.* New York: Foundation Press, 2003.

Sand, Peter. *Lessons Learned in Global Environmental Governance.* Washington, DC: World Resources Institute, June 1990.

Sax, Joseph. "Public Trust Doctrine in Natural Resource Law: Effective Judicial Intervention." *Michigan Law Review* 68 (January 1970): 490.

Schneider, Keith. "Ozone Depletion Harming Sea Life." *New York Times*, 16 November 1991, p. 6, col. 6.

Shellenberger, Michael, and Ted Nordhaus. "The Death of Environmentalism." http://www.thebreakthrough.org/images/Death_of_Environmentalism.pdf. 2004.

Sierra. "Casualty Friday." July/August 2004, 13.

Soroos, Marvin. "From Stockholm to Rio: The Evolution of Global Environmental Governance." In *Environmental Policy in the 1990s*, 2nd ed., edited by Norman Vig and Michael Kraft, 299–321. Washington, DC: CQ Press, 1994.

Sovacool, Benjamin. "The Coming Costs of Drilling in Arctic Refuge." *Roanoke* [Virginia] *Times*, 18 March 2003, 9.

Stevens, William K. "The 25th Anniversary of Earth Day: How Has the Environment Fared?" *New York Times*, 18 April 1995, B5.

Stoel Jr., Thomas B., Alan S. Miller, and Breck Milroy. *Fluorocarbon Regulation.* Lexington, MA: D. C. Heath, 1980. Cited in Benedick, *Ozone Diplomacy*, 28.

Stolarski, Richard, and Ralph Cicerone. "Stratospheric Chlorine: A Possible Sink for Ozone." *Canadian Journal of Chemistry* 52 (1974): 1610–1615. Cited in Benedick, *Ozone Diplomacy*, 10.

Sussman, Glen, Byron Daynes, and Jonathan West. *American Politics and the Environment*. New York: Longman, 2002.

Sussman, Karen. (Society for the Protection of Mustangs and Burros), quoted in Brett French, "Wild Horses' Fans Fear Roundup Will Weaken Herds." billingsgazette.com, (*Billings* [Montana] *Gazette*), 20 August 2005. http://www. billingsgazette.com/index.php?id=1&display=rednews/2005/08/20/build/ state/ 35-horses.inc (accessed 22 September 2005).

Switzer, Jacqueline Vaughn. *Environmental Politics: Domestic and Global Dimensions*. New York: St. Martin's Press, 1994.

Switzer, Jacqueline Vaughn. *Environmental Politics: Domestic and Global Dimensions*. 4th ed. Belmont, CA: Thomson/Wadsworth, 2004.

Symons, Jeremy. "How Bush and Co. Obscure the Science." *Washington Post*, 13 July 2003, B4.

Tampa [Florida] *Tribune*. "Developer Fined for Destroying Bald Eagle Nest." TBO.com NEWS, 8 September 2005. http://news.tbo.com/news/ MGB5YJ5DCDE.html (accessed 22 September 2004).

Tangley, Laura. "Bases Loaded." *National Wildlife*, October/November 2005, 38–45.

Thompson, Michael. "The Cultural Construction of Nature and the Natural Destruction of Culture." Working paper for International Institute for Applied Systems Analysis, Laxenberg, Austria, 1984.

Tinsley, V. Randall, and Larry Nielsen, "Interstate Fisheries Arrangements: Application of a Pragmatic Classification Scheme for Interstate Arrangements." *Virginia Journal of Natural Resources Law* 6 (2), Spring 1987: 265–321.

Tobin, Richard. "Environment, Population, and Economic Development." In *Environmental Policy in the 1990s*, 2nd ed., edited by Norman Vig and Michael Kraft, 275–297. Washington, DC: CQ Press, 1994.

Tripp, J. T. B., D. J. Dudek, and Michael Oppenheimer. "Equality and Ozone Protection." *Environment* 29, no. 6 (1987): 45. Cited in Benedick, *Ozone Diplomacy*, 28.

Trout, James. "A Land Manager's Commentary on the Public Trust Doctrine." In *The Public Trust Doctrine in Natural Resource Law and Management*, edited by Harrison Dunning, 169–177. Davis: University of California, 1981.

Union of Concerned Scientists. "Scientific Integrity in Policy Making." http://www.ucsusa.org/global_environment/rsi/page.cfm?page ID=1641 (accessed 23 July 2005).

Union of Concerned Scientists. "Specific Examples of the Abuse of Science." http://www.ucsusa.org/global_environment/rsi/page.cfm?page ID=1398 (accessed 23 July 2005).

Union of Concerned Scientists. "U.S. Fish & Wildlife Service Survey Summary." February 2005. http://www.ucsusa.org/global_environment/rsi/page.cfm? page ID=1601 (accessed 23 July 2005).

Union of Concerned Scientists. "Summary of National Oceanic & Atmospheric Administration Scientist Survey." http://www.ucsusa.org/global environment/rsi/page.cfm?page ID=1804 (accessed 23 July 2005).

U.S. Environmental Protection Agency. "Air Emissions Trends—Continued Progress through 2003." Washington DC: EPA, January 2005, www.epa.gov/airtrends/aqtrnd04/emissions.html.

U.S. Environmental Protection Agency. *Environmental Monitoring at Love Canal.* Washington, DC: USEPA, 1982.

U.S. Environmental Protection Agency. *Environmental Progress and Challenges: An EPA Perspective.* Washington, DC: Office of Management Systems and Evaluation CPM-222, June, 1984.

U.S. Environmental Protection Agency. *National Air Quality and Emissions Trends Report, 2003.* Washington, DC: EPA, September 2003, www.epa.gov/airtrends/reports.html.

U.S. Environmental Protection Agency. Science Advisory Board. *Reducing Risk: Setting Priorities for Environmental Protection.* Washington, DC: USEPA, September 1990.

U.S. Fish and Wildlife Service. "Deductions for Administration" http://federalasst.fws.gov/ financialinfo/deductionsforadmin.htm (accessed 16 September 2005).

U.S. Fish and Wildlife Service. "Federal Aid in Sport Fish Restoration." http://federalasst.fws.gov/sfr/fasfr.html (accessed 23 September 2005).

U.S. Fish and Wildlife Service. "Final Apportionment of Dingell-Johnson Sport Fish Restoration Funds for Fiscal Year 2005." http://federalasst.fws.gov/apport/SFRFINALApportionment2005.pdf (accessed 23 September 2005).

U.S. Fish and Wildlife Service. "Final apportionment of Pittman-Robertson Wildlife Restoration Funds for Fiscal Year 2005." http://federalasst.fws.gov/apport/WRFINALApportionment2005.pdf (accessed 23 September 2005).

U.S. Fish and Wildlife Service. *Restoring America's Wildlife* (brochure). Washington, DC: USGPO, June, 1992.

U.S. Fish and Wildlife Service. "Sport Fish Restoration Apportionment History." http://federalasst.fws.gov/apport/SFRAhistory.pdf (accessed 23 September 2005).

U.S. Fish and Wildlife Service. "Threatened and Endangered Species System (TESS)." http://ecos.fws.gov/tess_public/TESSBoxscore (accessed 25 September 2005).

U.S. Fish and Wildlife Service. "Wildlife Restoration Apportionment History." http://federalasst.fws.gov/apport/WRAhistory.pdf (accessed 23 September 2005).

U.S. Fish and Wildlife Service. *Restoring America's Wildlife, 1937–1987: The First 50 Years of the Federal Aid in Wildlife Restoration (Pittman-Robertson) Act.* Washington, DC: USGPO, 1987.

Vaughn, Ray. *Essentials of Environmental Law.* Rockville, MD: Government Institutes, 1994.

Vidal, John. "Revealed: How Oil Giant Influenced Bush." *Guardian* [Manchester, UK], 8 June 2005. http://www.guardian.co.uk/international/story/0,,1501632,00.html (accessed 2 July 2005).

Vig, Norman. "Presidential Leadership and the Environment." In *Environmental Policy: New Directions for the Twenty-First Century*, 6th ed., edited by Norman Vig and Michael Kraft, 100–123. Washington, DC: CQ Press, 2006.

Vig, Norman. "Presidential Leadership and the Environment: From Reagan and Bush to Clinton." In *Environmental Policy in the 1990s*, 2nd ed., edited by Norman Vig and Michael Kraft, 71–95. Washington, DC: CQ Press, 1994.

Vig, Norman, Michael Kraft, eds. *Environmental Policy in the 1980s: Reagan's New Agenda.* Washington, DC: Congressional Quarterly, 1984.

Vig, Norman, and Michael Kraft, eds. *Environmental Policy: New Directions for the Twenty-First Century.* 6th ed. Washington, DC: Congressional Quarterly, 2006.

Vig, Norman, and Michael Kraft. "Toward Sustainable Development?" In *Environmental Policy: New Directions for the Twenty-First Century*, 6th ed., edited by Norman Vig and Michael Kraft, 374–394. Washington, DC: CQ Press, 2006.

Walker, Jack. "Setting the Agenda in the U.S. Senate." *British Journal of Political Science* 7 (October 1977): 423–445.

Weber, Michael. "Marine Mammal Protection." In *Audubon Wildlife Report 1985*, edited by Roger Di Silvestro, 181–211. New York: National Audubon Society, 1985.

Werner, Erica Werner. "House to Act on Endangered Species Law." Washingtonpost.com, 29 September 2005. http://www.washingtonpost.com/wp-dyn/content/article/2005/09/29/AR2005092900295.html (accessed 2 October 2005).

Wilkinson, Charles. "Public Trust Doctrine in Public Land Law." In *The Public Trust Doctrine in Natural Resources Law and Management*, edited by Harrison Dunning. Davis: University of California, 1981.

Williams, Ted. "'Silent Spring' Revisited." *Modern Maturity*, October–November 1987, 46–50, 108.

Williamson, Lonnie. 1987. "Evolution of a Landmark Law." In *Restoring America's Wildlife 1937–1987: The First 50 Years of the Federal Aid in Wildlife Restoration (Pittman-Robertson) Act*, 1–17. Washington, DC: USGPO (Department of Interior, U.S. Fish and Wildlife Service), 1987.

Woltz, Charles. "Preface." *Administrative Procedure in Government Agencies.* Charlottesville, VA: University Press of Virginia, 1968.

Wright, Robert R., and Morton Gitelman. *Land Use in a Nutshell.* 4th ed. St. Paul, MN: West, 2000.

ABOUT THE AUTHOR

Susan Buck is associate professor of political science and director of Environmental Studies at the University of North Carolina at Greensboro. Before earning her PhD in public administration at Virginia Tech, she supervised the Wetlands Research Laboratory at the Virginia Institute of Marine Science. In addition to *Understanding Environmental Administration and Law*, she has written *The Global Commons* (Island Press, 1998), coauthored a text in public administration, and contributed numerous articles and book chapters on environmental policy and law. She is currently working on a book about federal-state relations in wildlife management. Dr. Buck lives in Greensboro, North Carolina.

INDEX

Abbey Dodge, The (1912), 147
Acid deposition/rain, 117, 208–209
Adjudication, 109, 114–115, 116
Administrative discretion, 60–61
Administrative hearings vs. court proceedings, 76
Administrative Procedure Act (1946): adjudication description, 109, 114–115, 116; agency rulemaking and, 7, 57; amendments to, 108; Attorney General's Report on, 107–108; benefit–cost analysis, 114; debate over/passage of, 106–108; description, 108; hearing components, 115; judicial review, 115–117; rule definition, 108–109; rulemaking description, 109; rulemaking guidelines, 108–114; rulemaking types/procedures, 111–114; rule types, 109–111; standing and, 79
Administrative rulemaking/procedures: constitution and, 7–8; legitimacy and, 57
Agreement on Straddling and Highly Migratory Fish Stocks ("U.N. Fish Stocks Agreement"), 204
Air pollution: air quality classes, 118; citizen suits and, 123; deaths from, 117; emissions trading program, 119–121, 122; hazardous air pollutants, 122; NAAQs-major pollutants, 118; new-source performance standards, 125;

overview, 117–125; pollutant types, 117, 118, 121, 122, 123; prevention of significant deterioration (PSD), 118; primary vs. secondary pollutants, 117; relationship between pollution–externalities–free riders, 119–121; sources of, 117; stationary sources vs. indirect sources, 123–124; tunnel ventilation systems, 123–124; vehicle emissions, 117, 118, 121, 123. *See also* Atmosphere (as global commons); *specific legislation*
Air Quality Act (1967), 117–118, 130
Airspace sovereignty, 90
Alaska National Interest Lands Conservation Act (1980), 180
Alaska Native Claims Settlement Act (1971), 27
Alienation (public trust doctrine), 97
Alliance of Small Island States (AOSIS), 214
Ambler Realty, Euclid v. (1926), 92
American Bar Association (ABA), 107, 108
American National Research Council, 47
American Revolution, 3
American Textile Manufacturers v. Donovan (1981), 7
Antarctica: as international commons, 192, 198, 199, 201; ozone hole, 211, 213
Antarctic Treaty System, 199
ANWR (Arctic National Wildlife Refuge), 34, 180